THE BEST NEW YORK SPORTS ARGUMENTS

THE 100 MOST CONTROVERSIAL, DEBATABLE QUESTIONS FOR DIE-HARD NEW YORK FANS

PETER HANDRINOS

SOURCEBOOKS, INC.®
NAPERVILLE, ILLINOIS

Published by Sourcebooks, Inc.
P.O. Box 4410, Naperville, Illinois 60567-4410
(630) 961-3900
Fax: (630) 961-2168
www.sourcebooks.com

Library of Congress Cataloging-in-Publication Data

Handrinos, Peter.
   The best New York sports arguments : the 100 most controversial, debatable questions for die-hard New York fans / Peter Handrinos.
      p. cm.
   Includes index.
   ISBN-13: 978-1-4022-0823-2
   ISBN-10: 1-4022-0823-5
   1. Sports--New York (State)--New York--Miscellanea. I. Title.

GV584.5.N4H36 2007
796.09747'1--dc22

                                                          2006032773

            Printed and bound in the United States of America.
                  CH 10 9 8 7 6 5 4 3 2

CONTENTS

THE BEST NEW YORK SPORTS ARGUMENTS

RINKS

CENTER COURTS

RINGS

TRACKS

SUPERLATIVES

FOREWORD

by Bob Wolff

In reading this book, I was struck by the immense privilege involved in being a New York sports fan.

Is there any sports town like it? We've got all four major sports, fielding nine franchises, as well as the best of the best in sports like tennis, boxing, and racing. So many splendid teams and athletes, all of them encompassing such rich histories, remarkable titles, and pioneering achievements. With no disrespect to the other great cities, New York is a sports fan's paradise. We've got it all.

In a completely unique city, Peter Handrinos has written a one-of-a-kind book. I've never seen a project take on so many topics in New York's incredible sports heritage, and do it with such preparation and joy. True sports fans seek both even-handed substance and spirited fun, and they might find plenty of both in *The Best New York Sports Arguments*.

And, most of all, the book provides some fresh perspectives. As a 60-year veteran of sports broadcasting, I pride myself on familiarity with most all aspects of the town's sports scene. More than a few times, I've been an eyewitness to its remarkable events and personalities. Even so, the book's many surprising facts and views made me feel I'd come across the topics for the first time.

All in all, *The Best New York Sports Arguments* is an immensely entertaining journey through "the greatest sports town in America." I hope and expect my fellow fans will enjoy it just as much as I did.

—**R.A.W.**
South Nyack, NY
August 2006

INTRODUCTION:
Do New York Sports Matter?

1 Yeah, it can all seem a little silly.

Anywhere two or more New Yorkers gather, you can frequently find fans talking and arguing about the in's and out's of baseball, football, basketball, hockey, tennis, boxing, and the rest. Not infrequently, fans' voices are raised, arms are waved, stray pretzels are tossed, and all over . . . what? No one's hammering out a peace plan for the Middle East or curing the common cold. They're obsessing on fun and games. All that passion and to-do is over a bunch of guys hitting a ball with a stick, carrying a ball over a line, shooting it through a hoop, etc., etc. Some pretty trivial stuff, it would seem.

But seeming isn't believing. There are very good reasons why sports are almost a secular religion in New York—athletics go to the heart of the city's restless identity and common causes alike.

Sports are relevant in this town mostly because they're all about competition and New Yorkers may be the most competitive people on earth. The most famous of our residents measure excellence in ratings points, blaring headlines, market shares, arbitrage fortunes, and electoral votes, but the truth is, competing is a way of life in all walks of city life.

There isn't a one in the eight million who hasn't clamored to hail the next passing cab, to make the next month's rent payment, to outpace next year's price hikes, to cope with the new era's threats and opportunities alike. Around here, staying solvent and sane can be a win in itself.

In New York's bustling energy, those who thrive must strive, and it isn't too difficult for them to recognize the striving chronicled on our favorite radio shows, broadcasts, papers, and sites. Of course we're big-time sports fans. We may not love some of the stress and excess to be found in either the city or its beloved athletics, but at the same time, we'd be lost without their drama and electricity. We'd be a Metropolis without Superman, a Gotham without Bruce Wayne.

No city lives sports-type competition like New York, and there's another thing—no other city needs sports' common language to unite its diverse populace, either.

The home of Ellis Island and the United Nations is, of course, packed with the proud representatives of every color, creed, culture, and class there is to be found in the spectrum of humanity. It's an entire world in itself, and that's before anyone gets into the inherent differences within greater New York, a mega-area that encompasses at least several million more souls situated through multiple counties and a hundred or more towns.

With all the fault lines running through the five boroughs and the tristate, sports can provide much-needed bridges. With just about every New Yorker interested in sports in some form or another, just about everyone can carry on a sports conversation in some form or another, and, whatever our respective views might be, at least we're united in that caring. In those conversations, it's not particularly relevant who's Jewish or Italian or black, who's a grocer or cop or stockbroker, and who's from Bed-Stuy or Roosevelt or Scarsdale. In those moments, we're citizens of one sports nation, indivisible.

Sometimes, maybe most of the time, sports provide just enough light conversation to pass the time, and that's useful enough to ease frictions among the city's strangers. At other times, though, arguing the ups and downs of the Yanks or Jets or Isles can create a noticeably greater kinship between acquaintances. At its very best, it can be a vital part of the communication that makes for close-knit friends and family, too. Regardless of the level of involvement, sports-based communication tends to make sometimes a hard and impersonal place just a little more livable and personal.

And, so, at the end of the day, the sports passions that can seem a bit silly may end up doing some very serious work. Get past all the arm-waving and pretzel-tossing, and in there's a highly relevant language of competition, one that's fluently spoken throughout a diverse but welcoming municipality. Our sports matter because they help make New York New York.

AROUND TOWN

WHAT ARE NEW YORK'S GREATEST SPORTS TRADITIONS?

2 Ever since New York was New Amsterdam, the town's accepted new arrivals and new ideas. Today it's defined by an ability to produce the next new thing in everything from fashion to finance, yet the sports scene features some of the well-established, home-grown traditions to be found anywhere. Classic customs include:

YANKEE OLD TIMERS' DAY

The returning ballplayers, ranging from their forties to their sixties, may vary from paunchy-n-slow to *very* paunchy-n-slow. A couple dozen retirees might be playing just hard enough to avoid groin pulls. The quality of the three inning exhibitions may resemble rec league tourneys.

But Yankee Old Timers' Day is definitely one of the best sports traditions around. It's the sweetest reunion in the National Pastime, an annual opportunity for an extended franchise family to pull together while tipping caps to fans' diamond memories. Those who value Yankee pride always mark the date.

DEE-FENSE!

The familiar chant was first heard during the Giants' march to the 1956 NFL title, as a special call out to star linebacker Sam Huff. (Those cute **D/Fence** signs didn't show up until much later, though.)

THE VERY GOOD SHEPPARD

You could say that Bob Sheppard's first game as Yankee Stadium's public announcer was a memorable one—April 17, 1951, also happened to be Joe DiMaggio's last opening day and Mickey Mantle's debut in the Bronx. Sheppard's outlasted generations of ballplayers since, of course, and his decades of service with the football Giants are legend.

To weigh Bob Sheppard's impact, just try to imagine Yankee Stadium without a familiar baritone delivering the words "Your Attention Please, Ladies and Gentlemen. . . ." Over the years, everyone's imitated The Voice of God. No one will ever match him.

THE BROADWAY SHOW LEAGUE

Every year for more than 50 years, some of the biggest stars of the Great White Way forget about Opening Night and start thinking about Opening Day.

The rec group, playing in Central Park's diamonds on a spring–fall schedule, features some of the most competitive amateur games to be found anywhere within city limits. Players range from stage hands to Oscar winners, with notable league alumni including Al Pacino, George C. Scott, John Lithgow, and Danny Aiello. Robert Redford (*The Natural*'s Roy Hobbs) once played ball in the Show League.

THE OPEN OPEN

For two weeks out of the year, the USTA National Tennis Center belongs to the U.S. Open and some of the most famous athletes in the world, but the rest of the time, it belongs to any tennis bum with a little spare cash and an appointment. The sites of Wimbledon, the Australian Open, and the French Open are monopolized by country club elites, but America's Grand Slam home has belonged to all the people since 1978.

THURMAN MUNSON'S MEMORIAL

As a silent tribute to #15's memory, Munson's corner locker was never cleaned out—the captain's equipment remains, still untouched, just as he left it before his tragic death in 1979. Thomas Boswell once wrote, "Ballplayers do not leave epitaphs, only memories and friends. Munson, the man who may have been baseball's ideal teammate, was rich in both."

HOMER JONES' SPIKE

There's some dispute over the originator of the spike, but Giants wide receiver Homer Jones definitely popularized it by disposing of touchdown balls with emphatic throw-downs in the late 1960s. Energetic without being too showy, it's still the best celebration in football.

THE METS' BEGINNING AND THE YANKS' ENDING

For more than 40 years "Meet the Mets" has been one of the most lively sports anthems of all time, an ever-familiar piece of audio fun:

> *Meet the Mets! /*
> *Meet the Mets! /*
> *Step right up and greet the Mets! /*
> *Bring your kiddies, bring your wife! /*
> *Guaranteed to have the time of your life! . . . /*

Frank Sinatra's ode to big-city ambition, "New York, New York," has been just as memorable for the Yanks since the late 1970s:

> *I want to wake up in a city, that doesn't sleep /*
> *And find I'm king of the hilltop of the heap . . . /*

Somehow, both tunes strike just the right chords.

THE YANKEES' UNIFORMS

The most famous franchise in sports has been atop the best-dressed lists since the 1930's, when its look came together in an interlocking "NY" logo, home pinstripes, road grays, and numerals. Babe Ruth and Lou Gehrig wore a uniform look that's still seen on new millennium Yankees. All those are great, but the single greatest New York sports tradition may be:

BROADWAY'S TICKER-TAPE PARADES

The city invented the confetti-tossing back in 1886, during spontaneous celebrations for the new Statue of Liberty, but it wasn't until 1954 that championship-winners first received the blowout treatment otherwise reserved for presidents, astronauts, and war heroes.

Other bergs have tried to imitate the tradition over the years, but why do they bother? The processions start where the city originated, the Battery, then take a spectacular "Canyon of Heroes" route through the Financial District, only to find a crush of delirious fans, crackling energy, a blizzard of dreamy bliss . . . nothing proclaims a distinctive New York success like a nice, slow stroll uptown. We do love a parade.

WHAT ARE NEW YORK'S WORST SPORTS TRADITIONS?

3 New Yorkers have long had to deal with packed rush hours, car-killing potholes, and stratospheric rents, not to mention freezing winters and scorching summers. Not all the Big Apple's most familiar traditions are welcomed traditions, and the same can be said for its sports. Certain bad habits have managed to hang around, with the worst including:

UNNECESSARY YANKEE NUMBER RETIREMENTS

If Ruth, Gehrig, DiMaggio, Mantle, and the rest were good enough for Cooperstown, they were good enough to have their numbers put away forever. No argument there.

The problem comes when some good/but-not-great ballplayers took the highest honor, too. Thurman Munson's tragic death and Elston Howard's pioneering role may have merited some special recognition, but what about guys like Don Mattingly and Ron Guidry? Both were good baseball players, but neither had the stats for the Hall of Fame, and many think Phil Rizzuto was borderline at best. They were popular guys, sure, but that shouldn't be enough for immortality.

THE ST. JOHN'S CRIME SPREE

In 2000, Erick Barkley's misdeeds brought down recruiting sanctions. In 2002, Sharif Fordham was imprisoned for selling crack. In 2004, Ron Artest was a ringleader in the Pacers-Pistons scrum, a.k.a. the worst brawl in NBA history. In 2004, Willie Shaw was arrested for buying marijuana along with former teammate Marcus Hatten. In 2004 (a horrible year, that one), six players were suspended or expelled over accusations of gang rape. In 2006, Jayson Williams was retried for charges related to a shooting death of his limo driver.

Once, St. John's students and alumni were associated with the Big East. Today they're more often associated with the Big House.

THE ELDEST-BORN SONS OF TEAM OWNERS

James (son of Charles) Dolan was named one of corporate America's worst managers by *BusinessWeek* even before he engineered the Knicks' ongoing disaster (#76). Jeff (son of Fred) Wilpon had his fingerprints all over the Scott Kazmir-for-Victor Zambrano trade. Hank (son of George) Steinbrenner has been quiet for a while now, but some suspect that he may have inherited some of dad's bad old ways (#50), too.

So much biological luck, so much managerial incompetence. Yes, there is a downside to family togetherness.

13

LAWRENCE TAYLOR, ACTOR

He was typecast as BJ Smith" in *Grand Theft Auto:Vice City*. He was stiff as Lamont in *Shaft*. He was over-the-top as Shark Lavay in *Any Given Sunday*. He was unconvincing as Lawrence Taylor in *The Waterboy*, *Wrestlemania*, and *The Sopranos*. This is one thespian who should be sacked.

THE BIGGEST JOHN STERLING FAN IN THE WORLD, JOHN STERLING

It isn't just the distracting way he drags out syllables ("aaaaaaand it's a fly ball to left"), or his never-ending supply of cornball catchphrases ("an A-bomb from A-Rod," "Bern-baby Bern" Williams). Or the constant hyperbole ("OHHHHHH, that's the play of the year! That's the most unbelievable play you'll ever see!"). Or the way he shamelessly breaks out the pom-poms to root for his paymasters ("Ball game over! The Yankees win! Theeeeeeeeeeeeeeeee Yankees Win!").

No, Sterling's such a bore because all the smug mugging constantly distracts attention from the Yankees and onto his strange little personality. Fans tune in for ball games but get an exhausting three hours of *The John Sterling Show* instead.

THE METS' LAME NEW THEME SONGS

For reasons known only to them, challengers have repeatedly attempted to overtake the chipper "Meet the Mets" anthem (#2) over the years. In 1969, it was the champion Mets, appearing as a lounge act in Vegas and recording an album of standards.

In 1985, it was a rap band called Starchild, releasing "You've Gotta Believe (Let's Go Mets)." They botched the phrase (it's "ya gotta believe," fellas) and things went downhill from there.

In 1986, it was various players putting out "Get Metsmerized," an unlistenable tribute to their own greatness (sample lyrics: "When they want a batter filled with terror / They call on me, Rick Aguilera,"). If they played like they rapped, they'd have lost 120 games.

In 2000, a novelty act's "Who Let the Dogs Out?" provided a rhetorical question for New York's playoff run. Few could forget (or escape) the "woof, woof, woof, woof, woof" ditty. Though many tried.

All those traditions are terrible, no doubt, but the worst of all may be:

THE NFL'S BAD DRAFT

When the NFL moves into the Madison Square Garden theatre or Radio City Music Hall in the spring, they put out a rotten show.

There's empty, ignorant talk (the endless blather about "quick feet" and "tremendous upsides"). There's completely inaccurate predictions (no one's ever come close to forecasting the first round). There are preening talking heads (the bombastic Chris Berman, the motor-mouthed Mel Kiper Jr.). There's the spin (the "inside information" that usually turns out to be generalities or outright lies). And there's the utter meaninglessness of it all (the cheers greeting first-round busts like Cedric Jones, the yawns meeting third-round superstars like Tom Brady).

Now there's a tradition with a little something for everyone to hate.

WHAT ARE NEW YORK'S BIGGEST SPORTS MYTHS?

4 The biggest city in America is teeming with hustling, fearless journalists—every last one of them dedicated to exposing the truth in their news and histories. It's also chock-full of urban myths. Some of the more popular ones include:

"THE CURSE OF THE BAMBINO"

Yep, Dan Shaughnessy was right—for over eight decades, the Ruth-less Red Sox were indeed cursed. By crony-dependent owners, racist general managers, tipsy advisors, dim-bulb managers, overpaid and underperforming ballplayers, an especially vicious media establishment, and a self-pitying, woe-is-me fan base that may actually deserve a major inferiority complex.

But Babe Ruth had nothing to do with their problems. The Bambino loved Boston, if not Harry Frazee, and said "the town's been good to me." He was a big-hearted party guy who couldn't hold a grudge to save his life and, besides, he didn't have a grudge to hold—things sort of worked out for him in the Bronx.

"NICE GUYS FINISH LAST"

Leo Durocher's famous phrase has always been jerks' favorite mantra, but it's complete nonsense.

Since it first made the rounds back in the '40s, some wonderful human beings have managed their way to championships. Think about the calm and steady Walt Alston. The gregarious Casey Stengel. The tough-but-fair Ralph Houk. The patient Gil Hodges. The beloved Bob Lemon. The bright and sociable Davey Johnson. St. Joe Torre. They didn't finish last, they finished first.

(By the way, Durocher, who had the personal morals of a rodent, only finished first three times in 25 seasons as a manager.)

JOE DIMAGGIO WAS A FIRST-BALLOT HALL OF FAMER

DiMaggio was introduced as "our greatest living ballplayer" for 30 years, but he didn't make it into Cooperstown until his third year of eligibility.

FIELD OF DREAMS = IOWA

The magical corn field was kind of incidental, when you get down to it. This was a New York movie through and through.

It's about a Brooklyn kid who grew up with bedtime stories of Ruth and Gehrig, but clashed with his Yankee-loving father over a true-blue allegiance to Brooklyn. Elsewhere, a brilliant writer grew up dreaming of Ebbets Field and Jackie Robinson, only to have his heart broken by their move out west. Eventually, he gave up on society, then moved to Boston.

The two baseball-loving New Yorkers started to rally, though, as soon as they left Fenway and met up with a former (a *really, really* former) Giant, an old guy who once played for John J. McGraw. The three found a ballfield featuring Mel Ott and Gil Hodges, among others, then lived happily ever after.

"YOGISMS"

Yogi Berra is the most quoted American of all time because he supposedly produced dozens of funny lines, like the time he said "nobody goes there anymore, it's too crowded." But most of them are mythic.

In the words of one baseball historian:

A reliable authority has revealed that the first few bon mots were legitimate, although in some cases with syntax adjusted for a boffo one-liner. This helped to create Yogi, the lovable folk hero, but most of what followed was generated by sportswriters and other aspiring wits, like comedy writers producing lines appropriate for a Jack Benny character, a Groucho Marx character, a Yogi Berra character. Few, if any, claim to have heard him utter most of the quotes. Berra himself states that he can't remember everything he said. Draw your own conclusions.

THAT WHITE PICKET-FENCE THING BEYOND CENTERFIELD AT YANKEE STADIUM IS A "FAÇADE"

Technically, a "façade" is the exterior face of a building. Architects call the 560-foot long white picket-fence thing a frieze.

THE JETS GOT THEIR NAME DUE TO FLYOVERS AT SHEA

Owner Sonny Werblin gave the Titans a new nickname in 1963, back when they were still playing football at the Polo Grounds. He liked the way it rhymed with Mets and evoked the early '60s jet age. LaGuardia's flight plans didn't have anything to do with it.

BABE RUTH VISITED A DYING LITTLE KID IN THE HOSPITAL

11-year-old Johnny Sylvester was laid up for weeks, but thankfully, the Bambino's No.1 fan (#5) walked out of the hospital in 1926, very much alive. He graduated from Princeton in 1937, served three years as a Navy lieutenant during World War II, and became a successful business executive in Long Island City. He didn't die until 1990, by which time he'd lived a long and happy 75 years.

BUCKY DENT'S HOME RUN BROKE THE RED SOX IN THE '78 PLAYOFF

For a famous game, this one isn't remembered very clearly at all.

Heading into the seventh inning of the AL East's single-game playoff, the Red Sox were leading the Yankees by a score of 2–0. Dent hit a memorable/improbable three-run home run over the Green Monster in the top of the inning, but that only gave the Yankees a one-run lead. The RBI's that decided the game for New York came afterwards, when Thurman Munson doubled in a run later in the seventh (making it 4–2 New York) and Reggie Jackson hit a one-run homer in the top of the eighth (making it 5–2 New York).

When Boston came back with their final two runs in the bottom of the eighth, they had the four runs they needed to overcome Dent's three-run homer, but not enough to over-come the follow-up RBIs. Bucky (F----n') Dent, a little No.9 banjo hitter, was identified with the win only because he made for a better story than Thurman (F----n') Munson or Reggie (F----n') Jackson.

"THE TUNA"

The story goes that, in the early '80's, a young Giants coach told a loafing player "who do you think I am, Charlie the Tuna?" The reference was to a none-too-bright cartoon character from the old Starkist commercials, so tagging an indisputably bright man with "Tuna" is about as appropriate as calling him "Slim." Duane Charles Parcells' nickname is "Bill."

All of the above were pretty good, but you could argue that the most popular myth in New York sports is this one:

THE 1962 METS HAVE THE WORST RECORD IN MODERN BASEBALL HISTORY

No post-1900 team has ever lost more than the Mets' 120 ball games, but that only made the Amazins the Majors' losingest ball club. The worst mark is based on something different—winning percentage (or losing percentage, if you want to put it that way). The worst teams are those who tend to lose the most on a day-in, day-out basis, regardless of their final loss total.

The '62 Mets' 40–120 mark produced an atrocious .250 winning percentage, true, but the 1935 Braves (38–115, .248) and 1916 Athletics (36–117, .235) sunk even lower over the course of the old 154-game schedule. It was close, but they were better at being worse.

FOUR!

In the 1977 World Series, Reggie Jackson hit three home runs on three swings against three different pitchers. He did. That was true as far as it goes, but it's not the whole story.

It's seldom remembered now, but Jackson hit a home run in his last at-bat in Game Five of the '77 Series, off the Dodgers' Don Sutton. Back in Yankee Stadium for Game Six, he walked in his first plate appearance and only then proceeded to blast three straight first-pitch homers (off LA's Burt Hooton, Elias Sosa, and Charlie Hough). If you count the last at-bat in Game Five and ignore the four-pitch walk to start Game Six, Reggie Jackson hit *four* straight home runs on *four* swings against *four* different pitchers.

WHO HAVE BEEN THE BEST FANS IN NEW YORK SPORTS HISTORY?

 Great athletic events wouldn't be great athletic events without the people's caring and energy. Some of the more memorable fans have included:

JOHNNY SYLVESTER

Few recognize the name but almost everyone's heard some version of the story.

When Sylvester, then 11 years old, fell from a horse in 1926, his uncle asked none other than Babe Ruth to send good wishes over to a hospital in Essex Falls, New Jersey. The Babe happily obliged, sending a signed baseball with a note promising "I'll hit a home run for you in Wednesday's game." Ruth promptly hit three homers in Game Four of the 1926 World Series, the first time that had ever been done in a playoff game.

Ruth later visited the kid in person, and the moment wasn't forgotten. More than 20 years later, Sylvester made his own visit to the dying Bambino's bedside, sharing memories and talkin' baseball.

THE CROWD AT TOOTS SHOR'S

It had competition from classy Manhattan gin joints like the Copa, Flamingo, and El Morocco, but during its 1940's/1950's heyday, Toots Shor's was the single greatest spot to see and be seen.

It was the place where Joe DiMaggio took Marilyn Monroe on their first date. Frank Sinatra once sat at a table with Bing Crosby, Jack Dempsey, and Babe Ruth. It was a favored hangout in Mickey Mantle's carousing with Whitey Ford and Billy Martin. Casey Stengel hammed it up at the circular bar.

A visitor to 51 West 51st could look around to see all the stars. Jocks (Frank Gifford) rubbed elbows with entertainers (Jackie Gleason, Charlie Chaplin), politicos (Dwight Eisenhower, John F. Kennedy), and journalists (Walter Cronkite, Mike Wallace, Edward R. Murrow). You could even find Jimmy Hoffa there, alive and well.

THE DODGER SYMPHONY

From 1938 to 1957, the unofficial house band for Ebbets Field was made up of half a dozen fans in the center field bleachers. Notable members include Brother Lou Soriano on drums and Jo Jo Delio, a midget who played the cymbals with his knees.

Red Barber said the self-taught symphony "couldn't play a note, they couldn't read a note," but that didn't stop them. They'd march up and down the aisles between innings and make "oomph-pah!" sound effects whenever a visiting ballplayer struck out. The umpires' introduction was "Three Blind Mice."

SAL DURANTE

Woody Allen once said that a big part of life is just showing up. Durante, then 19 years old, proved as much on Sunday, October 1st, 1961, when his right field seat (Number 3, Box 163D, Section 33) allowed him to grab Roger Maris' 61st home run on the last day of the season.

Durante offered to hand over the historic ball for nothing, but Maris told him "you can make some money from it," so Durante accepted a $5,000 offer from a California collector and used the money for his pending wedding. Decades later, he said that catching No.61 still ranked up there with his marriage and kids' births as the biggest thrills of his life.

KARL EHRHARDT

Ehrhardt is a Met fan known for displaying colorful, punny signs throughout Shea during the 1969 pennant run and years afterwards. When Frank Robinson struck out in the '69 World Series, for instance, Ehrhardt wrote up a poster-board saying **"BACK TO YOUR NEST, BIRD!"** The Sign Man's finest moment probably came in 1973, when he helped popularize Tug McGraw's "ya gotta believe" as words to live by.

MAYOR RUDY GIULIANI

Some agree with his politics, some don't, but no one disputes Hizzoner's devotion to his favorite baseball team.

Giuliani decided to follow the Yankees despite growing up surrounded by Dodger followers in Clinton Hill, Brooklyn and Met fans in Garden City, Queens. He's stuck with them ever since, even during ceremonial occasions at Shea. When the Subway Series came around in 2000, for instance, the Mayor tipped his cap to the opposition but didn't kid anybody about his rooting interests. Rudy can still be spotted at Yankee Stadium all the time. A single, outstanding exception to annoying politician/ "fans" (#6).

BARRY HALPER

Barry Halper's mom never cleaned the baseball card collection out from his closet, and the world is vastly better for it.

A New Jersey native and lifelong sports junkie, Halper started gathering memorabilia as a teenager and never stopped. By the time he sold a 45-year-old collection in 1998, he'd amassed the greatest treasure trove outside of Cooperstown—it included over 30,000 cards (including complete sets for every season since 1890), over 1,000 uniforms (including one for every Hall of Famer), and nearly 100,000 publications, pieces of equipment, and rare tchotchkes (press pins, buttons, tie clasps, etc.). The priceless collection cost $21.8 million at auction.

All of the above were great, but the greatest fans of all are:

PARENTS

Millions of 'em, throughout greater New York. All the biological parents and parental stand-in's who take an interest in kids' lives and use sports to help them develop.

Parents are the ones who serve as volunteer coaches, role models, spectators/cheerleaders, catch partners, equipment organizers, ticket buyers, rule instructors, task masters, character builders, and community ambassadors. They're the greatest sports fans in the world, the ones who ensure that the games do count.

WHO HAVE BEEN THE MOST ANNOYING FANS OF ALL TIME?

 The most annoying of the annoying:

POLITICIANS

My fellow Americans, politicians are never very likable, but it's when they bring their trademark posturing and pandering to sports that they get truly offensive.

There's wishy-washy Mayor David Dinkins, known for his habit of wearing a Mets cap at Shea and a Yanks cap in the House that Ruth Built. There's patrician Governor George Pataki, who sipped white wine as he gazed upon the 2000 World Series. There's Chicago-born Hillary Clinton, who grew up with the Cubs but later proclaimed an acute interest in the Bronx Bombers (and New York's Senate seat). There's Mayor Michael Bloomberg, a lifelong Bostonian who also developed new allegiances just around the time he started running for office.

And there was ill-fated presidential candidate John Kerry of Massachusetts, who once stopped off in a Manhattan fundraiser to offer congratulations to . . . the Red Sox's biggest rivals.

"FIREMAN ED" ANZALONE

Anzalone is an authentic member of New York's Bravest and there's no doubting his 27 years (and counting) of loyalty to Gang Green, not to mention his trusty #42 Bruce Harper jersey and green fireman's hat. So far, so good.

The annoyance comes in how Fireman Ed habitually uses his perch in Section 133, Lower Tier to rally the Jets crowds. He climbs atop his brother's shoulders, makes wild motions to stir up some noise, extends his arms to command silence, then twists and contorts himself as 70,000 or so football fanatics scream in unison:

J!
E!
T!
S!
JETS!
JETS!
JETS!

Nice try, but there's a reason why no other team has adopted cheering-by-spelling—visiting teams aren't particularly frightened by a mass effort to outline a four-letter word.

THE BLEACHER CREATURES

Perfectly OK fan behavior: getting tipsy and rowdy, giving out-of-towners a hard time, dishing out some lewd and crude heckling.

Not-So-OK behavior: getting falling-down drunk, getting rough (or worse) with rivals' fans, screaming obscene or homophobic chants, showering visiting outfielders with coins and batteries.

Too often, some bad apples cross the line into the not-OK, giving all Creatures a bad name.

HILDA CHESTER

Possibly the most obnoxious fan in baseball history.

Chester was a plump spinster who rooted for the Brooklyn Dodgers from the 1920s into the 1950s, instantly recognizable for the way her clanging cowbell and foghorn voice would echo throughout Ebbets Field. Pete Reiser once said "there could be 30,000 people there yelling at once, but Hilda was the one you'd hear."

No one, including the home team, wanted to get on her bad side, so she was treated as an eccentric quasi-celebrity on Bedford Avenue. The Dodger front office presented her with a trademark cowbell and free lifetime attendance. Even the ever-abrasive Leo Durocher made a point of meekly waving over at her.

CELEBRITIES

Hey, it's a free country. Jon Stewart and Jerry Seinfeld can hog up the box seats at Shea if they want to. Puffy Combs, Bryant Gumble, and Barbara Walters are at liberty to take up Yankee Stadium's front row. Ditto for Susan Sarandon and Tim Robbins, the celebrities in residence for the Rangers at Madison Square Garden.

The problem comes when the networks feel obligated to feature several, lingering shots of The Beautiful People in each and every broadcast. At some point TV honchos apparently decided that someone, somewhere is going to watch a new show because its actors are eating weenies along the third base line. Nobody cares. Everyone's annoyed.

LOU STILLMAN

One old-timer said "Stillman was no sitcom character, a crusty exterior with a heart of gold . . . he was all crust." Was he ever.

As owner/dictator of Stillman's Gym in the 1940s and 1950s, the bitter ex-cop terrorized the toughest boxers in New York as they trained, yelling commands at the top of his lungs ("Get the hell out of the ring!"), hurling every racist epithet in the book, and tossing out any trainer or spectator who dared say a word about it. He carried a loaded .38 in his jacket at all times.

30

For all of Stillman's influence in boxing, it would have been a stretch to call him a fan of anything. He apparently hated everything and everyone, including boxers.

BERNARD "TOOTS" SHOR

The King of the Hangers-On.

Shor's midtown restaurant was the acknowledged place to be for an array of famous athletes, ambitious politicians, and celebrities from 1939 into the 1950s (#5), and did he milk it for what it was worth. He provided mediocre service and food while discouraging "broads," ignoring "nobodies," and kissing up to the comfortable. He never tired of bragging about the times his close personal friend Joe D. took him for a walk around the block. Eventually, the IRS shut down Toots Shor's for income tax evasion.

All very annoying, but you could argue that the most annoying New York sports fan of all time is:

SHELTON LEE

Spike was a born hoops fanatic while growing up in Fort Greene, well before he got a hold of a Hollywood-sized ego and prime seats at the Garden. The combination has not been pretty.

Lee's the worst of the worst wannabe jocks, constantly prancing around in his seat and talking trash as if he's being paid to play instead of paying to watch—it's almost enough to make you feel sorry for those in the $1,700-a-game section. It's never a good idea to motivate visiting NBA stars with choke gestures, and Lee's cheap theatrics probably cost New York Game Five of the '94 playoffs against the Pacers. (Reggie Miller responded by shoving 25 fourth quarter points down Lee's throat.)

Spike Lee is the most annoying fan of all time because he works at it. In the 1980's he made those Mars Blackmon/Nike ads with a prime contender for public enemy No.1, Michael Jordan (#73). He was at courtside while his children were being born. He wrote a book entitled *The Best Seat in the House* but didn't make a decent movie between *Malcolm X* and *Inside Man*. He once said, "I have great faith in Isiah Thomas. Give him time, he WILL turn it around." This is a fan who demands your annoyance.

WHAT ARE THE MOST MEMORABLE SPORTS QUOTES OF ALL TIME?

6 Loud. Obnoxious. Pushy. Rude.

New Yorkers have been called all those things, and a few more unprintable terms besides, and, let's face it, there's some truth to the labels. From Riverdale down to Great Kills and from the Upper West Side over to

South Jamaica, city residents can be found passionately arguing over their sports . . . and politics . . . and religion . . . and culture . . . and you name it. It's a way of life. Sports figures aren't prone to the same kind of talk, though, mostly because they know that reporters may toss bulletin-board fodder right back at them at the worst possible time. Still, in certain unguarded moments, they stop delivering safe, cliché-ridden commentaries and start echoing the outspoken fans around them. Over the years memorable quotes have included:

Stan has more friends than Leo Durocher has enemies.
—An opponent on the ethical, laid-back Stan Hack
*
We figured we'd better let them win one or they'd leave town.
And they left town anyway.
—Phil Rizzuto on the Dodgers' first-ever Subway Series victory in 1955
*
It was like having the girl you love tell you she's marrying
another guy because he has more money and
a new house in San Francisco.
—Vic Ziegel on the Giants' move in 1957
*
Her name is Mrs. Coleman and she likes me.
—'62 Met Choo Choo Coleman, when asked "What's your wife's name and what's she like?"
*
Reporter: What do you think is happening to the team?
The ship be sinking.
Reporter: How far can it sink?
Sky's the limit.
—Micheal Ray Richardson on the 1981–82 Knicks

Playing for Yogi was like playing for your father. Playing for Billy is like playing for your father-in-law.

—Don Baylor on the differences between managers Berra and Martin

*

Well, Merry F-----' Christmas to you, too.

—Jets backup quarterback Pat Ryan, after coach Joe Walton's post-practice diatribe on December 25th, 1986

*

Aren't they already?

—Lawrence Taylor, when asked, "Would you like drugs legalized?"

*

I've waited 20 years, 20 long years for this.

—Coney Island's Stephon Marbury reacts to his being drafted in the NBA. He was 19 years old at the time

*

Oakley is a-hackin' and a-wackin' and a-houndin' and a-poundin.'

—Clyde Frazier

A ZOO

The "Bronx Zoo" Yankees of 1977–78 must have been the most quotable team in sports history. Nothing and nobody was safe. Some of their gems:

Get it immediately, if not sooner.

—George Steinbrenner

*

The phone would ring in the middle of the night and you knew it was either Mr. Steinbrenner or a death in the family. After a while, you started to root for a death in the family.

—former public relations executive Harvey Greene

*

There's nothing quite so limited as being a limited partner of George Steinbrenner's.

—John McMullen

Lots of people look up to Billy Martin. That's because he just knocked them down.

—Jim Bouton

*

It's not that Billy [Martin] drinks a lot. It's just that he fights a lot when he drinks a little.

—*Daily News* columnist Dick Young

*

Me and George and Billy are two of a kind.

—Mickey Rivers

*

He quit baseball to become a star.

—Lou Piniella on backup catcher-turned-broadcaster Fran Healy

*

I didn't come to New York to be a star. I brought my star with me.

—Reggie Jackson

*

Well, you better stop readin' and writin' and start hittin'.'

—Mickey Rivers to Reggie Jackson. He'd just told Rivers, "I must be crazy. I've got an IQ of 160 and I'm arguing with a man who can't read or write."

*

It was an insurance homer—that's why I hit it half way to the Prudential Building.

—Reggie Jackson, on his RBI in the 1978 playoff against Boston

*

I unwrapped it and it told me how good it was.

—Catfish Hunter on the "Reggie" candy bar

*

If they want a third baseman they have me. If they want an entertainer, they should get George Jessel.

—Graig Nettles, after being fined for missing an organizational banquet. Jessel later sent him a telegram thanking him for the publicity

*

Cy Young to Sayonara.

—Graig Nettles on Sparky Lyle, an award winner in 1977 and trade bait in 1978

They were the most intense team I've ever seen. It was like being
in a bathtub with Jaws.
—Red Sox starter Bill Lee on the Boston Massacre series of September '78
*

Ain't no sense worrying about things you got no control over, 'cause if
you got no control over them, ain't no sense in worrying. And ain't no
sense worrying about things you got control over, 'cause if you got
control over them, ain't no sense worrying.
—Mickey Rivers on life

DIAMONDS

WAS MERKLE TO BLAME FOR MERKLE'S BONER?

8 Everyone's had the daydream at one time or another—you make the big play to break open a big game in the late innings. A 19-year-old rookie named Fred Merkle probably had that dream, too. Only, when he joined the New York Giants in 1908, his reality turned out differently.

In Merkle's big ball game, the first-place Giants were leading the Chicago Cubs by half a game in the ninth inning of a crucial pennant showdown. With Moose McCormick as the runner on third base and Merkle on first, Al Bridwell hit a two-out single well into the Polo Grounds' outfield gap. Merkle, spotting McCormick score the winning run at home plate, jogged off the field without bothering to advance to second base. He didn't have to, since the game was over.

Or so he thought.

Cubs infielder Charlie Evers hastily retrieved the ball, touched second base, and asked umpire Hank O'Day to call the absent Merkle out on a forceout. When O'Day obliged, the Cubs registered the third out of the inning, negating the Bridwell RBI, and pushing the contest into extra innings. With darkness approaching in the pre-lights Polo Grounds, the game was called as a tie, and what had been a Giants win became a lost opportunity.

Enraged New Yorkers immediately appealed O'Day's ruling to National League President Harry Pulliam, only to be denied. The tie game stood and turned out to be the crucial margin for the season when the Cubs and Giants finished with a flat-out tie in the standings (they both finished at 98-55 and split their season series at 11-11). When the two clubs met to finally decide matters on October 8th, the Cubs prevailed by a score of 4-2, so, when all was said and done, the September 23rd game cost New York a pennant.

Fred Merkle was immediately tagged with blame for the Giants' lost season (the *Times* called his baserunning "censurable stupidity"), but you could argue that he wasn't the main culprit, not at all.

To understand what happened, it's important to remember that, in those days, trailing runners rarely, if ever, bothered to touch the next bag on a winning run. It was almost always unnecessary to a game's outcome, of course, particularly on something like Bridwell's single, which was so well-hit that touching second would have been a mere formality.

The best confirmation of the standard practice came, ironically enough, from Evers and O'Day themselves. As it happened, Evers tried the same trick play with the umpire three weeks before, in a Cubs game against Pittsburgh, but O'Day, relying on the universally-accepted custom, refused to call out the Pirate runner. Exactly why O'Day had a sudden change of heart for the Giants-Cubs game is a complete mystery. At minimum, he should have given fair warning about his brand-new interpretation before he single-handedly decided the biggest game of the season.

Some might say, all right, though, you can't hand O'Day all the blame. Even if everyone played according to certain de facto rules, John J. McGraw and his Giants should have known that the formal guidelines required Merkle to touch second.

Technically, that's so. You can always insist that absolutely everything be done by the book every time, no matter what. That's theory, but then there's baseball.

Think of how modern Major Leaguers openly violate the letter of the rules as a matter of routine. For double plays, almost all middle infielders touch second base from the next zip code over, and catchers always block the third base line on a close throw at the plate. Both are flagrant and important violations, but all real-world players and umpires long worked out a silent agreement to allow something else. In those situations, custom still says no harm/no call, and there is no call.

If O'Day was completely out of line in his sudden insistence on formalities instead of well-established custom, an almost equal share of the blame has to go to NL President

Pulliam. Like O'Day, who faced down a hometown mob after the ball game, the Manhattan-based Pulliam showed a lot of gumption in upholding the decision. Unfortunately, though, courage wasn't much of a substitute for common sense. Pulliam should have been the one to insist that the Giants gain credit for a win they'd rightfully taken through their prowess on the field.

This would have taken some explanation on Pulliam's part, and undoubtedly made some enemies over in Chicago, but it would have been a triumph of common sense, much like the "Pine Tar Game" of July 1983. As New York fans well remember, George Brett's game-winning homer against the Yanks was nullified due to an illegal bat, but AL President Lee MacPhail promptly overruled the umpires' call on the field. To those who insisted "a rule is a rule is a rule," MacPhail found that the violation didn't matter to the natural course of the game, and that was the single most important factor. "Games should be won and lost through skill on the playing field—not through technicalities of the rules," he said and, in time, that good sense was vindicated.

Pulliam could have shown the same wisdom by applying the intent and spirit of the rules back in 1908. If he did, he would have saved Hank O'Day from his misjudgment, the New York Giants from second place, and poor Fred Merkle from some very unfair blame.

A HARSH FATE

The so-called Merkle's Boner incident, like the Buckner Game in the '86 World Series, has gone down as one of the signature events in the history of baseball. It turned out to be an exceptionally sad episode for everyone involved.

After the game, Fred Merkle said he "wished that a large, roomy, and comfortable hole would open up and swallow" him. He was called Bonehead for the rest of an unexceptional 16-year Major League career and avoided the Polo Grounds for decades after his retirement. When he passed away in 1956, age 68, his Associated Press obituary mentioned the September 23rd, 1908, disaster in the first paragraph.

It was a harsh fate, but it wasn't the worst one to come out of the Cubs-Giants contest.

After Chicago won the hotly disputed pennant of 1908 they beat the Detroit Tigers in a five-game World Series, but the Cub Nation has been waiting for another championship ever since. It's been the longest title draught in the history of American sports.

Finally, the fallout from the Merkle incident caused National League President Harry Pulliam, already under strain due to owner infighting, to slip into a deep depression. The 40-year-old suffered a nervous breakdown during the annual NL banquet a few months later, and he never did recover. On July 28, 1909, Pulliam checked into a room in the New York Athletic Club and took his own life.

WHO WAS THE BIGGEST YANKEE HATER OF THEM ALL?

9 It is possible to win too much and make too much money while doing it. No doubt about it.

The New York Yankees are living proof. They've earned 26 World Championships, a billion-dollar franchise valuation, and some bitter enemies over the years. The dominating do tend to arouse bad feelings over the dominated, and rivals have never particularly appreciated the Yankees' big-money, too-much-isn't-enough habits.

The Yankees have ill will in every corner of the National Pastime it seems, especially the Red Sox Nation and Metropolis, so picking out the single biggest Yankee hater should be one tough assignment. It isn't. This much is certain—no one ever hated, hated, hated the New York Yankees as much as old John J. McGraw.

The trouble started when McGraw served as player/manager for the Baltimore Orioles during the American League's inaugural season of 1901. Little Napoleon's confrontational ways and umpire-baiting soon sparked a feud with AL President Ban Johnson, and McGraw struck back by conspiring with John T. Brush, owner of the rival National League's

Giants, to entice Oriole stars to abandon their team. When the players all signed on with New York, McGraw effectively crippled Johnson's outpost in Baltimore. McGraw then quit and joined the Giants as manager in 1902.

Unfortunately for McGraw, revenge didn't prove very sweet, or long-lasting, either. Johnson opened peace talks with the NL during the 1902–03 off-season, offering to end the AL's own bidding wars in exchange for the rights to a new team in Gotham. When the National Leaguers took the deal, the remaining roster from the old Baltimore Orioles became the first New York Highlanders in 1903 (they'd change their name to Yankees a decade later).

Little Napoleon's Giants won the 1904 NL pennant but boycotted the World Series against the AL, leading to the only Series cancellation for 90 years. In the end, however, there was nothing he could do. McGraw's new ball club suddenly had some new competition. From McGraw's old ball club.

Strike One: The early Highlanders/Yankees foiled McGraw's plan to monopolize New York baseball outside Brooklyn.

In the first two decades of the twentieth century McGraw established himself as one of the most successful managers in baseball by employing what modern commentators would call "small ball"—he manufactured runs with walks, bunts, hit-and-runs, and stolen bases, that sort of thing. Unfortunately for McGraw, Yankees owner Jacob Ruppert noticed that a Red Sox player named Babe Ruth was playing a different game, one based on incredible home run production. Ruppert paid off the Sox and brought the Big Bam into town for the 1920 season.

McGraw railed and railed against Ruth's booming power game, saying that it was ruining baseball's fundamentals. He repeatedly claimed that the Bambino was overrated ("we pitch to better hitters in the National League"), too. It was to no avail. Gradually, the Major Leagues gave up on McGraw's push-'em-over-style and started going for the Yankees' brand of long ball.

Strike Two: The Yankees ruined McGraw's brand of "scientific baseball."

Before Babe Ruth showed up, Christy Mathewson and other stars helped the Giants finish in either first or second place in the NL for 13 of 17 years, even as their lowly neighbors mostly confined themselves to the second division. By 1912, the Yankees were so unpopular and broke that they were forced to move from old Hilltop Park (165th & Broadway) and into the Polo Grounds. The Yankees forked over 10 cents per fan to become cotenants/very junior partners to the mighty Giants.

Ruth's Yankees soon turned the tables on McGraw, however, winning their first pennant in the Bambino's first year. The 1920 Yankees also blew away the Giants' Major League record for paid attendance, becoming the first franchise to ever draw one million-plus in a season.

Suddenly, the pennant-winning Giants were the second most popular attraction in their own building, and a furious McGraw promptly evicted the upstarts, helpfully suggesting that they "move to some out-of-the-way place like Queens." The Yanks thought better of it, though, and decided to move a mere half-mile across the Harlem River. The Bronx Bombers dominated the Giants in attendance, year-in and year-out, for decades afterwards, and if you guessed most of those new Yankee fans were former Giants followers, you'd be right.

Strike Three: The Yankees took away McGraw's status as the most powerful team in baseball.

In the year of Yankee Stadium's debut, 1923, the Giants met them for the city's first Subway Series. McGraw refused to have the players dress in the Stadium locker room—the Giants dressed in the Polo Grounds, then took cabs to the Bronx.

Spite didn't do McGraw any good, however. After winning the 1921 and 1922 World Series over the Yankees, McGraw finally lost in '23. The black and orange, which had won eight pennants and three titles since 1904, ended up winning a single championship (1924) in his nine remaining years with the Giants, even as the plush, celebrated Yankees won four pennants and three titles. They were on their way to many, many more.

Strike Four: The dynastic Yankees took away from McGraw's championship aura.

For more than 20 years, McGraw's 1905 Giants—who fielded five future Hall of Famers and won 105 games while leading the league in runs per game, stolen bases, and fielding—were discussed as one of the greatest ball clubs of all time. When the 1927 Yanks came along, though, they put an end to all of that.

Strike Five: The stupendously great '27 Yankees made baseball forget McGraw's great '05 Giants.

McGraw retired in 1932 and died shortly afterwards, but the Yankees weren't finished with the Giants yet. They continued to outshine the "other" New York team, year after year, both in regular season standings and the Subway Series of 1936, 1937, and 1951 (they won a combined 12 games to the Giants' five). The last of the Series, in '51, came up in a rare year when the Giants made it past the Brooklyn Dodgers, only a former McGraw protégé named Casey Stengel skippered a certain pinstriped dynasty to an easy Series victory.

Finally, with McGraw too dead to do anything about it, a fed-up team owner up and left for California (#24). The widowed Mrs. McGraw was there, at the last home game, on September 29th, 1957, crying her eyes out. John McGraw's New York Giants had ceased to exist.

Strike Six: The Yankees helped Horace Stoneham wipe out McGraw's memory.

So, if and when the Yankees manage to destroy someone else's hometown lock ... style ... popularity ... championships ... glory ... and their very franchise, then historians can argue about the biggest Yankee hater of them all. Until then, the line starts behind the angry ghost of old John J. McGraw.

DID THE YANKEES' CARL MAYS COMMIT AN ON-FIELD MANSLAUGHTER?

10 **The time and place:** August 16th, 1920, the Polo Grounds, Morningside Heights, Manhattan.

The suspect: Carl William Mays, RHP, New York Yankees.

The victim: Raymond Johnson Chapman, SS, Cleveland Indians.

The incident: Mays, the Yankee starter, faced Chapman, the Indians' leadoff batter, in the fifth inning of a 3–0 game. After going to a 1–1 count, Mays' inside fastball struck Chapman, a right handed hitter, in the left temple.

Ray Chapman was rushed to nearby St. Lawrence Hospital with massive bleeding to the skull, but never regained consciousness. He was pronounced dead the following morning.

The witnesses: Players for both teams stated that Mays' submarine-style pitch was just on the edge of the strike zone, a hard fastball that tailed up and in as it crossed home plate.

Witnesses generally agreed that Chapman was crouching and crowding very near the plate at the moment of impact. Several players, including Yankee catcher Muddy Ruel, claimed the batter was positioned almost on top of the plate when he was struck.

The suspect's testimony: During interviews with the Manhattan District Attorney's Office, Mays repeatedly expressed great regret for Chapman's death but denied any attempt to knock him down or hit him. Mays declared he'd done nothing wrong.

The possible charge: Manslaughter—the unlawful killing of one human by another without express or implied intent to do injury (in other words, carelessness leading to a death).

Analysis: In the years before the beaning incident Carl Mays had established a notorious personal and professional reputation.

Former teammates from the Red Sox frequently complained about his antisocial and confrontational attitude. He had numerous disputes or fights with players like Ty Cobb and was reportedly one of the most reviled players in baseball. Some suspected Mays' teammates intentionally lost his starts in order to force his trade out of Boston.

Mays was well-known as an aggressive inside pitcher as well. He was first or second in AL hit batsmen in 1917, 1918, and 1919 and, prior to the 1920 season, he'd beaned 49 batters in 1,225 career innings pitched (roughly one batter for every 25 innings). It was one of the highest rates in Major League history, so if Mays did make a conscious attempt to throw at Chapman, the decision would hardly have been out of character. At least one ballplayer warned he could kill someone someday.

For all that, though, there are no solid reasons to believe Carl Mays wanted to hit Ray Chapman, and several reasons to believe he was trying to avoid it.

By all accounts, Ray Chapman was one of the best-liked players in the American League, and Mays and Chapman didn't have any previous run-ins. Chapman was primarily known as an able fielder and base runner and, while he hit well for average (.303 in 111 games in 1920), he didn't have extra-base power (.423 slugging on the year). Few pitchers feared Chapman enough to brush him back from the plate.

If anything, the details and circumstances of the game indicate that Mays was being careful to *avoid* hitting Chapman. The Yankees were almost tied for first place in the American League on August 16th, so a win was vital to the team. With Mays trailing by three runs in the game, he couldn't afford to hit Chapman and allow a new base runner/RBI opportunity for Indian sluggers like Tris Speaker.

Other factors in Chapman's background and game conditions indicate an accident.

Teammates from the Indians stated that Chapman had a reputation for crowding the plate, only dodging away from inside pitches at the last possible moment. He had reportedly frozen during his other beanings and, from the eyewitness accounts, that's exactly what happened during the Yankees-Indians game—Chapman made almost no move to get away from the ball. Mays' unusual submarine style may have contributed to the incident, and some believe Chapman's spikes may have caught in the batter's box.

In addition, unfavorable game conditions probably played an important role in the beaning.

The Major Leagues forced umpires to use the same baseballs throughout ball games and didn't have any rules providing for a clear hitting background at the ballpark. If they'd replaced the dirty old game ball, or given Chapman a better field of vision, he would have had a much better chance of picking up the ball's flight. As it was, he didn't have quite enough time to pick up the ball on a gray, drizzly afternoon.

Conclusion: No charges.

Carl Mays may have been an unpleasant person and an intimidating pitcher, but there's no evidence to believe that he acted recklessly. Ray Chapman's death was a terrible baseball tragedy, but it wasn't a crime.

THE BABE & BARRY— WHO WAS THE BETTER HITTER?

11 Only Home Depot has a hardware collection comparable to those of George Herman Ruth or Barry Lamar Bonds.

A charter member of the Hall of Fame, Babe Ruth defined the image of a Major League power hitter, retiring with the honors associated with no less than 56 Major League records. Ted Williams and Lou Gehrig, among many others, called him the best slugger who ever lived. More than 70 years after Ruth's last Major League game in 1935, the majority of present-day commentators agree.

Barry Bonds' resume has been similarly unapproachable in our own time. He's won a record seven Most Valuable Player trophies in the process of breaking Ruth's records for home runs in a season and a career, among other marks. In the new millennium, several experts have hailed Bonds as the greatest hitter alive, so if anyone can take on the Babe's Ruthian reputation, he's the one.

So, suppose you had a Major League ball club, a time machine, and a run to score. Which player should you chose? The Babe and Barry—who was the better hitter?

There are various ways to assess power hitters relative merits, but the best ways avoid unfair comparisons in career totals or skewed stats like home runs and RBIs. Career slugging percentage is a better measure, and it favors Ruth by a huge margin.

Ruth retired with a record .690 career slugging percentage that he blew away the AL's .397 slugging average for the years he played at least half a season as hitter (1919 to 1934). The Babe could be counted on to deliver 73.8 percent more extra-base power than the average AL hitter for sixteen years. He was that good.

Bonds was great, but he's never reached the Bambino's heights. From his rookie year of 1986 to the end of the 2005 season, Bonds' career slugging percentage of .611 has lagged behind Ruth, along with Ted Williams (.634), Lou Gehrig (.632), and Albert Pujols (.621). As the National League's slugging percentage has averaged .401 over that period, Bonds' numbers give him a smaller advantage, 52.4 percent, over the prototypical contemporary.

At his peak, Ruth also towered over his fellow ballplayers in a way that Bonds couldn't approach. For instance, in Ruth's best five-year period of 1920 to 1924, the Yankee slugger averaged a .774 slugging percentage. In an era where .396 was the AL norm, his slugging was 95.5 percent higher than the AL average. The Giants' Bonds did put up a higher (.782) slugging percentage in his 2000 to 2004 peak, but he did it in a hitter's era when the NL average stood at .425, so he didn't have the same relative advantage (84 percent) over his peers.

What about the second half of a hitter's job—his ability to get on base in the first place? Well, here again, Ruth and Bonds are in the same general ballpark, but the Bambino deserves the nod as the once and future king.

Ruth's .474 career on-base percentage is second only to Williams on the all-time list and comfortably ahead of Bonds' mark of .442. Ruth hit in an era where other hitters averaged a .349 OBP, meaning he made it on base about 35.8 percent more often. Bonds hit in an era where other league hitters averaged an OBP of .327, so, for all his patience at the plate, he got on base 35.1 percent more often over the course of his career.

The one thing that can be said in Bonds' favor is that his peak on-base performance surpassed Ruth's very best years. In the five-year stretch when Ruth was at his very best, he hit, walked, or otherwise got on base at a .501 clip, as opposed to the AL average of .352. Bonds outdid him in that, getting on base at a .535 clip versus the NL's average of .334. While the Babe was on base 42.3 percent more than the average player, Bonds surpassed his fellow hitters by 60.2 percent.

Whether due to lack of protection in the San Francisco lineup or an incredible eye for balls and strikes, peak-era Bonds succeeded in getting on base even more often than Ruth. With all those intentional and semi-intentional walks, it's fair to say Bonds may have been the most feared ballplayer of all time, at least in comparison to follow-up hitters like Benito Santiago or Pedro Feliz.

Finally, there's a single number that may make the clearest comparison between Ruth and Bonds. The invaluable Baseball Reference site has a metric called OPS ("on base plus slugging"), which combines career power and on base numbers. In those catchall numbers, Ruth's career OPS stood at 1.164 with Bonds behind at 1.053. In OPS+, which adjusts OPS for different ballparks' effects and standardizes them against league averages, Ruth outperformed the historic major-league average more than two times over. He's the only one who's ever done that.

An old-timer named Jimmy Reese once said that Babe Ruth was "the only man who ever lived up to his reputation." Maybe so. He is the one who put up effectively unbeatable career numbers, so while Barry Bonds may end up as the second best power hitter of all time, the No. 1 spot is still reserved for the Yanks' ole' #3.

THE BABE & BARRY— DO THE NUMBERS SPEAK FOR THEMSELVES?

When you pass someone, that makes you better. . . . . The numbers speak for themselves.
—Barry Bonds

Not so fast, BB.

Honestly, numbers don't speak for themselves. They never utter so much as a peep. They just lie there on a book page or computer screen. Nope, the numbers need people to speak for them, and people have to be guided by a sense of what the numbers really mean.

In Barry Bonds' case, passing Babe Ruth on the home run list certainly didn't mean he was better at hitting home runs on a day-to-day basis—if he was, Bonds wouldn't have needed an additional 800 at bats to pass Ruth's 714 career total. No, Bonds passed Ruth because he was nearly as good as Ruth for a much longer time. Like Hank Aaron, he only caught up to the Babe's total because he had so many extra chances to catch up to the Babe's total.

Nothing in the preceding chapter refers to career totals, and it's for that reason that career numbers are unfairly skewed by varying career lengths. The fact that one player happened to play more games than the other (Barry's 2,730 handily surpasses the Babe's 2,503) isn't nearly as significant as what he did on a daily basis.

In assessing power, it's also good to avoid tradition-bound measures like home runs and RBIs. Both power-hitting stats are somewhat useful in telling us how productive a slugger may be, but they both provide woefully incomplete pictures.

As writers like Bill James have pointed out, homers are the single most valuable play in the game, but an exclusive focus on them overlooks how a slugger can make important contributions through triples and doubles. RBI numbers, similarly, tell us that a hitter's doing an important job in driving in runs, but those stats can't account for the way productive teammates boost a particular player's stats while relatively weak lineups decrease them. Only slugging percentage tells us how many bases a hitter picks up in the average at bat, so that's a better measure of a player's all-around power hitting.

Finally, batting average and hits aren't very useful in assessing a player's ability to get on base, because those are incomplete and deceptive statistics, as well. A player's job isn't to hit safely as often as possible, but to reach base safely as often as possible, and that can come through bases or balls or times hit by a pitch. Little League coaches love hits, of course, but also advise that "a walk's as good as a hit" and players sometimes have to "take one for the team." Because they're exactly right, it's a good idea to

57

bypass batting average for the more comprehensive "on-base percentage" (OBP).

THE BABE & BARRY— WHO WAS THE BETTER ALL-AROUND PLAYER?

13 So Babe Ruth was a better hitter than Barry Bonds. End of the argument? Hardly. More like the beginning.

After all, there are more facets to the game than hitting. There's baserunning, fielding, and pitching, to name three, and even if Bonds falls short of Ruth at the plate, he can still, theoretically, make up for that with superior numbers on the base paths, outfield, and mound. Bonds can still establish himself as the better overall player, if not the better hitter.

And, as fate would have it, Bonds has displayed marked superiority over Ruth in a couple aspects of the game, starting with baserunning.

It may not be well remembered in his muscle-bound, lumbering presence, but it was a lanky Barry Bonds who came up to the major leagues as leadoff hitter for the Pirates. In time, he eclipsed his godfather, Willie Mays, as the greatest combination of speed and power the game has ever seen.

When Bonds debuted in 1986, there had been only 11 occasions when a player had hit as many as 30 home runs while stealing 30 or more bases (five of those seasons came from Barry's father, Bobby). By the time Bonds had played 16 full seasons, though, he'd averaged more than 30 stolen bases and 35 home runs a year. To date Bonds is the only man to hit more than 500 major league home runs while stealing more than 500 bases. In fact, he's the only major leaguer to hit as many as *400* homers while stealing *400* or more bases. He's been the only one to out-slug every runner and out-run every slugger.

Bonds redefined the art of theft in the context of the power game largely because he was so heady. He's only been caught stealing 141 times in 647 attempts, giving him a gaudy 78.2 percent success rate that compares favorably with Tim Raines and Rickey Henderson—among the best of all time. The ultimate testament to Bonds' prodigious power may be the fact that his remarkable speed isn't remarked upon more often.

The fact is, Ruth wasn't anywhere in Bonds' league as a man of steal. Blame it on exhaustion from big swings or those surprisingly thin legs, but the Babe only stole 123 bases from 1918 to 1934 and, even worse, his 51.3 percent success rate ranks him as one of the dumbest runners of all time (67–72 percent or so is considered a minimum for productive runners). Babe Ruth wasn't all that bad a runner—he was atrocious.

While Bonds effectively used his running to convert more than 500 singles into doubles or doubles into triples, thereby enhancing his power numbers to even greater heights, Ruth's running game only hurt his offensive presence. If he wasn't touring the bases on a leisurely home run trot, he spent his time on base either A) staying put/clogging up the base paths, or B) running/wiping out potential runs by being caught. There are no reliable stats on double plays for the 1920's and 1930's, but it's more than likely that Ruth's slowness led to more than a few twin killings, too.

Barry Bonds used his legs to outpace Babe Ruth in another important aspect of his game, and that's defense.

There are excellent reasons why Barry has eight Gold Gloves in his trophy case, tied for fifth among all major league outfielders. Playing the overwhelming majority of his games in left field, he had a career fielding percentage of .985 as compared to a NL average of .981 (he was more sure-handed than the average NL outfielder in 17 of his 20 career seasons). Moreover, Bonds got to a lot of balls, too. Bonds' range factor, calculated by assists and put-outs per game, comes out to 2.24 in comparison to the NL average of 1.92. To put that in context, Bonds' range factor differential of .32 sets him dead even with Brooks Robinson. Granted, left field isn't as important a defensive position as third base, but, clearly, Bonds has been one of the superior outfielders of his time.

Ruth, again, flunks when it comes to defense. In six of 17 years where he played at least half a season in the field, the Babe's fielding percentage was lower than the AL average. He made enough errors that his mediocre .968 mark barely outpaced the .966 league average. Even worse, Ruth had bad putout and assist numbers, putting up a 2.07 range factor as a right fielder as compared to the AL's average of 2.22 (he was below average in 11 of 15 full seasons). While Bonds spent a lot of his time in the outfield running down line drives, cutting off extra bases, and gunning down runners, Ruth apparently spent a lot of his time in the outfield standing in the outfield.

Perhaps the big guy just couldn't run or perhaps he considered his job finished when he walloped balls way over the field of play. Either way, there's little doubt that Ruth's mediocre-to-terrible defense was a huge liability. When contemporary writer Grantland Rice called his hero "a star defensive outfielder who could be rated with the best," he must have been preoccupied with the Bambino's lumber rather than his leather.

So there you have it. With Barry Bonds dominating Babe Ruth as a base stealer and a fielder, the Giant has a compelling case as a better all-around . . .

Oh, wait a second.

There's one last thing to consider.

Pitching.

As lopsided as the Bonds-Ruth comparisons may be in baserunning and fielding, they're completely one-sided in terms of pitching. Multitalented as Bonds might have been through his two decades, he hasn't thrown an inning as a major league hurler. Babe Ruth threw 1,221 of them, and he did so in awe-inspiring fashion.

As just about every fan knows, Ruth originally came up as a Red Sox pitcher in 1914 and, if not for his batting talents, he surely would have established himself as a Hall of Famer. It's hard to overemphasize just how good the man was.

In his first full year, 1915, Ruth already distinguished himself among league leaders in wins (18), winning percentage (.692), hits allowed per nine innings (6.86), and strikeouts per nine (4.63). By his second year, 1916, he set a still-standing AL record by putting up nine complete game shutouts while leading the league in ERA (1.75) while finishing among league leaders in hits per nine innings (6.17) and strikeouts (170). In 1917 and 1918, his last years as a full-time pitcher, it was much the same, with a very young Ruth ranking alongside veterans like Walter Johnson and Pete Alexander as the best pitchers in baseball.

Babe Ruth gave up pitching only because his superstardom in a four-man rotation yielded to something like super-super-stardom in an everyday lineup, and that's the difficulty in the comparisons. With Barry Bonds taking such a commanding lead in stolen bases and fielding stats, and the Babe taking an equally formidable lead in pitching, the two were completely apples-and-oranges in their skills away from the plate.

Still, if numbers don't resolve the mess, maybe common sense can.

Imagine, hypothetically, you were presenting scouting reports on two young players who were exact equals as hitters. However, Player A can give you world-beater speed and defense over the course of his career. Player B will always exhibit subpar speed and defense, but can offer four plus years of service as a Cy Young-caliber pitcher. Which player would you expect a canny talent evaluator to prefer?

Perhaps some would choose Player A, Bonds, but my guess is that the majority would opt for Player B, Ruth. The Bambino would win. Perhaps it would be a draw between the two, but if that's the case, Ruth still wins, because it's up to Bonds to overcome the Babe's big advantage in hitting. For those reasons, you could argue that Babe Ruth is still the greatest baseballplayer of all time. As Mike Schmidt once said, "He'll always be the guy."

THE BABE & BARRY— WHAT ABOUT THE DIFFERENT HISTORICAL ERAS?

14 No one compares the twenty-first century's cars to 1920s-vintage Model T's.

No one's out there detailing the culture, or politics, or the anything from today in relation to those of their great-grandparents' days. Certainly, no one compares football or basketball players across the generations. That's too ridiculous to merit an effort.

So why compare baseball players?

After all, no one can deny that baseball's off-field conditions have changed drastically over seven or eight decades. In the days before Jackie Robinson, white ballplayers never had to face-off against quality ballplayers from minority communities. Modern-day conditioning was unknown, and pitchers hadn't invented pitches like sliders and split-finger fastballs. Bat and ball equipment has undergone drastic changes in the last eight decades. In the 1920s, also, teams played a 154-game schedule that didn't include night games.

With all those changes in play, it shouldn't make any sense to compare a 1920s/1930s-era player like Babe Ruth to a new millennium ballplayer like Barry Bonds.

But it does.

The game of baseball has changed over the years, that's for certain, but it's done so in relatively predictable, manageable ways. Comparisons across time are always debatable, but they're also open to some pretty informed, if imperfect, judgments.

Take the argument that Babe Ruth's records deserve an unofficial asterisk because he never competed against the best of the best African-American and dark-skinned Latino players of his era. With all-white baseball cut off from so many talented ballplayers, some say that Ruth's numbers should be discounted relative to the fully diversified, international game of today.

It's possible to make that call, but it's just as valid to assume that Ruth would have ended up with roughly the same numbers no matter who he played against.

The fact is, Ruth did play against dark-skinned players on dozens of important occasions—during his many off-season barnstorming tours across the United States and in Cuba. The integrated games may not have counted in the major-league standings, but they surely mattered to the minority-community players and audiences involved. For them, the Babe's visits may have amounted to an unofficial World Series.

How did Ruth do in those integrated-game performances? Fantastic, as usual. One historian has come across detailed accounts of 60 Ruth at bats and found that the Bambino hit .400 with 11 home runs and a contemporary, Negro Leaguer Judy Johnson, laughed at the notion that black pitchers could have done much to stop the Bambino. Ruth was an equal-opportunity slugger.

Would a born talent like the Babe have fallen behind modern-day athletes who routinely work out in everything from weight lifting to isometric stretching? Again, there's a little room for doubt, but plenty of reason to give Ruth the benefit of the doubt.

Young George H. Ruth grew up with an iron constitution and barrel-chested physique, so what were often mistaken for out-of-control habits and flab were closer to oversized appetites and a uniquely stout, muscle-bound build. There have always been tall tales matching Ruth's rowdy off-field hedonism to his on-field exploits, but he certainly wasn't a John Goodman-type fat man—he spent most of his career carrying an estimated 235–240 lbs. on a 6'2"/6'3" frame. From what we know, he was a fairly disciplined athlete, too. It's rarely mentioned, but he was one of the first Major Leaguers to hire a pro trainer and work out on a fairly regular schedule during the off-season.

The best proof of Ruth's work ethic was the fact that he was one of the most durable young pitchers (averaging nearly 40 games per year) and hitters of his era (averaging more than 140 games per year from 1920 to 1934, with the exception of a surgery year in 1925). If Ruth was gorging on various meat products 10 hours a day, there's no way he would have outlasted all but a handful of his contemporaries over the course of a 22-year career. As it was, he was still the third best hitter in the American League at the fairly ancient age of 39.

Ruth's push-up-and-jumping-jack routines had nothing on today's workouts, of course, but that cuts both ways, doesn't it? Just imagine what he could have done if he had access to the modern weight equipment and the nine-figure contract incentives to make the most of it. There's every reason to believe he would have ended towering over today's players much the same way he towered over yesterday's players.

The story goes on like that, all down the line. For all the points against Ruth's greatness, there are just as many counterpoints boosting his case:

• The Sultan of Swat never faced-off against competitors drawn from today's global talent pool, but he did play at a time when the game attracted an unprecedented percentage of available athletes. Since baseball was almost the only big-money sports option for aspiring athletes in the 1920s and 1930s, a disproportionate number of great athletes tried their hand at the National Pastime back then.

- The Babe never faced-off against relief specialists, but the starting pitchers of his era utilized softer game balls and benefited from significantly deeper ballpark power alleys. Historian John Thorn once estimated that nearly 800 Ruthian blasts would have landed beyond the fences of twenty-first century ballparks.

- Ruth never had to face down sliders, but he did face down legal spitballs. (They were banned in 1920, but grandfathered AL pitchers were allowed to use them for the rest of their careers.)

- The Bambino didn't play a 162-game season, but his 154-game season was filled with multiple off day exhibitions that were all but mandatory for the biggest gate attraction in American sports.

- Ruth never played a night game, but he did have to battle against intense daytime heat, expanding afternoon shadows, and dim hitting backgrounds. And just imagine what he would have done with modern-day batting helmets, body armor, and sculpted, rock-hard bats.

The Bambino's career was a product of a very different time, and we'll never know what one would have done in another era, not in any definitive way. Still, there are a lot of solid reasons to believe Ruth would have overcome the modern day's playing challenges, largely through the modern day's competitive advantages. In all probability, the greatest hitter of all time would have been great in any time.

THE BABE & BARRY— WHAT ABOUT THE STEROIDS MESS?

15 There's another reason why many commentators believe that Babe Ruth and Barry Bonds can't be compared, and that has to do with Bonds' alleged dabbling in modern chemistry.

The steroid issue deserves a thorough book in its own right, so this is hardly the cramped little space to settle anything. I'd just note the following, which are too often hidden in plain sight:

1. Despite three years, two grand juries, and millions of taxpayer dollars spent, there's still no hard evidence that Bonds intentionally took steroids—no prescriptions, no physical evidence, no payments. The witnesses testifying against him range from vengeful ex-girlfriends to ex-employees to leaking, anonymous cops.
2. Bonds has been tested for steroids on multiple occasions. He's passed every time.
3. Bonds has never been charged with a thing.

All that is verifiable and knowable, as are the many reasons why Bonds has been playing clean. He's talked about his father's All Star genes, his childhood apprenticeship among Major Leaguers, his career-long track record for hitting greatness, his work in an unprecedented hitter's era, his well-documented workouts, his perfectly legal nutrition aids, his phenomenal batting eye, and his reputation as "the smartest ballplayer in the game."

At the very least, there's no conclusive evidence against Bonds, and in the absence of conclusive evidence, you shouldn't pronounce a man guilty until proven innocent. That may be a minority view, but it is in line with the best American principles for fairness. For now, at least, Barry Bonds' numbers should stand.

LOU & CAL JR.—WHO WAS TOUGHER?

16 Long before Cal Ripken Jr. broke Lou Gehrig's decades-long record for 2,130 consecutive games played in 1995, both ballplayers were known for always showing up to play, every game and every year. Their names will always be linked—Gehrig & Ripken, Ripken & Gehrig, two iron men representing the gold standard of durability in the longest, most grueling schedule in sports.

At the end of the day, Gehrig's 2,130 and, later, Ripken's 2,632 represented more than streaks, or even their authors' stubborn refusal to give in or give up. Because they played thousands of games in a row, they represented their authors' claim to being the toughest of all Hall of Famers. But, superlatives being superlatives, only one player can be No. 1.

So . . . Cal Ripken Jr. and Henry Louis Gehrig—who was the toughest ballplayer of all time?

In the first, most obvious, comparison, Ripken simply blows Gehrig away. It's important to note that Ripken didn't break Gehrig's record as much as shatter it, playing as he did three straight years after he had the consecutive game record all to himself. In compiling more than 2,600 straight games from May 30, 1982, to September 20, 1998, he extended Gehrig's original mark by another 501 games, or more than 23 percent.

To put gap in perspective, consider it in comparison to other elite career records. For some future power hitter to overtake Hank Aaron's home run record in the way that Cal outlasted Lou, for instance, he'd have to hit 930 home runs (more than twice as many as Hall of Famer Duke Snider). For a pitcher to overtake Nolan Ryan's career strikeout total by a similar margin, he'd have to ring up 7,038 K's (more than twice as many as, say, Cooperstown's Walter Johnson). Not for nothing has analyst Pete Palmer called Ripken's final games-played total the most unbeatable major league record out there.

Without a doubt, Ripken stands alone in overall durability, but that doesn't have to be the be-all-and-end-all in the debate. Everyone knows that ALS disease cut down Gehrig, ending not only his streak, but his career and, eventually, his young life.

The terrible irony is that the one of the toughest of Hall of Famers was the youngest to pass away, and it just feels wrong to dismiss Gehrig's achievements, not due to any shortage of will and work, but terrible luck. He played his last full season at age 35 and, if given the blessing of good health, there's every reason to believe that he'd have played at least as long as Ripken, maybe longer.

If it's not fair to make a direct comparison based on Ripken's final game record, it does seem fair to ask which ballplayer had to endure more while playing on a daily basis. A rough, indirect sense of that can be gained from the players' batting and fielding numbers.

Consider the offensive stats. Ripken, as you'd expect, blows Gehrig away in career at-bats (11,551 vs. 8,001), but Gehrig still achieved far more at the plate on a game-by-game basis. Ripken's lifetime .340 on-base percentage lags far behind the Yankee's .447 OBP, which means that Ripken garnered significantly fewer hits and walks per game (1.437 vs. 1.954).

Power hitting comparisons are even more lopsided in Gehrig's favor, with Ripken's .447 lifetime slugging percentage up against Gehrig's phenomenal .632 average.

Ripken's relative lack of power meant that he ran to fewer total bases per game (1.722 vs. 2.338) and, not so coincidentally, he scored fewer runs per game, too (0.549 vs. 0.872). To top it off, Ripken was a lead-footed runner, with only 36 career stolen bases in 39 attempts, while Gehrig stole 102 bases in 203 attempts.

Gehrig's superior hitting wasn't just evidence of superior skill, but good evidence of superior toughness as well. Hitting for percentage and power meant that Gehrig inevitably legged out far more hits, took far more extra bases, suffered far more collisions, and tore up far more base paths. With the typical ball game taking more out of him, it's fair to say that the Yankee captain displayed more toughness on a day-in, day-out basis, too.

Unfortunately, if Gehrig has a clear-cut edge over Ripken in his offense, the fielding comparison isn't nearly as simple. Ripken split his time between shortstop (2,302 games) and third base (675 games), with the former involving all kinds of double play relays/collisions while the latter spot called for less contact but even more diving and relays. Gehrig, meanwhile, played all but 10 out of 2,147 career games at first base, which meant that he had to hustle after far more balls put in play. As you might expect, Ripken put up far more assists (8,214 vs. 1,087) and completed an impressive 1,565 double plays, but lagged way behind Gehrig in career putouts (4,112 vs. 19,525).

Basically, the defensive comparison is a toss-up based on

judgment calls. If you believe diving after ground balls, throwing across the diamond, and facing down base runners on double plays makes for the better test for physical toughness, you've got to favor Ripken. He may have played more demanding defensive positions on the left side of the infield. If you put more emphasis on the hustle involved in a first baseman's fielding and constant hustle, though, then you have to favor Gehrig.

To be honest, neither side has a monopoly on the merits. It's a toss up.

During his record-breaking game, Ripken took a victory lap around Camden Yards and made an eloquent speech to salute Gehrig. On the memorable night of September 6th, 1995, he stated, "I believe our true link is a common motivation, a love of the game of baseball, a passion for our team, and a desire to compete at the highest level." No one was about to disagree, then or now, and Cal Ripken Jr. will always be bound to Gehrig in those values.

Now, getting a sense of their relative greatness, that's the tough part.

LOU & CAL JR.— DOES IT MAKE SENSE TO COMPARE THEM?

17 There's no denying that Lou Gehrig and Cal Ripken Jr. played in vastly different eras, which means comparing them has to account for some vastly different playing conditions.

When Gehrig was active from 1923 to 1939, he played 154-game seasons, started games in the daytime, and made do without modern medical assistance. All that had changed by the time of Ripken's playing career in the 1980's and 1990's, and that's the divergence that creates all sorts of complications.

How much credit should Ripken receive for playing eight extra contests in a 162-game season, or for making dozens of extra coast-to-coast road trips? Should you salute his maintaining a blue-collar work ethic despite his guaranteed multimillion dollar contracts?

On Gehrig's side, how much credit should you give for his survival without modern medical assistance? The man didn't have highly-paid, highly-trained pros to care for his countless bumps and bruises, stiffness and soreness, strains and sprains, tweaks and tears, etc. When he retired, doctors found he'd suffered 17 fractures in the bones of his hands, all of them untreated. And how can you account for his enduring all those extra ball games in the hot, bright sunlight anyway?

Neither player played every inning of every game, or played according to the same rules as far as the designated hitter. Should those details count in the comparison?

At the end of the day, there are no definitive answers for any of the above, and anyone who tells you otherwise is lying. In setting Ripken and Gehrig side-by-side, you have to ignore some of the realities of their respective eras or, perhaps, hope that the varying conditions more or less cancel each other out. Either option will work.

WHAT WOULD HAVE HAPPENED IF JACKIE ROBINSON FAILED?

18 Everyone knows the success story.

When General Manager Branch Rickey gave Jackie Robinson the opportunity to become the first black ballplayer in the twenieth century, the second baseman faced down racists' vicious resistance to erase baseball's color line. From 1947 on, Robinson became a standout Brooklyn Dodger, a Hall of Famer, and a pioneer for generations of minority athletes. In time, his name became synonymous with the possibilities in American courage and American opportunity. A Jackie Robinson is a groundbreaking leader.

Everybody knows Jackie Robinson. He succeeded. What we'll never know is what would have happened if the story turned out differently.

Imagine, just for a minute, if Robinson didn't maintain his poise against the constant abuse he endured from opposing players and opposing fans. What would have happened if he fought back against his tormenters with equally violent words or actions? Major league pitching was enough to crack any 28-year-old rookie, even if he didn't have to deal with a barrage of beanballs and off-field death threats. What if he washed out in that summer of '47? What would have happened if Jackie Robinson failed?

Robinson would have been dismissed.

He would have been labeled an outside activist and/or hothead. Undoubtedly, the editors of *The Sporting News* (baseball's bible) would have concluded they were vindicated in saying blacks didn't have the intelligence or inner fortitude to succeed on the highest level.

An estimated 60 percent of the Major Leaguers of 1947 were white southerners who'd never known anything but racial segregation, and every one of them, including high-profile players like Enos Slaugher, Dixie Walker, and Bobby Bragan, would have been treated as heroes for calling anti-Robinson boycotts. Those who had stood with Robinson, the Pee Wee Reeses of the world, would have been the marginalized ones.

It wouldn't have been long before repercussions from the failure reached Rickey. In January 1947, he fought a unanimous establishment on the race question—team owners voted 15–1 against Negro League recruiting, claiming that mixed rosters would ruin the business of baseball. With a Robinson failure, those hard-liners would have only been emboldened, even as the Dodgers became even more outcast in areas like scouting. In a worst case scenario, owner Walter O'Malley would have fired Rickey altogether.

A Robinson embarrassment would have also set back a whole generation of Brooklyn players, too. The reaction would have encouraged even more hostility and controversy around blacks, so it's highly unlikely that the team would have tried again, at least not for years to come. The heart of the 1940's and 1950's Dodgers—Roy Campanella, Don Newcombe, Joe Black, Junior Gilliam—would have been shut out of the big club, and without them, it would have been highly-unlikely-going-on-impossible for the Dodgers to win six pennants and a world championship over the next decade.

Jackie Robinson's failure would have been portrayed as the failure of integration as a whole, and its fallout would have extended to all minority ballplayers. They would have been told they were better off among their own kind, then shuttled off to the Negro Leagues' cut-rate wages, second-rate ballparks, third-rate facilities, and fourth-rate crowds. Doors would have slammed shut once again. No matter how hardworking or talented, dark-skinned players throughout America and the world would never compete against the best white players.

With Robinson out of the way, the major leagues would have reverted to the 60-plus years when an unwritten gentleman's agreement kept all rosters all white. It was founded on a centuries-old American tradition, the one that said that the races were better left separated and unequal. The color line would have been held up as the natural order of things, in baseball and football and basketball, too. In all walks of life. "The coloreds have to know their place," it was said. The whole context of American achievement would have been unchanged, so baseball wouldn't have aided civil rights, not in any meaningful sense. Without Robinson, a college student named Martin Luther King would have lost one of his great heroes.

New York would have been a different place if Jackie Robinson failed. The "I'm for Jackie!" buttons of April '47 would have become novelties. The most ethnically diverse city in the world wouldn't have been exposed to daily reminders of the way the races could work together as a whole, united by a shared commitment to excellence. That bond wouldn't exist. White kids would have had their white role models, black kids would have had their black role models. Just like before, just like always.

It's tempting to think all the above is an extreme, nightmare scenario for Jackie Robinson's failure, but history gives many reasons to believe it would have been all too likely.

Jackie Robinson was an extraordinary man, perhaps the only one who could have stood up to the pain and stress involved in defying the worst racism of the late 1940's. If Robinson couldn't have born the burden, even for one weak moment, then his attackers would have had all the excuse they needed to exclude him, and from then on, history would have taken a very different course. The absurd status quo would have grown even stronger, and the progress and positives of the great experiment would have become its lost momentum and frustrations. Color would have defeated character.

Changes couldn't have been denied forever, but Robinson's failure would have deferred them indefinitely. Rickey believed that it would have set the game back 20 years or more, and there's little reason to believe he was exaggerating. Even as it was, respectable, nay, legendary, sports figures like Adolph Rupp and Bear Bryant were maintaining an institutional color line well into the late 1960s, claiming those who believed in anything else were radicals and agitators.

Robinson's real-world impact has been so great and so positive that it's tempting to take for granted. Modern society, as imperfect as it may be, has steadily moved toward far more tolerance and diversity in the years after 1947. Jackie Robinson changed baseball and he changed America. Today, everyone knows he succeeded.

WHO WAS THE MOST UNDERRATED STAR IN YANKEE HISTORY?

19 Ballplayers in markets smaller than New York have always griped that they don't get the attention and respect they deserve. Stars supposedly benefit from oversized reputations in the Big Apple, what with all that media capital of the world thing going on, and great players just don't expect the same treatment in Oakland and St. Petersburg.

You know, there might be some truth to the pro-New York bias. The guys down the street from all the newspapers and TV cameras do tend to get more ink and face time. Many Pastime historians believe that New York-based athletes from Dave Bancroft to Phil Rizzuto have made it into the Hall of Fame based more on good, plentiful press than Hall-worthy numbers.

Still, it's possible that at least one New York mainstay has remained overlooked through the years, so much so that he's been denied in his own Cooperstown credentials. That would be one Allie Pierce Reynolds, the most underrated star in New York Yankees history.

Reynolds put up a workmanlike 51–47 career record with the Cleveland Indians by the time he was traded to the Yanks before the 1947 season, but he transformed from so-so to star in the Bronx, utilizing plus-fastballs, sharp sliders, and slow curves to put up a spectacular 131–60 record in eight straight winning seasons. In six of those campaigns, Reynolds placed among American League leaders in wins. More than 50 years after his 1954 retirement, he still ranks among the top 50 in all-time winning percentage.

Without a doubt, Reynolds' winning was helped along by his teams' strong lineups. There's no denying that a pitcher's life gets easier when he's backed by the likes of Joe DiMaggio and Mickey Mantle, but Reynolds' career numbers are just as good as they look.

The fact is, Reynolds' teams were winners largely *because* Reynolds was a winner—his career .686 win percentage in pinstripes was far superior to his fellow pitchers' .636 overall average. Put another way: when someone other than Allie Reynolds picked up the decision, the 1947–54 Yankees won at a rate that would work out to 96 wins over a 154-game schedule. When Reynolds decided the ball game, though, they played at a clip that would amount to an average 106 wins per season. This despite Casey Stengel's habit of saving his ace for the toughest pitchers in the league.

The fact is, it was Reynolds' record that made champions look good, not the other way around. It's impossible to say what would have happened if he wasn't in the rotation—the Yanks might have found another diamond from some other rough—but as it happened, Reynolds' strong performances were the foundations for several pennant runs.

And he got even better in October.

SuperChief lived up to the nickname in the World Series between 1947 and 1953. Reynolds put up a 7–2 record and 2.79 ERA, with two complete game shutouts in nine post-season starts. Today Reynolds still ranks No. 2 in all-time World Series wins (Whitey Ford won three more but played an additional seven games), No. 3 in strikeouts, and No. 5 in winning percentage for those with 50 or more innings pitched.

The trio of Reynolds, Eddie Lopat, and Vic Raschi were collectively known as the Big Three but, based on those numbers, it would be more accurate to call Allie the Big One. It's no wonder that the teammate that knew him best, Hall of Famer Yogi Berra, once said "I thought that Allie was as tough a money pitcher as there ever was." Coincidentally or not, Reynolds' Yanks went 6-0 in their Series against Brooklyn, Philadelphia, and the New York Giants.

The secret to Reynolds' success was in his superior combination of power and control—he consistently produced strikeouts (five finishes among the AL leaders in K's per nine innings) while rarely giving away free passes (six straight seasons among league leaders in walk to strikeout ratio). Batters were forced to hit their way on, but they rarely did, as Reynolds led AL pitchers in opponent batting average five times. That's why few were surprised when Reynolds threw two no-hitters in the same season (1951), something that's only been done four times in the last 130 years.

As incredible as Allie Reynolds' performances may have been, he was probably even more impressive in his durability and versatility. Reynolds was a workhorse—he averaged nearly 30 starts per season from 1947 to 1952, finished among league leaders in complete games three times, and racked up 36 complete game shutouts. However, he was so good and so strong that Casey Stengel frequently brought him in on the off days between starts. Reynolds was spectacular in those save situations, too, putting up a 15–9 record with 41 saves and 2.87 ERA in the regular season to go along with four saves in five World Series chances.

In effect, Allie Reynolds was both an ace starter/lights-out reliever for years on end, and how unique was that? Stengel, who was in and around the Majors for over 50 years, once said, "he's the best at the two things that I've ever seen." Stats guru Bill James agreed, saying that no one's been better in switching back and forth between the rotation and the bullpen.

It's safe to say that today's babied starters will never attempt that kind of pitching punishment, much less succeed in it. And, yet, here again, Reynolds may have been punished for his success. Reynolds didn't reach 200 career wins, but we'll never know what kind of totals the ace would have put up if he was fully rested. Anyway, forget the numbers for a sec. Who wouldn't want a pitcher who was, in effect, two pitchers in one, a guy selfless and durable enough to pull out games in both starts and relief appearances?

So, in conclusion, Allie Reynolds' career featured superb winning, clutch performance, power and control, versatility . . . and no Hall of Fame recognition. He hasn't come close. Why?

It's tempting to blame a lack of knowledge. The voters may not realize that Reynolds' career winning percentage places him ahead of more than a dozen Hall of Famers, including the likes of Bob Feller and Cy Young. They may not be aware of his acknowledged leadership in one of the greatest baseball dynasties or some of the most spectacu-lar World Series numbers of all time. It's possible they overlooked all his league-leading stats and forgot about his once-in-a-lifetime versatility, too.

It may all be some big mistake. Or anti-New York bias.

CHUCK DRESSEN—WAS HE THE REAL GOAT OF THE '51 DODGERS' PENNANT COLLAPSE?

20 Ralph Branca was doomed. He's always been blamed.

When Branca came in as relief for the Brooklyn Dodgers during the third and final game of the 1951 National League playoffs, his job was simple—maintain a 4–2 lead over the arch-rival Giants. Put away slugger Bobby Thomson, or at least keep him in the ballpark. Just get a couple outs to finish off the ninth inning, win the ball game, and take the NL pennant.

But Branca was doomed.

An inside 0-1 pitch ended up as a middle-of-the-plate offering and, 315 feet later, flew into memory as one of the most famous home runs of all time, the fabled Shot Heard 'Round the World. In the words of broadcaster Russ Hodges, "The Giants win the pennant, the Giants win the pennant, the Giants win the pennant . . ."

OK, OK. Branca didn't get the job done. If goat status is all about being the wrong guy at the wrong time, then he was the goat. No argument there. But that's not to say that Branca bore central responsibility for the Dodgers' squandered season. To find the real culprit, you'd have to look past the mound and into the dugout—you'd have to take a good, long look at Brooklyn manager Chuck Dressen.

Dressen's first huge mistake was confidence. He had way, way too much of it.

When the Dodgers pulled away with a big early lead in '51, Dressen didn't motivate his players to finish off their bitter rivals. New York had a talented ball club (preseason polls predicted they'd win the pennant) but Dressen told his ballplayers that .500 ball would be a good enough record for the stretch run. In almost any other year, he would have been right but, then again, champions, unlike the '51 Dodgers, don't take any chances—they play all-out all the time. As it turned out, the Bums' 26–24 finish was good enough for a 96-58 record, but wasn't quite good enough to avoid a year-end playoff series.

By all accounts, the height of Dressen's disrespect for the competition came in August '51. After sweeping a crucial three game set in the Polo Grounds, Jackie Robinson and Carl Furillo decided to taunt Giants manager Leo Durocher in his own clubhouse, knocking on the adjacent room's flimsy doors and shouting, "You'll never win this year, you son of a bitch." Dressen, far from reining them in, actually joined in on the fun, shouting and singing, "Roll the barrel, we got the Giants on the run."

Just try to imagine a proven winner, a Joe Torre or a Tony LaRussa, pulling a cheap stunt like that.

As it turned out, Dressen did provide plenty of motivation—for the other side. While Brooklyn was busy muddling through their stretch run, the fired-up Giants stormed out to a 39–8 streak through August and September. The also-ran ball club that went 3–12 against Brooklyn before the clubhouse incident matched up at 6–1 afterwards.

When the Giants and Dodgers tied at the end of the regular season, the Dodgers won the official coin toss to determine home field for the special three-game playoff series. They decided to give it away. The exact reasoning is a mystery, but in the annals of baseball incompetence, the call was the equivalent of screwing up a one-car parade. Has anyone else, from Little League on up, *ever* passed up home field advantage?

And, yet, for all of their leader's complacency, arrogance, and bungling, the Dodgers entered Game Three with a shot to pull it out. That is, before Dressen got to work.

It all started in Game Two. As the Dodgers evened the series by romping to a 10–0 victory, Dressen didn't pull team ERA leader Clem Labine in the late innings. Apparently, nailing a complete game blowout was more important than retaining a relief option in the biggest game of the season. Labine was completely unavailable for Game Three.

The next day, during that final game, Dressen was still hard at work, carefully evening the odds for the Giants. The moment of truth came when New York put runners at second and third and one out in the ninth inning. The Dodgers had the opportunity to walk Bobby Thomson to the open base and then pitch to the next hitter, a rookie named Willie Mays. They passed it up.

Putting Thomson on base with the winning run would have been an unconventional move, but consider the situation. Thomson was a steely six-year veteran and the Giants' hottest hitter during their torrid stretch run (he hit .357 over the last 47 games of the season). He was also the Giants' top power hitter and run producer (32 home runs, 101 RBI) on the year.

Pitching around Thomson would have set up a play at every base and, more importantly, would have forced the Giants' follow-up hitter to win the game. It was a sound option. It may be hard to remember nowadays, but in 1951 a 20-year-old Willie Mays was still only beginning to show flashes of his dazzling promise. Still wet behind the ears, he'd slumped for a good portion of the season and didn't match Thomson's current hitting or year-end power numbers (Thomson hit for .514 slugging while Mays came in with .472).

Yet Dressen, confronted with the choice between pitching to the confident, power-hitting veteran and the shaky new guy, decided to take on . . . the confident, power-hitting

89

veteran. After the game, the elated Durocher stated that he "never got a bigger or better surprise in my life."

Still, even then, the Dodgers' Chuck Dressen, the Giants' best friend, wasn't finished.

It's often forgotten, but Dressen had a good bullpen option when Thomson strode up to home plate. Even if Labine was effectively out of the equation and Carl Erskine didn't have a good handle on his curve ball, the Dodgers could have gone to reliever Bud Podbielan, who had done well against the Giants (2–0 on the year). Podbielan had a lukewarm 3.50 ERA during the regular season, but he'd already proven himself under pressure by nailing down the all-important season finale versus Philadelphia. Podbielan was rested and ready, too, not having pitched in three days.

But Bud never did get his chance. We have to remember, the captain of the *Titanic* was at the helm.

The manager's choice was Ralph Branca. On the third day of the tenth month, Dressen decided to bring in #13.

Branca was a good pitcher in 1951 (13–12 record, 3.26 ERA), but any first-guesser could see that he was the wrong man for that particular situation—in six starts against the Giants, he'd lost five games while giving up 11 home runs. His latest, most devastating gopher ball came just two days before, in Game One of the series, a blast he gave up to someone named . . . Bobby Thomson. Think about it—in an all or nothing, win-or-go-home spot, when a home run would represent the end of the world, Dressen brought in a fastball pitcher to face a fastball hitter.

Fans always come to ball games to see players play and never come to see managers manage, so it's predictable for commentators to focus attention on what went wrong out on the field on the autumn afternoon of October 3rd, 1951. Sure, Ralph Branca gets the blame for throwing a bad pitch, but he was set up to fail. By a goat named Chuck Dressen.

CHUCK DRESSEN— WAS HE EVEN DUMBER THAN HE LOOKED?

21 The more you examine Chuck Dressen's performance in the 1951 pennant race, the worse he looks.

Dressen was known as a preening overmanager, the kind who would tell his players to "stay close to 'em. I'll think of something." In '51, he assumed the pennant as early as the 4th of July, when he was quoted as saying, "We knocked [the Giants] out. They'll never bother us again."

Dressen's arrogance, bad enough in itself, was matched by a distinct sense of incompetence. While Giants outfielder

Monte Irvin and others stated that Leo Durocher probably won an additional five or six games during the season through superior game tactics, Dressen always stuck with convention. Coincidence or not, the Giants' final record outperformed expectations (based on runs scored/runs allowed) by five games, while the Dodgers won a single extra game.

Even as the Giants were beating the odds with superior tactics, Dressen was evening them with willful ignorance. Years after the fact, it was revealed that Durocher had set up an elaborate sign-stealing operation in the center field area of the Polo Grounds. Dressen had no idea what his old boss was up to. The Dodgers' pioneering statistician, Allan Roth, begged the manager to take a look at the numbers he'd compiled on pitcher/batter matchups. Dressen didn't bother to look up Roth's dire analysis on Branca vs. Thomson. Labine, the team's best reliever, feuded with management over the last few weeks of the season. Dressen sat him even as Brooklyn's lead dwindled down to nothing.

Finally, let's remember just how unforgivably stupid it was for Dressen's Dodgers to give away home field for the playoff series.

Forget the fact that they actually volunteered to confront hostile crowds in the most decisive games of the season—by playing Game Two and Three in the Giants' Polo Grounds, the Dodgers were flanked by the most home-run friendly outfield porches in the Major Leagues (279 feet from home plate), and they made all the difference. If the Dodgers were, rightly, back home in Ebbets Field, Thomson's 315-foot drive would have fallen far short of the 343-foot left field wall. "The most theatrical home run in baseball history" would have ended up as a long, loud sacrifice fly, and the Dodgers may have ended up as winners.

Because of Dressen, we'll never know.

WAS DON LARSEN'S PERFECT GAME THE MOST SHOCKING EVENT IN BASEBALL HISTORY?

 ## THE PERFECT GAME

Anyone who thinks it's impossible to be shocked on an everyday basis should try watching baseball for a while.

There's a lifetime of surprises in the National Pastime. One game can finish 2–1 and the next 11–9. It doesn't cause any great comment when a front line starter gets racked up while a mop-up man throws six scoreless. Cleanup hitters can go 0 for 5 in the same game where utility players go 3 for 4. It's no big deal when the best team in the league loses to the worst one, not in a game where champions blow more than 65 games a year and cellar dwellers win as many.

Of all baseball surprises, though, perfect games are the most surprising. There have been exactly 14 examples in baseball's post-1903 era, translating to one perfecto for about every 30,000 major league starts.

Fielders' unassisted triple plays (12) are more rare than perfect games, true, but their rarity doesn't necessarily make them more shocking. The play is mostly about the random luck involved in being at the exact right place at the exact right moment. Perfect games, in contrast, are based on the skill involved in shutting down 27 straight batters and throwing nearly 100 dead-on pitches. They're much, much more difficult than ordinary no-hitters even, because they make absolutely no allowance for walks or errors.

Actually, in an important way, perfect games should be impossibilities.

In theory, pitchers are always trying to shut down the opposition, but the working reality has them "pitching to contact"—throwing enough filthy strikes that batters hit weak drives to the fielders. Hurlers will gladly concede the occasional bloop or four-bounce grounder through the middle, just as long as their teammates handle the other chances and put-outs. That's why Pete Alexander, Lefty Grove, Bob Feller, Whitey Ford, Steve Carlton, and dozens of other Hall of Famers haven't pitched a single no-hitter, let alone a perfect game, through hundreds of career starts. It's far too hard. They don't even try for it.

THE PITCHER

Don Larsen stands almost alone among the perfect games' authors.

Of the 14 pitchers who've done it, five (Catfish Hunter, Sandy Koufax, Jim Bunning, Addie Joss, and Cy Young) made it to Cooperstown, while another will be a first-ballot inductee just as soon as he retires (Randy Johnson). No one was completely jarred when one of those all-timers accomplished pitching's all-time feat.

Four others pitched a perfect game over the course of very solid careers. Kenny Rogers, Dennis Martinez, David Wells, and David Cone all finished in league ERA leader boards at least three times in their careers, with all but Rogers receiving Cy Young Award votes at least twice. No one expects perfect games, but with those pitchers enjoying more than their share of great days, it wasn't a tremendous shock when they enjoyed the greatest possible day. Likewise with three good-but-not-great pitchers (Len Barker, Mike Witt, and Tom Browning), who had league-leading numbers in strikeouts or hits-and-walks per nine innings at the time of their feats.

And then there was Don Larsen.

Before October 1956 Larsen's off-field drinking was better known than his on-field pitching. "Gooney Bird" went 7–12 as a rookie, then lost 21 games in his sophomore year before the Orioles tossed him into a 15-player trade with the Yankees. Going into September '56, he struggled to nail down a rotation spot as a third or fourth starter. Larsen finished relatively strong, but in overall makeup, track record, and stuff, general managers probably wouldn't have taken him in an even-up trade for New York's Whitey Ford, Johnny Kucks, Bob Grim, and Tom Sturdivant, or Brooklyn's Don Newcombe, Carl Erskine, Don Drysdale, and Koufax.

Forget the Hall of Fame-, star-, and league leader-good. Don Larsen just wasn't that good, period.

Some would argue that Charlie Robertson was an even more middling pitcher than Larsen, and thus a more unlikely candidate for a perfect game performance. There might have been something to that. Robertson was Larsen's inferior in career games (166 to 422), ERA (4.44 to 3.78), walks and hits per nine innings pitched (1.518 to 1.400), and wins (49 to 81). All that's true, but Don Larsen's perfect game was even more unlikely than Charlie Robertson's perfect game due to the pressure involved (see below).

THE HITTERS

When Gooney Bird faced off against the 1956 Dodgers, he faced one of the greatest lineups to be victimized by a perfecto. The '56 Brooklyns fielded four future Hall of Famers in Roy Campanella, Jackie Robinson, Pee Wee Reese, and Duke Snider, along with an eight-time All Star in Gil Hodges and a career .299 hitter in Carl Furillo. A seventh hitter, Junior Gilliam, hit .300 in 1956. Collectively, the offense averaged 8.5 hits and 4.7 runs per game during the regular season, second only to the 1922 Tigers among the teams victimized by a perfect game.

That era's Dodgers were so good, in fact, that they deserve a mention among the best offenses of all time. Three years before meeting Larsen, in 1953, the group had helped compile the 14th best on-base percentage in the twentieth century relative to their league average (Brooklyn's .362 was a hefty 9 percent higher than the NL's .332). The year before the Larsen game, the World Champion Dodgers led their league in OBP, batting average, home runs, and runs scored.

With apologies to the other team in town, the Dodgers were giants.

THE PRESSURE

All but one of the major leagues' perfect games were pitched during the regular season, and most involved little more than the pride of winning on a given day. Joss' effort did come late in a tight 1908 season, but Cleveland still had another five games to decide the pennant.

Don Larsen's perfecto was achieved in a very different situation.

It goes without saying that World Series games are always among the most tense, hard-fought contests of the year. Well, the Dodgers-Yankees Subway Series were among the most tense, hard-fought of World Series, since they involved bragging rights among millions of New Yorkers. To top it off, 1956 was arguably the most tense, hard-fought of Subway Series, what with the Brooklyns seeking a repeat of their first-ever world championship and the Yankees seeking revenge for their loss the previous October.

The tensions only increased as Larsen took the ball for Game Five. The Yankees split the previous four contests, but desperately needed another win in Yankee Stadium before heading back to finish the Series at Ebbets Field. A lost Game Five would have likely meant a lost championship, since the Dodgers were 18–8 at home in October. They'd already won Games One and Two in Flatbush by a combined score of 19–11.

Gooney seemed like the last man to provide the Yankees' must-win, since he'd been knocked out of his previous start, Game Two, in the 2nd inning (the Dodgers ended up scoring 13 runs on the day). Still, Casey Stengel had no alternatives on his exhausted staff.

And . . . these words are being written because somehow, Larsen found a way to overcome it all. A pitcher who had given away an average of 11.47 walks and hits per game allowed zero walks and hits. A sloppy defensive team that had committed 135 errors on the year didn't make a single mistake. Hitters who had averaged 8.8 hits and 6.0 runs over the previous few games came up with nothing at all.

When Vin Scully said "Let's take a deep breath as we go to the most dramatic ninth inning in the history of baseball," he wasn't hyping the situation one bit.

Don Larsen's best day has become such an accepted piece of Pastime lore that it's hard to appreciate how incredible it was in its own time. He overcame the greatest possible odds, with almost the least possible talent, against some of the toughest possible opposition under the most possible pressure.

Despite it all, on October 8th, 1956, Don Larsen shocked the baseball world. He was perfect.

DID BROOKLYN ABANDON THE DODGERS?

 Many people hated Walter O'Malley at first sight, just so they could save the time and effort in getting to know him.

The man led a Grinch-like life. As an up-and-comer, O'Malley was heartless enough to foreclose on dozens of hard-luck businessmen during the Great Depression. As a Dodger owner, he was unscrupulous enough to chisel star ballplayers out of fair wages. As an executive, he was small-minded enough to push out the brilliant Branch Rickey and fire the popular Red Barber.

Oh, O'Malley double-talked. He didn't know any good jokes. He didn't pick up the check at lunch. He was jowly and had beady little eyes. He was a lawyer.

The man had many personal faults and flaws. But he was not stupid. Far from it.

In the mid-1950's, O'Malley was, in many ways, the sharpest operator in baseball. Despite their outdated reputation as perennial losers, the 1940's/1950's Dodgers were the class of the National League, putting together 16 winning seasons in the 17 years from 1941 to 1957, including seven pennant winners from 1941 to 1956. When the team wasn't winning, it was innovating, bringing New York its first baseball broadcasting (radio and TV), batting helmets, and minority players. Some estimates had the super-efficient Dodgers' leading the league in annual profits, and insiders called their brain trust the most respected in sports.

For all his success and smarts, though, O'Malley could see the Dodgers' future prospects declining. At barely over 32,000 in seating capacity, Ebbets Field was the tiniest venue in major league baseball and, even as the Dodgers won pennant after pennant, their attendance lagged behind NL-leading Milwaukee by about a million fans per year. By 1956, the 44-year-old Ebbets, with its urinal troughs, obstructed views, and crumbling infrastructure, was a relic held together by peeling paint, rotting wood, rusting metal, and mildew. Worst of all, Flatbush's almost nonexistent parking was turning off more and more suburbanite fans.

O'Malley saw that his franchise desperately needed a new ballpark, and he did his best to make it happen. He picked out the perfect site at Atlantic Terminal, one which bypassed traffic and parking crises by accessing mass transportation lines. He drew up state-of-the art designs for a new venue and its surrounding area, then arranged to finance them on his own dime. All O'Malley needed was for the city to get out of the way.

An everyday fan, as much as he might have disliked the heartless, unscrupulous, small-minded Walter O'Malley, could have readily seen that the new ballpark was a pretty good deal. Heck, a not-so-bright politician could have seen the self-interest in locking up the heroic Dodgers' long-term future in the borough. Unfortunately, neither common-sense fans nor not-so-bright politicos were in charge of the Dodgers' future. An unelected, dictatorial bureaucrat named Robert Moses was in charge.

As Michael Shapiro recounts in his *Last Good Season* bestseller, Moses had virtually unchecked power as New York's construction czar in the mid-1950's, effectively overruling the Mayor and City Council when it came to municipal building projects. He was the one with the final say-so over the Dodgers' future in Brooklyn, and he did everything in his vast power to kill it.

Moses strung along the O'Malley ballpark negotiations for months and years. He refused to define the new Atlantic Street site as a "public purpose" or allow any rezoning. He didn't lift a finger to grant the highest taxed team in baseball any financial relief. Moses tried to strong-arm them over to Queens, then ignored O'Malley's backup planning for California. No, he didn't spell out the words *"D-R-O-P D-E-A-D,"* but, then again, he didn't need to.

To this day, no one knows the reasons for Moses' high-handed fumbling. He was responsible for building the Northern State Parkway and Lincoln Center, among other projects, so he must have preferred commuting to baserunning and/or operas to Opening Days. Like czars of the Russian variety, Moses answered to no one and explained to anyone. The true motives behind his obstruction are still a mystery.

One way or the other, though, O'Malley finally got Moses' message. By early 1958, the LA Dodgers were born.

It was unsurprising that the exceptionally unlikable O'Malley would be blamed for the Los Angeles move, since he was the one who had to pull the trigger on it. It was unsurprising, but unfair.

Think about it—for O'Malley, Brooklyn was a sure thing, representing a well-established history, a huge fan base, and settled families (including his own, on Park Slope). Los Angeles, on the other hand, was a big question mark, one representing startup costs, cross-country travel expenses, a still-unsettled ballpark situation, uprooted ballplayers, and thousands of enraged Brooklynites. If one of the smartest operators in baseball had been given any real choice in the matter, clearly, he would have chosen Brooklyn.

Contra the stale old joke, Walter O'Malley wasn't Hitler or Stalin, but a canny businessman who tried to gain a workable business deal. Ultimately, he failed, but that didn't mean his Dodgers abandoned Brooklyn. It was Robert Moses who abandoned the Dodgers.

The Brooklyn Dodgers, Stickball, and Doo-Wop

New York chronicler Pete Hamill once said the Dodgers' move out west represented a change of consciousness for New Yorkers, more than anything else. Afterwards, conversations included the words, "before the Dodgers moved ..."

There's no denying the point. The Brooklyn Dodgers did play in a special era—an era when kids played all-day stickball, teenagers sang street-corner doo-wop, vendors sold 25 cent hot dogs, gentlemen wore fedoras, and Ralph Kramden and Ed Norton supplied the laughs. Looking back, the team and times did merge into the image of a sweeter and better city. "Before the Dodgers moved ..." was a better time, at least in comparison to the strife to come in the 1960's and 1970's.

The Dodgers' departure appeared to destroy the '50s idylls, but quite obviously, it had nothing to do with later changes. Larger social forces produced Brooklyn's spiraling crime rate, unemployment, taxes, and racial tensions over the coming years. It was those forces that turned blue-collar neighborhoods into slums, chased away small businesses, messed up the schools, closed the navy yards, and shuttered grand old buildings. Far too many Dodger fans were eventually forced to follow their heroes, away from the borough they once knew.

It's tempting to suppose, if a cherished old ball club had stayed home, they might have headed off the bad times. If only that were true.

WHAT WAS THE DUMBEST MOVE IN THE HISTORY OF NEW YORK SPORTS?

24 The Jets hired Rich Kotite after he'd lost seven straight games.

The Yankees fired Dick Howser after he'd won 103.

The Mets gave up on Nolan Ryan before he'd posted 324 career wins.

The Nets invested in Yinka Dare before he sank 233 career points.

In the history of New York sports, mistakes have been made. Major mistakes have been made. *Titanic-* and *Hindenburg*-sized mistakes have been made.

And yet, over the long run, even the worst moves and the dumbest misjudgments can be forgiven. We're all human. Team executives are looking for opportunities and trying to reward their fan bases. When worst comes to worst, a dumb front office might cost itself a few bad years. There's always hope for a better tomorrow.

To cross the line from very bad mistake to complete debacle, you need a much, much more. You have to give up a once-in-a-lifetime opportunity while betraying your fan

105

base, all in one fell swoop. You have to cost yourself the future. You have to eliminate all hope for a better tomorrow.

You have to be Horace Stoneham, the owner who moved the New York Giants to San Francisco in 1957.

To appreciate the sheer, breathtaking stupidity in Stoneham's move, consider his Giants' enviable position in 1956. They were winners who'd taken a championship two years before and the National League pennant five years before. They were relatively popular, too, having finished in the top half of NL attendance from 1951 to 1954 while surpassing the era's million-fan benchmark in an average year. Finally, the Giants had a very bright future, with a 25-year-old Willie Mays in centerfield and future Hall of Famers Willie McCovey, Juan Marichal, and Orlando Cepeda all signed to the farm system.

And that wasn't the best news.

In 1956 the Giants' toughest competition, the hated Brooklyn Dodgers, were beginning the process of . . . moving . . . out of town! The Dodgers, who had finished ahead of New York in eight of the previous 10 seasons. The Dodgers, who had finished in front of the Giants in attendance in eight of 10 years. Yes, those Dodgers were prepared to make amends for their past domination, leaving for LA and handing the Giants a monopoly as the only NL team remaining in New York. The Giants were poised to become the new favorites to every Yankee-hater living in the tristate area.

The Giants were on the brink of finally, truly living up to the name through exploding performance and popularity alike. With the Dodgers gone, an embarrassed City Hall would've been strongly inclined to give all sorts of help in upgrading the 44-year-old Polo Grounds or, if need be, moving to a new ballpark over in someplace called Flushing, Queens. The future was incredibly bright.

But none of it was to be. A not-quite-foolproof future encountered a fool named Horace Stoneham.

Stoneham, incredibly, decided to ignore the crystal-clear potential in his horizon. Rather, Stoneham skedaddled from the best sports market in the country without so much as a single Dodger-free season. He went so far as to take Walter O'Malley's "friendly" advice to move from Coogan's Hollow and over to San Francisco just as the Dodgers were decamping for California in '57.

It's hard to express just how idiotic Stoneham's move was. Consider what he tossed away on the ride over to San Fran:

- Instead of drawing from half of New York, with a city-limits population of 7.8 million, the Giants found themselves making do in a city of little more than 740,000. They shrunk their potential fan base more than five times over.
- Instead of benefiting from the coverage of over a dozen local newspapers, the Giants were covered by two.

• Instead of playing in the spacious Polo Grounds, they played in a tiny minor league ballpark (capacity: 22,900), soon to be followed by the detested Candlestick Park, a.k.a. "the Cave of the Winds."

With Stoneham's debacle in place, the new San Francisco Giants soon headed for eminently predictable decline. Over 40 seasons, the Giants reached two million in attendance only three times, and constant money struggles had them threatening to pull up stakes once again, well into the 1990's. Nearly 50 years on, they still haven't brought a World Series title to the city by the bay.

The very worst part, though? The part that affixed a permanent dunce cap on Stoneham? It was his betrayal of some irreplaceable New York traditions.

Stoneham cut off the oldest professional sports organization in New York, one with roots tracing back to 1883. Stoneham dustbinned an orange-and-black identity forged by all-time greats like John J. McGraw and Iron Joe McGinnity and Christy Mathewson and Bill Terry and Carl Hubbell and Mel Ott and Leo Durocher. He cut off millions of fans from dear memories ranging from "The Catch" to "The Shot Heard 'Round the World" to the 1930's Subway Series and farther on back. He condemned a beautiful, utterly unique old venue that might have become as revered as Wrigley Field and Fenway Park are today. And he denied the greatest player in the game, Willie Mays, a stage in the greatest city in the game.

All that was left behind when the New York Giants made their last road trip away from 8th Avenue & 155th Street, and for no good reason.

Historians tend to skip over the Giants' move when they focus on the trauma inflicted by the Brooklyn Dodgers' move out to California. That was painful enough, but it shouldn't continue to overshadow an even worse debacle. While others have lost games and seasons, Horace Stoneham threw away an entire New York franchise.

MARIS IN '61— HOW DID HE MATCH UP TO BABE RUTH?

25 When Billy Crystal's *61* film came out in 2001, it represented a remarkable new revision of some old perceptions. Roger Maris' effort to break Babe Ruth's record for home runs in a season had long been shrouded in criticism and negativity, but the new film's portrayal version worked to reverse all that.

Crystal should have stuck to the original story, though. The many charges associated with Maris' '61 in '61 homer chase were right from the beginning:

* **It was completely fair to compare Roger Maris to Babe Ruth.** They donned the same Yankee uniform, hit from the left side, batted number three in the lineup, challenged the short porch at the Stadium, and played in right field. It would be impossible *not* to compare the two. Roger Maris wasn't eclipsing Joe Shlabotnik's most famous number.

* **It was a darn shame that a mediocre player like Maris broke Ruth's record.** No need to embarrass Maris by comparing his 12 years in the bigs to the Bambino's awe-inspiring career. Better to picture a midget at the bottom of the Grand Canyon.

When the 61st homer was hit, a vastly inferior player, inevitably, diminished a vastly superior player's standing in the record books. It was a darn shame.

* **Maris' '61 season wasn't nearly as good as Ruth's season in '27.** Leaving aside more lively baseballs and smaller ballparks, Maris' good numbers in '61 shouldn't have overshadowed Ruth's numbers in '27.

Despite playing in fewer games (151 to Maris' 161), taking fewer at-bats (540 to 590), and making fewer plate appearances (678 to 684), Ruth managed to compile many more hits (192 to 159), doubles (29 to 16), triples (8 to 4), and total bases (417 to 366) on his merry way to a higher batting average (.356 to .269), higher on-base percentage (.486 to .372), and slugging percentage (.772 to .620). Playing in a career year, Maris still couldn't overtake Ruth's routine greatness.

MARIS IN '61— DID HE HAVE UNFAIR ADVANTAGES IN BREAKING THE RECORD?

26 * **Maris had an unfair advantage in playing a 162-game season instead of Ruth's 154-game season.** Babe Ruth may have had the most astounding month of his astounding career in September 1927, hitting 17 round-trippers in 27 games played. If he benefited from an additional eight ball games against exhausted pitching staffs, it's likely he would have hit . . . how many on the season? 65? Even more? The record would have been well out of Maris' reach.

Commissioner Ford Frick's past friendship with the Babe may have rendered him biased in separating out the 1927 and 1961 home run records, but he had a completely valid point when he said, "You can't break the 100-meter record in a 100-yard dash." 100 meters isn't 100 yards and a 162-game record isn't a 154-game record.*

> * Until 1991, the record books listed two separate single-season homer records. That's it. The so-called asterisk never existed.

* Maris had an unfair advantage in facing expansion-year pitching. The eight American League teams of 1960 were joined by new franchises in Washington and Los Angeles in '61, meaning dozens of unready rookies, over-the-hill veterans, and career Minor Leaguers snuck on to Major League staffs. While Babe Ruth faced experienced, authentic Major Leaguers in 1927, Maris could feast on two full staffs' worth of new scrubs in 1961. Think that made a difference?

Expansion caused a completely unprecedented power surge throughout the AL—non-expansion teams' average home run production jumped from 132 up to 153 (16 percent) in a single year. There's never been another one-year increase like it, even in the homer-happy 1990's, and Maris was the single most famous beneficiary of the league-wide hitting bonanza. In the year before expansion diluted the pitching, he had 39 homers. When things settled down a year afterwards, he had 33. He never again swatted more than 26.

* Maris had an unfair advantage in lineup protection. True, Ruth did have the second-best slugger in the Pastime, Lou Gehrig, hitting behind, just as Maris had Mickey Mantle protecting him during his season-long home run derby. Both sluggers saw more strikes and fastballs as a result, but that's where the comparisons end.

Ruth was a monster power hitter with or without Gehrig—his five peak years (1920–24) actually came before The Iron Horse's first full season (1925). Maris was a whole different story, however. In five seasons without Mantle (ages

22 to 24, then 32 and 33), Maris never hit more than 28 round-trippers in a season. During the magical 1961 season, he had a .682 slugging percentage in 152 games with The Mick's protection, but a dismal .365 in the nine games without. It's true—Roger Maris' record was Mickey Mantle's creation.

MARIS IN '61—DID HE DESERVE A HARD TIME FROM THE MEDIA?

27

* **If there was justice in the world, Mickey Mantle would have taken the record instead.** If ever there was such a thing as a true Yankee, Mickey Mantle was a true Yankee.

In the early 1960's, Mantle was in his second decade in the Bronx, playing in the only uniform he would ever wear, well on his way to playing in the most games anyone would ever play in pinstripes. He helped win five World Series before Maris first arrived via a salary-dump trade with the Athletics. Mantle's name was all over the Bombers' season- and career-record book, as it still is.

If there was anyone to take away the ultimate Yankee home run record, Mantle should have done it. Those who knew the M&M boys best—their teammates—liked Maris well enough, but made no bones about favoring their cleanup hitter.

* Mantle had a better year in 1961. Despite manning a more demanding centerfield position and playing with serious injuries, the switch-hitting dynamo had more power (a .687 slugging percentage to Maris' .620), more hits (163 to 159), a higher on-base percentage (.448 to .372), and more stolen bases (12 to 0). Forget about the all-time greats—Roger Maris wasn't even the best-hitting Yankee outfielder in 1961.

* Maris was a mean guy. It's hard to avoid sympathizing for someone who receives stacks of hate mail basically because he's trying to do his job, but let's be honest. The living Roger Maris wasn't exactly a prince.

"I was born surly," Rajah once said, "and I'm going to stay that way." He didn't answer fan mail ("I got enough work to do without writing letters."), avoided fan autographs ("I don't want to get one of their pencils in my eye."), and didn't believe in that charity nonsense, either ("The club shouldn't expect you to go to hospitals. They don't ask, and I don't go"). He made no secret of his preference for Kansas City over New York City and once said "I'd have played college football if I'd been smart enough to get into school."

When spectators, somewhat predictably, decided to boo Maris, he responded by jeering them right back ("How much are you making?"). He once bought an oversized plastic hand with the middle finger extended in the air.

Billy Crystal portrayed a celluloid Maris as a wide-eyed, flat-topped country boy in the urban jungle, but his real-life values weren't exactly innocent. "If I could make more money down in the zinc mines, I'd be mining zinc," he declared; and, apparently, he meant it. Rog was money-conscious enough to stage frequent contract holdouts, peddle cigarettes, and appear in cheesy fare like *The Perry Como Show* and the *Safe at Home* movie. His one moment of generosity may have come at the very end of the season, when he turned down a fan's offer to turn over his record-breaking baseball.

Roger Maris once declared, "I don't give a damn about being a hero." No kidding.

✱ The media didn't hound Maris. Again, it's no fun for a player to become a talker for hours on end, especially since the situation was so poisonous to begin with. At one point, famously, Maris' hair fell out in clumps, but was that solely a comment on the media? The guy was a brooder by nature. Before and after he went through his season-long ordeal, #9 would often sit in front of his locker drinking cans of beer and chain-smoking cigarettes (he ended up dying of lung cancer at age 51).

Reporters didn't belong to the same good ole' boys' club by the time Maris came around, granted, but let's remember—it was still 1961. The Camelot-age papers would've been more than happy to sell a feel-good storyline about an underdog's homering his way into our hearts, if only their cover boy would play along. Maris wasn't interested. On good days he'd be blah and bland; on bad days he'd snap off a "How the f---do I know?" and "You've got to be a f---ing idiot."

Despite it all (despite Mantle's superior year, even!), beat reporters voted "Rude Roger" a second straight MVP award at year's end.

* **It was the public that rejected Maris' record.** Opinion polls showed widespread disfavor over the final outcome in the Maris-Mantle home run chase. There were 23,000 in attendance when Maris hit his 61st on October 1st, 1961, and even that meager number was somewhat inflated—an extra couple of thousand or so filled the cheap seats just to snag a $5,000 prize for the record-breaking ball.

It was the New York public that rejected Roger Maris, and why was that? Well, in the *61 film, Crystal portrayed his fellow fans as a bunch of dim-witted, mean-spirited bigots. Not nice. Here's a different explanation:

It was a darn shame that a mediocre player like Roger Maris broke Babe Ruth's record. His '61 season wasn't nearly as good as Ruth's season in '27, and, anyway, he had unfair advantages in a 162-game season, expansion-year pitching, and lineup protection. If there was justice in the world, Mickey Mantle would have taken the record instead. He had a better year, and Maris was a mean guy.

WERE THE NEW METS THE OLD DODGERS?

28 Sure, in certain ways, the Brooklyn Dodgers did leave New York in 1957. It's undeniable.

The old cast of characters frolicked on the Left Coast in 1958, playing in the LA sunshine even as old Ebbets stood idle. Back in Kings County, jilted fans fumed and sport sections thinned. The only National Leaguers passing through town that year were the Milwaukee Braves, and they were being hosted by the Yankees during the World Series.

All that was true, but that didn't necessarily mean that the Dodgers completely disappeared when they left New York. After all, the power in their presence went beyond their players, their ballpark, and their ball games. It was a matter of identity. For years, in the Bronx and in Brooklyn, New York witnessed the Yankees and the anti-Yankees.

While the Yanks played in the very first stadium grand enough to include three tiers, the Dodgers played in an antique bandbox. When the Bronx saw a parade of pennant winners for generation after generation, Flatbush saw a string of losers called the Daffiness Boys and Bums. As Yankee fans gloated over multiple champions in the 1940's and 1950's, Dodger followers mourned over seven straight World Series losses prior to 1955. At River Avenue & 161st Street, nearly every

117

year was a very good year, but around Sullivan Place it was wait 'til next year.

The Dodgers' presence was about an underdog spirit, and that spirit wasn't necessarily packed up for Walter O'Malley's trip to the West Coast. It was reborn, in 1962, when much of the old Dodgers' essence transferred over to the new Mets. The karma just took slightly different forms.

Once again, there was a team lacking the Yankees' button-down tradition, but making up for it in charm and light-hearted humor. The Sym-phony at Ebbets became Stengelese and Banner Day at Shea. The franchise may not have been the team to beat, but they knew how to stick it out through the tough times. "Dem Bums" morphed into the '62 Mets and their successors. The National Leaguers may not have had as many wins, but their comebacks could make it worth the wait. The celebrated champions of 1955 found heirs in the Amazin's of 1969.

The Metropolitan Baseball Club of New York, which welcomed so many of the Dodgers' old followers, welcomed much of their character, too. They attracted a more down-to-earth crowd, the kind whose love of the game didn't fluctuate with the standings. No one could accuse them of being pompous or arrogant. They knew New York was a tough town, one whose rewards could be found in Dodger-style persistence and perseverance more often than Yankee-style glory and glamour.

Now, Mets/Dodgers spirituality aside, a lot of material things were lost in the move in '57, and it would be silly to pretend otherwise. Flushing, Queens wasn't Flatbush, Brooklyn. Shea Stadium wasn't picturesque Ebbets Field, either, any more than adjacent World's Fair grounds were the same as the Fort Greene neighborhood. Interleague games and one New York/New York World Series in 2000 never made up for lost Subway Series.

Many of the external traces of the old Dodgers fled. But not all of them.

If you look around, some of the old Dodgers' signs and symbols still live on. In 2001, for instance, the Mets debuted a popular Minor League club in Coney Island, one sporting familiar B caps and blue-and-white uniforms. Fans tour the Dodgers Hall of Fame before dozens of home games per year and, on promotional nights, they welcome back ballplayers from way back when, pre-'57. The whole thing's been a huge hit with the Brooklynites.

And there are other hints of what used to be. The Jackie Robinson Foundation still directs more than a dozen New York charities and scholarship programs. Mrs. Rachel Robinson is still treated as visiting royalty at Shea Stadium celebrations and commemorations. Sandy Koufax still shows up at the Mets' Spring Training camp, year in and year out. The Boys of Summer never did leave baseball's bookshelves, and throwback Dodgers merchandise still does brisk business, too. By some measures, it's more popular than it was 50 years ago.

New Yorkers still remember, and they've always included Dodger memories in their present and future. The single best example is in a Borough Park kid named Fred Wilpon, who tossed batting practice for the Bums in 1953, grew up to make a fortune in real estate, and eventually bought the Mets. He's opening a new ballpark in 2009, and Wilpon promises it will bear a strong resemblance to a certain beauteous ballpark from his youth. Ebbets Field may be long gone, but it'll never been forgotten.

WERE THE '62 METS THE WORST TEAM OF ALL TIME?

29 It's a long way down.

To make history as a loser, a ball club has to sink far, far beyond ordinary incompetence and thud up against rock bottom. Its bats must resemble toothpicks, its pitches have to look like volley balls, its gloves must consist of tin. The hitters have to be untimely, the pitchers have to open up, the fielders have to forget the fundamentals.

Not easy to do, but the 1962 Mets once did it all in the process of posting 120 losses in a season. As John Helyar once wrote of the first-year expansion team, "The town wanted National League baseball back in the worst way, and got just that." The '62 Mets were the '27 Yankees in reverse.

If the stumbling, newborn Mets were certainly among the worst baseball teams of all time, do they take the booby prize as the very worst? Well, there are five contenders for the distinction, those with the puniest winning percentages in the last 100 years—the Amazin's, 1916 Athletics, 1935 Braves, 1952 Pirates, and 2003 Tigers. The test of an unchampion breaks down into 1) Embarrassing Record, 2) Futility, 3) Incompetence, 4) Feeble Hitting, 5) Helpless Pitching, and 6) Crummy Fielding.

Let the losing commence:

1. EMBARRASSING RECORD

As noted elsewhere, the '62 Mets were utterly unique as the losingest team of the twentieth century (#4). Their 120 losses set them apart from even dismal, 100-loss teams in the same way that dismal, 100-loss teams are below 80-loss teams. Even so, New York didn't have the worst winning percentage of all time:

Team	Win/Loss	Winning Percent
1916 Athletics	36-117	.235
1935 Braves	38-115	.248
1962 Mets	40-120	.250
2003 Tigers	43-119	.265
1952 Pirates	42-112	.273

To be fair, the Mets were terrible, but the '16 Athletics were notably worse in terms of day-in, day-out losing, and would have certainly sunk even lower still if they had a 162-game schedule to work with. They're on top (or the bottom) in the early going.

2. FUTILITY

The Mets' woes were sometimes blamed for their status as first-year team, but the other new expansion clubs of 1961–62 (Houston, Washington, the LA Angels) averaged a not-horrid 65 losses in their inaugural campaigns. New York's low standing was completely unique in its era, but not in Major League history:

Team	Games Out of First Place
1935 Braves	61.5
1962 Mets	60.5
1952 Pirates	54.5
1916 Athletics	54.5
2003 Tigers	47

Score one for the '35 Braves. Athletics 1, Braves 1.

3. INCOMPETENCE

One of Bill James' statistical innovations was something he called a Pythagorean Score, which calculates expected win totals based on total runs scored and total runs allowed. The idea is to explain how outside factors altered teams' final records, beyond what would have been expected based solely on offensive production, pitching, and defense. For losers, the Pythagorean differential puts a number on bad luck and/or incompetence:

Team	Actual Win/Loss	Pythagorean Win/Loss	Differential
1935 Braves	38-115	50-103	-12
1962 Mets	40-120	50-110	-10
2003 Tigers	43-119	49-113	-6
1952 Pirates	42-112	48-106	-6
1916 Athletics	36-117	41-112	-5

None-but-the-Braves go ahead of the Athletics, 2–1.

4. FEEBLE HITTING

The best measures of team offense involve the ability to get on base and hit for power, which are reflected in an on-base-plus-slugging average (OPS+) stat that also takes into account overall league offense and home ballparks.

The OPS+ number comes courtesy of the "Baseball Reference" site, and keep in mind that the lower a club sinks below the 100 median, the worse it is:

Team	OBP	Slugging	OPS+	R/game
1952 Pirates	.297	.331	79	3.34
2003 Tigers	.300	.378	81	3.65
1962 Mets	.317	.361	88	3.86
1935 Braves	.309	.362	91	3.76
1916 Athletics	.299	.313	96	2.90

It's becoming clear that the '62 Mets were a fraud. Compared to their fellow losers, they got on base more, hit for middling power, matched up OK against the league, and scored some runs. Why, Frank Thomas hit 34 homers on the year and Richie Ashburn got on base at a .424 clip! That's downright good.

As for the true losers . . . while the 1952 Pirates scored more than the 1916 A's of the dead ball era, they were even more pathetic in getting on base and in relative offense. They win.

Or lose. This is getting confusing.

Braves 2, Athletics 1, Pirates 1.

5. HELPLESS PITCHING

Pitching effectiveness can best be expressed in earned run average and what Baseball Reference calls ERA+, which is the ratio of the league's ERA to that of the ball club after the numbers are adjusted to account for the team's home ballpark. As with OPS+, the lower the score, the worse the performance:

124

Team	ERA	ERA+
1916 Athletics	3.92	73
1935 Braves	4.93	77
2003 Tigers	5.30	81
1962 Mets	5.04	83
1952 Pirates	4.61	86

The '62 Mets may have trotted out two 20-loss pitchers and an NL-record 5.04 ERA, but they didn't create quite the same impression as the 1916 Athletics—the A's giving up nearly four earned runs per game in the dink-and-bunt days was the equivalent of allowing 6.62 runs per game in last year's American League. Now there was a horrendous pitching staff. Braves 2, Athletics 2, Pirates 1.

6. CRUMMY FIELDING

It was said that the Mets had a defensive backstop who couldn't catch. But did his teammates hold up their end of the bargain?

Team	Unearned Runs
1916 Athletics	191
1962 Mets	147
1935 Braves	123
1952 Pirates	89
2003 Tigers	81

Casey Stengel's team misses one last chance to live down to its reputation. All A's, once again. Athletics 3, Braves 2, Pirates 1.

The final tally has the 1916 Athletics (Embarrassing Record, Helpless Pitching, Crummy Fielding) beating out the 1935 Braves (Futility, Incompetence) as The Worst Team of All Time, with the 1952 Pirates getting a single dishonorable mention (Feeble Hitting).

Once again, the '62 Mets are shut out.

CASEY STENGEL—WAS HE ALL THAT FUNNY?

30 Let's not kid ourselves. Casey Stengel wasn't all laughs.

Even friends allowed that the Stengel could be combative, temperamental, and sarcastic. Well into his sixties and seventies, as manager of the Yankees and Mets, he badgered umpires and feuded with opponents. Certain key players never did appreciate some of Stengel's more impatient and cocky ways. Before the 1950's brought black ballplayers into the game, the old man was suspected of harboring some of the racist attitudes he grew up with in late 19th century.

None of that was light or funny, but it was there. Casey Stengel was an imperfect person. At the same time, he was an almost perfect baseball comedian.

On one level, Charles Dillon Stengel simply had a natural, God-given gift for fun and games. He was a sworn enemy of boredom from his earliest days, a quick-witted jokester and irreverent comic who could keep his friends in stitches. Casey dropped out of school and never did spend much time in church, instead devoting his energy to partying, gambling, talking with the boys, and flirting with the girls. He once won a wrestling match with a greased pig.

By the time Stengel made it up as a Brooklyn Dodger in 1912, he'd developed a reputation as a bona fide eccentric. He didn't own up to it, but Stengel may have engineered one of the most legendary pranks in baseball history in 1915 when he goaded Dodgers manager Wilbert Robinson into catching a baseball tossed from a passing airplane. Robinson caught the "baseball" on the fly, only to find a juicy grapefruit exploding all over him. Another time, Stengel scooped up a dazed little bird in the outfield and quickly hid it away. A couple minutes later, a tip of the cap allowed a sudden flight into the Ebbets sky. Some lambasted him, but Casey pointed out he had three hits on the day. "I figure I'm showing a more serious attitude than players with no sparrows in their hats," he said.

Stengel had an innate theatricality that could have played to a Broadway audience as easily as ballpark grandstands, and maintained a taste for flamboyant sights throughout his long life. As a young manager in the 1930's, he mocked umpires' refusal to call a rain delay by carrying an umbrella out to the third base coach's box. Everyone broke up. When Comiskey Park's exploding scoreboard debuted in the late 1950's, the restless Stengel lit a sparkler and danced a little jig in front of the dugout. The crowd went nuts. When he was nearly 80 years old, a publicity stunt had him riding around Shea Stadium in a chariot. Huge cheers again.

There were a dozen more incidents. Stengel was a one-of-a-kind character in his day, and it's safe to say there'll never be another like him. Just try to imagine anyone in the dead-serious Majors of today daring anything along those lines. Classy as he may be, expect to see Willie Randolph dancing a little jig if and when his pants are on fire.

Some might say that some light-hearted fun is an end in itself, but it would be easy to overlook the hidden agenda in Stengel's various pranks. Laughing ball clubs tend to be loose ball clubs, the kind most prepared to deal with the inevitable ups and downs of a 162-game season. While teammates and players testified as to Stengel's tactical brilliance or second-to-none competitiveness, the man knew that winning wasn't everything. Even in the 1950's, when Stengel led the most staid organization in the Majors, he appreciated how both intensity and comic relief were indispensable to bouncing back from the game's inevitable setbacks.

Stengel's most memorable fusion of fun and purpose came in his invention of a mangled form of English dubbed "Stengelese." In talking to the press, he'd give long, screwball responses featuring mixed grammar and word games along with endless digressions into every topic and no topic in particular. Very often, "Stengelese" lines fit into a self-created, word-tripping character ("Some people my age are dead at the present time," "My health is good enough above the shoulders"). At times, the syntax contained a double meaning that reporters could choose to see either way ("I'm outta baseball and I was in it for a long time and it don't have to be forever").

There was always a very careful sense behind the Stengelese nonsense, though. As it happened, the Ole' Perfessor was more than capable of speaking in crystal-clear, succinct sentences (his protégé, Whitey Herzog, once called him the most intelligent man he'd ever met). Stengel chose to ply reporters with colorful quotes instead because they provided a convenient means to stay away from serious, unfavorable topics—every minute he kept beat reporters chuckling and scratching their heads was another minute he didn't have to talk about benching a player, an injury problem, a losing streak, or any one of a dozen other not-so-light subjects.

The greatest example of Stengel's humor-as-distraction may have come when he was called to testify before Congress in 1958. The controversy at hand was federal regulation over baseball, but Stengel instead regaled the Senators and scribes with an impossibly disjointed 45-minute ramble through his life and his living, from Shelbyville, Kentucky to New York City, from night games to the minors, from pensions to payrolls . . . he just rollicked on and on, making just enough sense to be coherent but never enough to be understandable. By the time he was finished, the Senate Subcommittee on Antitrust had long forgotten their boring law thing. Just as Stengel had intended all along.

The very peak of Stengel's comedy career, by all accounts, came in his days as Mets manager from 1962 to 1965. Due to his past Yankee championships and solid investments, the elderly skipper had rock-solid professional credentials and financial security, and no one was too eager to talk about the Mets' horrid on-field record anyway. Stengel was secure and free enough to act as a resident folk hero instead, and he succeeded in presenting the young Mets the wisecracking, fun alternative to the pinstriped dynasty in the Bronx. He may have been old enough to be a great-grandfather, but he'd saddle up to bars and regale with impromptu orations for five, six hours on end, well into the morning hours. Every time he did, he made more friends and the young Mets won more fans.

Hall of Fame sportswriter Red Smith once stated that Casey Stengel was no clown. "He is something else entirely," Smith wrote. "A competitor who always had fun competing, a fighter with a gift of laughter." For millions, Stengel was the game of baseball at its very best, and it's hard to imagine a more enduring, more positive legacy.

Seriously.

CASEY STENGEL— WHAT WERE THE 18 FUNNIEST THINGS HE EVER SAID?

31

The paths of glory lead but to the Braves.

—On his second division ball club

*

Good pitching will stop good hitting and vice versa.

They say you can never do that, but he is, and it's a good idea, but sometimes it doesn't always work.

—On a rival's controversial managerial move

*

That fella is a tree hitter. Everything he hits is in the trees.

He's a hard-nosed, big-nosed kind of player.

—On Billy Martin

*

I think you look like Tyrone Power.

—To Yogi Berra, after a game-winning home run

*

Nobody knows this [yet], but one of us has just been traded to Kansas City.

—To Bob Cerv. They were alone at the time

THE BEST NEW YORK SPORTS ARGUMENTS

Now, there's three things you can do in a baseball game: you can win or you can lose or it can rain. So far.

—When asked if Don Larsen's perfect game was the best he'd ever done

*

I couldn't have done it without my players.

—On his Yankee championships

*

The Mets is a very good thing. They give everybody a job. Just like the WPA.

—On the '62 Amazin's

*

You look over at the Cincinnati dugout and what do you see? All mahogany. Then you look over at our bench and all you see is driftwood. I got this kid who's nineteen, and in 10 years he has a chance to be twenty nine.

—On prospect Greg Goosen, who did play his last Major League game at age 24

*

We gotta trade him while he's hot.

—On Don Zimmer, who'd just broken a 0 for 34 slump with a couple of hits. Zimmer *was* traded a few days later

*

I feel greatly honored to have a ballpark named after me, especially after I've been thrown out of so many.

—On the dedication of Stengel-Huggins Field

*

They had two languages I couldn't speak—French and English.

—On Montreal

*

I'll tell you something. They examined all my organs. Some of them are quite remarkable, and others are not so good. A lot of museums are bidding for them.

—On his health at age 70

*

There comes a time in every man's life, and I've had plenty of them.

—His tombstone inscription

MATTY, WHITEY, & TOM TERRIFIC—WHO WAS NEW YORK'S GREATEST PITCHER?

32 First there was Christy Mathewson.

From 1900 to 1916, the Giants' ace tore through strike zones with a fastball, knuckleball, and variety of curves, all complimented by his pioneering "fadeaway" (screwball) pitch. Despite the sharp movement on his pitches, Matty was among the most precise and durable right-handers of all time, and the off-field Mathewson may have been one of the most admired Americans of his day, too. "He talks like a Harvard graduate, looks like an actor, acts like a businessman, and impresses you as an all-around gentleman," it was said.

Then there was Whitey Ford.

The Yankee foiled American League hitters of the 1950's and 1960's with a repertoire of fastballs, curves, change-ups, and sliders, all thrown from a bewildering variety of arm angles and speeds. "The Chairman of the Board" had dozens of different lefty pitches, in effect, and always delivered them with an uncanny professionalism. Roger Angell once wrote that Ford "stands on the mound like a Wall Street bank president. Tight-lipped, absolutely still between pitches, all business and concentration, he personifies the emotionless perfection of his team."

Finally, there was Tom Seaver.

From the late 1960's into the 1980's, the Mets' Tom Terrific utilized a rising fastball, slider, curve, and change-up to shut down opposing batsmen, and may have been just as well-known for the phenomenal control in his righty power pitching. For his grasp of technique and personal maturity, an opposing manager once said, "Tom Seaver has a 35-year-old head on top of a 21-year-old body."

Christy Mathewson, Whitey Ford, and Tom Seaver were very different professionals and personalities, working for three separate franchises and eras. What they shared was even more important, though—all of them deserve consideration as the best pitcher in the history of New York baseball.

The city has never seen winners like them. With 373 career wins, Mathewson tied Pete Alexander as the most winning National League pitcher of the twentieth century. Ford, by winning at a .690 rate (236–106) over his career, leads all Major League pitchers with 200 or more decisions. Finally, Seaver's 14 consecutive years with 10 or more wins distinguish him as one of the most consistent hurlers of all time.

To single out any one of the three Hall of Famers as New York's finest pitcher, it makes sense to assess their career performance, peak performance, impact on team winning, and postseason numbers.

While wins and ERA are often used to measure pitcher performance, Baseball Reference has developed a more objective stat called "ERA+" [see the following chapter], one that adjusts pitching performance to home ballparks and sets a ratio to league averages. With 100 representing the league average, the higher score represents the better performance.

Here's how Mathewson, Ford, and Seaver compared for their careers:

	Career	Career ERA+
Matty	1900–16	135
Whitey	1950, 1953–67	132
Terrific	1967–86	144

Tom Seaver did put up a higher career ERA (2.86) than either Christy Mathewson (2.13) or Whitey Ford (2.75), but that was largely due to his playing in relatively unfavorable times for pitchers. His ERA marks were extremely stingy compared to his contemporaries, so he gave his teammates better opportunities to win. Seaver takes the early lead, 1–0.

Of Mathewson, Ford, and Seaver, who was best when he was in the prime of his career? Here are their ERA+ for the aces' best five consecutive years:

	Five-Year Peak	Peak ERA+
Matty	1908–12	175
Whitey	1954–58	147
Terrific	1969–73	158

Ford and Seaver were extremely good, but when Mathewson was at his best from 1908 to 1912, almost no one was ever better—his 1.71 ERA was more than 1.00 earned run below the league average in four of five years, and he averaged 1.24 earned run superiority over the league's already-low ERA. Matty and Seaver tie at 1–1.

Next, it's worthwhile to see how the golden trio did as winners.

The very best pitchers should be difference-makers, the ones capable of lifting their teammates to greater heights. If one can assume that hitting support and bullpen help are much the same for all starting pitchers, the differential between the pitchers' win percentage and team win percentage can measure their individual impact on team fortunes (the way they improved the team's chances to win).

Among Mathewson, Ford, and Seaver, the career numbers break down as follows:

Pitcher	Win %	Team Win %	Differential
Matty (1900–14)	.665	.590	+.075
Whitey (1950, 1953–65)	.690	.593	+.097
Terrific (1967–86)	.614	.483	+.131

(The above pitcher percentages only count full seasons where they made 20 or more starts while the above team percentages count only the games where the starter in question didn't pitch.)

Mathewson and Ford can't compete with Seaver in this respect—no one has ever carried more Major League teams to victory. To take just one example, a rookie Tom Terrific had 18 complete games, 170 strikeouts, and a 2.76 ERA on a 1967 Mets team that went 61-101 while finishing dead last in NL team scoring. He went 16–13, but imagine what he could have done with some decent run support. It's Seaver 2, Matty 1.

Finally, the playoffs.

Postseason pitching numbers are notoriously unreliable, since they're based on such a small number of games, but it's fair to consider them for pitchers due to the all-important nature of their position. In October, aces don't have the luxury of establishing themselves over several starts—they absolutely must perform at their best for their teammates to win a short series. All their postseason games are clutch games. For that reason, it's fair to evaluate them based on ERA, innings pitched per game, and win/loss in October.

THE NUMBERS:

	W/L	ERA	IP/G
Matty	5–5	0.97	9.27
Whitey	10–8	2.71	6.64
Seaver	3–3	2.77	7.71

The Ford's 10 wins place him among the top six playoff pitchers of all time, and he still holds the all-time World Series record for consecutive scoreless innings (32), but he wasn't superlative in the way Mathewson was superlative. Despite his final 5–5 record in the 1905, 1911, 1912, and 1913 World Series, Matty had a sub-1.00 ERA and completed every one of his 11 postseason starts. It's highly doubtful that his '05 Series, featuring three complete game shutouts, will ever be surpassed as the greatest World Series pitching of all time.

In the final tally, then, Tom Seaver comes out ahead for consistent ERA excellence and impact on team winning, but Christy Mathewson wins out as a peak-performer and playoff hero. Either one may have been the single greatest pitcher New York's ever seen. Flip a coin.

MATTY, WHITEY, & TOM TERRIFIC— HOW SHOULD THEIR ERA'S AND ERAS BE COMPARED?

33 Depending on who you listen to, commentators can account for pitching greatness in relation to awards or stats like wins, strikeouts, walks, and hits allowed. Unfortunately, none of the criteria are very reliable.

Voters have all sorts of kooky reasons for handing out awards, and win totals/winning percentages can be wildly deceptive due to their dependence on teamwork. A mediocre starting pitcher can notch a lot of W's by working with potent run support and a strong bullpen, for example, while an above-average starter can lose more than his share due to his team's weak hitting and relievers' blown saves.

Strikeouts, walks and hits allowed stats reveal more about a pitcher's work, but they're fragmentary. The idea isn't to strike out the side or prevent hits, after all, but to deny opponents' runs. Plenty of strikeout pitchers, for instance, fail because they're susceptible to walks. Similarly, a low

139

"walk and hit per nine inning" number may not be very helpful if the hits allowed result in home run trots.

Earned run average is a far more useful catchall number for pitching performance, but it's not without its own limitation. Over the years, Major League conditions have changed in factors from mound height and strike zone to ballpark dimensions and ball configuration, and those changes rendered some periods notably more favorable to hitters (the 1930's, 1990's) and others more favorable to pitchers (1910's, 1960's).

Pitchers' numbers have to be adjusted for those shifting contexts, and "Baseball Reference's" ERA+ tends to take the guesswork out of those adjustments.

The statistic takes a pitcher's earned run number, adjusts for his home ballpark, and then sets it to a ratio with the league average. The result is a relatively objective look at how the pitcher did relative to those who worked under the same prevailing conditions. By using ERA+, we can measure how Matty, Whitey, and Tom Terrific performed in their own times, then compare them for all time.

THE '69 METS—WHY WERE THEY THE MOST AMAZIN' STORY IN BASEBALL HISTORY?

34 Amazin.'

It's an adjective signifying "greatly surprising" ("The dog was capable of amazing tricks") or "inspiring awe or admiration or wonder" ("New York is an amazing city").

That's how one dictionary defines the word. Baseball defines it by a ball club—the World Champion Mets of 1969. They stand alone. No team has ever improved more to win a title or broken so completely with a legacy of utter failure. No other champions have staged the same kind of late season rally, and played so far over their heads, despite such inexperience. And no one's pulled off the same kind of World Series upset, either.

"Greatly surprising?" You might say so.

1. One-Year Improvement

Almost all World Series champions have been good-to-great before stepping up to the highest level. Exceptions have been few and far between, but the Mets were the most exceptional of the exceptions.

141

At the end of the 2005 season, only 10 of 101 World Series winners improved by as many as 18 regular season wins (or .115 in regular season winning percentage) from the previous year. One of them, the 1919 Reds, was playing against a "Black Sox" team that wasn't even trying to win, so the nine true comeback clubs have included:

	Pr. Yr.'s Wins	Title Yr.'s Wins	Win Differential
1969 Mets	73	100	+27
1912 Red Sox	78	105	27
1954 Giants	70	97	27
1914 Braves	69	94	25
2002 Angels	75	99	24
1988 Dodgers	73	94	21
1933 Giants	72	91	19
1927 Yankees	91	110	19
1967 Cardinals	83	101	18

The '12 Sox and '54 Giants match them, but no World Series winner has ever surpassed the '69 Mets for one-year improvement.

2. Overcoming the Past

Common sense says that a team can't expect to win it all before gaining at least some respectability, and that's almost always been the case. Almost every one of the comeback clubs listed above, for instance, took a title after coming from success or, at worst, mediocrity. A few (the '54 Giants, '88 Dodgers, '27 Yankees, and '67 Cardinals) had won league championships within the previous three years. Others (the '12 Red Sox, '02 Angels, and '33 Giants) had multiple winning seasons. They may have made a big one-year jump, but they were on a very solid success cycle beforehand.

The 1969 New York Mets stood apart from all that—they weren't coming back from a bad year in 1968, but a bad existence dating back to 1962.

From the epic losers of the inaugural season (#29) through '68, the Mets had averaged a .348 winning percentage translating to a 56–106 record. In the previous seven years they suffered through five 10th place finishes and two 9th place finishes. In all but 1966 and 1968, they were the very worst franchise in the Major Leagues. In spring training '69, their manager, incorrigible optimist Gil Hodges, was hoping for a huge 12-game improvement, all the way up to 85 regular season wins. That would have been enough for the first winning season the Mets had ever seen.

Of all the World Series-winning teams, only the Braves of 1914 begin to compare to the Mets in prior long-term futility, but even they fall short. The Braves had a higher winning percentage (.457 to the Mets' .451) in the year before the championship and a better winning percentage (.361 to .348) over the previous seven years. Also, they were the worst ball club in baseball just once, three years before.

No one's come back from a tradition of losing equal to the old Mets. In one incredible year, the franchise went from the very bottom to the very top.

3. Late Season Rally

No champion has ever come back in a late season dogfight like the '69 Mets.

In the game's pre-wild card era (before 1995), the Mets are the only team to win the World Series after being as far as 9.5 games out of first place on August 15th, or as far as five games out on September 1st. No other champion took its first lead of the year as late as September 10th, either. As Casey Stengel once said, "they came slow but fast."

The Braves, again, come close to the Mets, but they weren't quite as miraculous as the boys from Shea. The Braves were within 2.5 games by August 15th of their big year, and they already led by .5 games on September 1st.

4. Playing above Their Heads

Team runs scored and runs allowed generally correlate very strongly with team wins, so when a club scores 632 total runs while allowing 541 total runs, theory forecasts a Pythagorean Record of 92–70. The '69 Mets' reality saw an 100–62 record. If they played according to the numbers, the Mets would have tied the Cubs in the NL East, but ultimately, they scrapped, scratched, and clawed their way to enough close wins to beat Chicago by seven.

Don't bother looking for a more fortunate, gritty World Series champion in the last 103 years—no one's ever exceeded the Mets' plus-eight wins, including their fellow comeback champs:

	Pythagorean Record	Actual Record	Win Differential
1969 Mets	92–70	100–62	+8
1914 Braves	89–67	94–59	+5
1967 Cardinals	97–64	101–61	+4
1988 Dodgers	91–70	94–67	+3
1912 Red Sox	102–50	105–47	+3
1933 Giants	90–62	91–61	+1
1927 Yankees	109–45	110–44	+1
1954 Giants	97–57	97–57	0
2002 Angels	101–61	99–63	-2

5. Overcoming Inexperience

Once the Fall Classic was established as a baseball institution in the early years of the twentieth century, virtually all its winners featured multiple players with experience in the playoffs and, if not the playoffs, then pennant races. At the very least, their rosters included mature players who'd gone through winning seasons. "Experienced leadership" has always been a byword for sound ball clubs.

Well, almost always.

The fact is that no one on the very young Mets' starting lineup—no one—had played a playoff game before October 1969. They didn't know how to deal with playoff pressure because they didn't know what playoff pressure was. Only Tommy Agee and Don Cardwell had seen a winning season on the Major League level.

Manager Hodges did win pennants and a World Series as a player for the Dodgers, but, likewise, he'd never won a thing as a manager. Before opening day 1969, he'd had six losing seasons in six years with the Senators and Mets. His career managerial mark stood at 139 games below .500 (394–533).

In short, the Met players shouldn't have known how to play at the highest level, and their manager shouldn't have known how to manage them to the highest level. They kept winning anyway. Apparently, just once, ignorance was bliss.

6. The Upset

Forget all the other ways the '69 Mets were completely unique. Forget how much ground they made up. Or their break with so much failure. Or their furious late rally. Or their daunting numbers. Or their complete inexperience. Forget all that. If nothing else, the '69 Mets were a once-in-a-lifetime team in the way they took a World Series that should have been a complete mismatch.

The 1969 Baltimore Orioles answered the Mets' one great leap forward with consistent excellence. They answered New York's tradition of league-worst losers with the best record in Major League Baseball from 1962 to 1969. They answered the Mets' late, desperate rally with a five-month grip on first place.

They matched the Mets' anemic 3.9 runs per game (eighth in the National League) with a robust 4.81 runs per game (second in the American League). They matched the Mets' low 2.99 team ERA with an even more stingy 2.83. They matched the Mets' complete lack of experience with proven World Series winners like Frank Robinson, Brooks Robinson, Jim Palmer, and Boog Powell, among others. And they matched Hodges' woeful managerial record with a future Hall of Famer in Earl Weaver.

The Mets-Orioles World Series, by rights, should have been a blowout, a complete blowout. No other champion—not the 2003 Marlins, not the 1988 Dodgers, not the 1987 Twins, not the 1954 Giants—has ever overcome so many disadvantages up and down the line.

No one except the '69 Mets. That's why they were so "greatly surprising." That's why they were Amazin.'

THE '69 METS—HOW DID THEY PULL IT OFF?

35 How did the Mets beat preseason experts' 100-to-1 odds?

Well, they had a lousy offense, one that finished no higher than eighth in the NL for runs scored, on-base percentage, slugging, and stolen bases, but they could overcome it through dominant pitching. With the very young Tom Seaver, Jerry Koosman, Gary Gentry, and Nolan Ryan making up a staff that led the league in ERA and shutouts, the Mets kept games close and prayed for the best.

Often enough, their prayers were answered. "We had deep depth," said coach Yogi Berra, and he was right—an unprecedented 20 different players knocked in game-winning runs for the Mets over the course of the year, with the fireworks coming from slap-hitters like Ed Charles (.207 batting average), Al Weis (.215), and Wayne Garrett (.218). They found a way. Miracles do happen.

"MR. OCTOBER"—WHO WAS THE YANKEES' GREATEST PLAYOFF HITTER?

36 In a sense, some of the greatest Yankee playoff performances of all time were delivered by the modest bats of Bobby Richardson, Brian Doyle, and Scott Brosius.

The 1960 World Series was Richardson's showcase, as he hit .387 while slugging .667, hitting two doubles, two triples, and a home run in 30 at-bats. Doyle, playing in the '78 Series, hit .438 while knocking in two runs and scoring another couple. In the 1998 Fall Classic, Brosius got hot at exactly the right time, too, putting up a .471 batting average while slugging .824 and driving in six.

They were true Bronx Bombers, all. But none were among the greatest Yankee playoff hitters of all time.

Richardson, Doyle, Brosius—and many others—have been great for one short series, but one short series does not a legend make. To be the greatest Yankee playoff hitter of all time, a player has to display greatness over multiple postseasons. At his best, he has to completely dominate, and, even at his worst, he has to do well enough to instill fear in opponent pitching staffs. He has to help carry his teams to victory, too.

The Yanks' many happy autumns have been produced by rosters featuring Hall of Famers like Yogi Berra, Joe DiMaggio, Lou Gehrig, Reggie Jackson, Mickey Mantle, and Babe Ruth. All six Hall of Famers played at least seven play-off series (and 119 or more at-bats) for the Bombers, and, notwithstanding the brash Mr. Jackson's trademark, each put up the kind of numbers to stake a claim as the single, authentic "Mr. October."

The first qualification is in career playoff effectiveness. The best stats for it are on-base percentage, which accounts for walks as well as hits, and slugging percentage, which accounts for doubles and triples as well as home runs. Most analysts combine the numbers in a catchall on-base-plus-slugging (OPS) number.

Purely for the sake of context, regular season OPS is included below to show how the hitters' did in comparison to their regular season standards. The parentheses next to OBP, SLG, and OPS indicate a status among all-time leaders in the Major Leagues' postseason history:

	OBP	SLG	Playoff OPS	Reg. Season OPS
1. Ruth	.467 (9)	.744 (4)	1.211 (4)	1.164
2. Gehrig	.477 (8)	.731 (6)	1.208 (5)	1.080
3. Jackson	.432	.672	1.104	.846
4. Mantle	.374	.535	.909	.977
5. Berra	.359	.452	.811	.830
6. DiMaggio	.338	.422	.760	.977

There's a six-of-one/half-dozen of the other difference in the stats between Ruth and Gehrig, but, even in this group, they're clearly men among boys. Jackson stepped up in the playoffs, too, but not like them. Mantle and Berra actually underperformed in October, as compared to April through September, and given DiMaggio's reputation in the clutch, his below-average Octobers are fairly shocking. Ruth 1, Gehrig 1.

Apart from their overall totals, how did the sluggers compare at their very best? Here are the two best postseason series from each player:

	Years	OBP	SLG	OPS
1. Gehrig	1928	.706 (7)	1.727 (2)	2.433 (2)
	1932	.600	1.118	1.718
2. Ruth	1928	.647	1.375 (4)	2.022 (5)
	1923	.556	1.000	1.556
3. Jackson	1977	.542	1.250 (9)	1.792
	1978	.529	1.000	1.529
4. Mantle	1960	.545	.800	1.345
	1964	.467	.792	1.259
5. Berra	1956	.448	.800	1.248
	1953	.538	.619	1.157
6. DiMaggio	1950	.471	.615	1.086
	1939	.353	.500	.853

All the above stats came in the World Series, with the exception of Jackson's 1978 performance, which came in the AL Championship Series against Kansas City.

It's worth noting that Jackson's 1977 World Series (featuring those three-homers-on-three swings in Game Six) was probably the most publicized power hitting of all time, but that didn't make it the most outstanding power-hitting Series of all time—in the pre-television age of the 1928 World Series, both Lou Gehrig and Babe Ruth were even better. Since Gehrig's very best performances beat Ruth's best, The Iron Horse takes the lead. Gehrig 2, Ruth 1.

Next, it's worth asking which of the Yankee all-timers could hit in the playoffs even when they weren't at their very best. Here are the two most subpar series in which the sluggers had more than six at-bats:

	Years	OBP	SLG	OPS
1. Gehrig	1926	.464	.435	.899
	1938	.375	.286	.661
2. Ruth	1921	.476	.500	.976
	1922	.250	.176	.426
3. DiMaggio	1941	.333	.333	.666
	1949	.278	.238	.516
4. Jackson	1980	.333	.364	.697
	1977	.222	.125	.347
5. Mantle	1963	.188	.333	.521
	1962	.241	.160	.401
6. Berra	1947	.200	.316	.516
	1949	.118	.062	.180

Jackson's numbers come from the 1977 ALCS and 1980 ALCS, while the rest came from the World Series.

Again, here, Gehrig is a man apart, a slugger that could scare opposing pitching staffs even when he wasn't at the top of his game—even if you include the illness-induced slump in the '38 Series, his worst two playoff series were more effective, on balance, than those from Ruth and the rest. Gehrig 3, Ruth 1.

Finally, there's the win/loss records for the postseasons in which the "Mr. October" candidates had more than six at-bats:

	Wins	Losses	Winning %
1. DiMaggio	9	1	.900
2. Gehrig	6	1	.857
3. Jackson	5	2	.714
4. Berra	8	4	.667
5. Ruth	4	3	.571
6. Mantle	5	5	.500

Gehrig 3, Ruth 1, DiMaggio 1.

The team-oriented DiMaggio once said, of all his career achievements, he was proudest of the nine wins in 10 Series, and it does stand out as one of those records that may never be broken. Even so, all of Joltin' Joe's winning can't make up for his former teammate's unsurpassed numbers. It was the unforgettable Lou Gehrig who was the real "Mr. October."

37 Yogi Berra may not have the greatest statistics among the October Yankees, but he was the greatest winner.

When a 22-year-old Berra saw his first significant playing time in 1947, the Yankees hadn't won a World Series in three years, which tied for their worst dry spell of the post-1920 (Babe Ruth) era. In Berra's rookie season, though, they won a world championship, then another nine more over the next 16 years—by far the greatest sustained period of success the Yankees, or any other American sports team, has ever had.

When Berra was hired as Yankee manager in 1964, his aging ball club was considered an underdog to repeat as a pennant winner. In his first season at the helm, the Yanks won the pennant, then came within one game of yet another championship. Yogi was fired, though, and the ball club dropped to sixth place, then last place, over the next two seasons.

When Berra was hired as a Met coach in 1965, they were the worst team in the Major Leagues. Within four years, they were World Champions.

When Berra was hired as Met manager in 1972, they had muddled through two straight .500 seasons. Within a couple years, they went to Game Seven of the World Series. Yogi was fired not long after, though, and Shea didn't see another winning season for eight years.

When Berra was hired as a Yankee coach for the 1976 season, they hadn't made the playoffs in 12 years. Within six years, they'd won two world championships and four pennants.

When Yogi was hired as Yankee manager in 1984, they hadn't put together back-to-back winning seasons for six years. That year, they did. Yogi was fired, though, and Yankee Stadium didn't see another playoff club for another 11 years.

Casey Stengel said his "assistant manager" could reach into a sewer and pull out a gold watch, and luck had a lot to do with all those twists and turns. No one can win (or lose) on his own, but the facts remain. Every time Yogi Berra walked in the door, major successes followed. As soon as he left, disaster.

WHAT WAS THE SADDEST FAREWELL IN NEW YORK SPORTS?

38 When Karl Spooner played for the 1954 Brooklyn Dodgers, he blew away 15 batters in his debut game and 27 batters in his first 18 innings pitched, but blew out his arm. He left the bigs after only 31 games and hardly more than a glimpse of his full potential.

An aging Mickey Mantle went through his last two years in pinstripes, 1967 and 1968, not as a power-hitting outfielder, but a diminished, limping first baseman. After losing his career .300 average with .245 and .237 seasons, the 38-year-old Mantle finally retired in the spring of 1969.

When Willie Mays returned to New York for one final season, he was a shadow of the Hall of Famer he'd been over the previous 20 years. With a 1973 batting average and slugging percentage more than 100 points below career norms, he was forced out of the game, too.

Yeah, New York's seen some special talents leaving baseball through some sad departures, but none of the above players represented the saddest possible farewells. It's the way of the baseball world that some youngsters will get hurt while some veterans fade away. Not good times, but it happens.

The worst possible exit stood outside of that. A legend left at the very height of his powers for reasons that combined self-destructive penny-pinching and a complete disregard for fan sentiment. The saddest farewell in New York baseball was George Thomas Seaver's trade away from the Mets in the summer of 1977.

In his 10½ years with the Amazin's, Tom Seaver was simply the best pitcher in baseball. From 1967 to 1977, he finished among National League leaders in earned run average, shutouts, complete games, and strikeouts eight or more times each, winning three Cy Young Awards and making 10 All Star Game appearances in the process. The 1977 Mets may have been in last place, but on every fifth game, with Seaver on the mound, they had a fighting chance to be the best team in baseball.

The conflict between Seaver and Mets honcho M. Donald Grant wasn't based on performances, but dollars. It started when Seaver had the nerve to request a market-rate salary, ensuring that one of the best players in baseball would be among the best-compensated employees in the game. Grant, a stockbroker-turned-executive, claimed to be outraged by the outburst of baseball capitalism and refused to offer a new contract, portraying Seaver's request for a raise as a shameful display of greed.

To justify his penny-pinching, Grant enlisted a hard-drinking, profanity-spewing columnist named Dick Young. He went so far as to put Young's son-in-law on the Met payroll, just to make sure their mouthpiece delivered, and soon enough, multiple *Daily News* pieces condemned the supposed sin in the renegotiation. The final straw may have come when Young's confidential, inside source claimed the contract impasse was actually motivated by Nancy Seaver's personal jealousy toward Nolan and Ruth Ryan. Young's confidential, inside source? M. Donald Grant.

The next day, an infuriated Seaver demanded a trade out of town and, all too soon, the organization followed through. In the infamous "Midnight Massacre" of June 15, 1977, the New York Mets dealt him to the Cincinnati Reds in exchange for four spare parts. Aside from a single, ill-fated season in 1983, Tom Seaver spent the remaining 10 years of a brilliant career outside New York.

The Seaver trade caused an unprecedented fan furor in 1977. It didn't seem to make an ounce of sense. Nearly 30 years later, it still doesn't.

Leave aside the notion that Pat Zachry, Doug Flynn, Dan Norman, and Steve Henderson (and a dozen of their best friends) could begin to equal the best pitcher in New York history—even in money-first, financial terms, the transaction was absurd.

"The Franchise" brought an additional 4,000 live fans per game for his starts, and his greatness kept countless more involved in the team's future. The Mets' skimping on his contract cost them irreplaceable ticket sales. Worse still, turning out his proven talent was an unmistakable, toxic confirmation that the front office was unwilling to pony up for the cost of business in the free agency era. And, worst of all, the Mets' cheap-skatery was coming at a time when the cross-town Yankees were winning championships by spending big bucks.

Met fans had plenty of experience in supporting the Amazin's through some lean years, but even the diehards couldn't miss the message in the Seaver trade. The Big Apple's big market, Seaver's Greenwich home, his oft-repeated desire to stay, his past greatness, his years of future greatness . . . none of it meant anything. Suddenly, the franchise's losing was anything but lovable. "I WAS A BELIEVER BUT NOW WE'VE LOST SEAVER," one banner read in June '77. Millions grieved and agreed and, for the first time ever, the bottom fell out in the Met standings and attendance alike.

It would be hard to overstate the charisma deficit created by the move, too. Beyond the numbers, Seaver was the lionized heart of the '69 World Champions, one of the last active reminders of what the team was capable of at their best. He was as clean-cut, handsome, and intelligent as any ballplayer alive, too, and shipping him off to the Midwest meant tossing away an irreplaceable sense of spirit. The front office didn't just trade away the greatest Met of all time—in a sense, it gave away the fans' abiding sense of hope and possibility.

There was a gloom in the Seaver trade, and, strange as it is to say, the gloom traveled far beyond Shea. Around that time, the very fabric of the city started unraveling.

The summer of 1977 was a sweltering, chaotic one in New York. Hundreds of arson fires raged throughout working class neighborhoods, and those who weren't fleeing flames were terrorized by the "Son of Sam" mass murders. Within a month of the "Midnight Massacre," Queens was, literally, plunged into darkness through a massive ConEd blackout. Some of the worst rioting and looting in city history followed. Those were the years when Hollywood started producing basket-case portrayals of the inner city— *Taxi Driver, The Warriors, Escape from New York*, etc. For a while there, it was Hell by the Hudson.

It would be foolish to link those disasters to the stupidest of stupid trades, not in any cold, logical way at least. Still, at the time, all the bad news certainly seemed to be of a piece. With Tom Seaver's sad farewell, a lot of New Yorkers were losing.

JETER & A-ROD— WHO'S THE BETTER CLUTCH HITTER?

39 In some ways, Alex Rodriguez and Derek Jeter have led parallel lives.

They were born less than a year (1974–75) and 30 miles from each other, one in Washington Heights and the other in Pequannock, New Jersey. They grew up rooting for New York teams and playing shortstop. They turned down college to submit to the Minor League draft in 1993 and 1992. When they first saw significant action in the 1995 season, they were two of the three youngest players in the Majors. From their rookie season on, they were mentioned in the debate over the best shortstop in the American League. By 2001, they were among the highest-paid athletes in sports. Finally, after a trade brought Rodriguez from the Texas Rangers to Jeter's Yankees in 2004, they played on the left side of the same infield.

With A-Rod's arrival in New York, however, things changed. A number of commentators became fixated on his differences with Jeter, and, most often, the contrast was pretty unflattering. The consensus from the tabloids and sports radio said that Alex Rodriguez didn't come through for the team, at least not in the way Jeter came through.

The chatter may be popular in some quarters, but that doesn't make it true. In fact, the Empire State Building will launch into orbit before anyone makes a solid, evidence-based argument that Alex Rodriguez takes a backseat to Jeter in the ability to hit for power, get on, run the bases, and stay healthy while doing all the above. Despite their superficial similarities, A-Rod has always been in another league when it comes to hitting.

After 10 full seasons, 1996 to 2005, A-Rod is running almost neck-and-neck with Jeter in on-base percentage (.385 to 386) and batting average (.307 to .314), but completely blows away his rival in power (.577 to .461). Arod has had eight seasons that top Jeter's personal best in slugging (.552) and nine with more than Jeter's high in home runs (24). Through 10 full seasons, he's had a superior on-base-plus-slugging (OPS) number every year, with a yawning difference of .100 or more points in most years. His *eighth* best all-around effort, in 1998, was better than all but two of Jeter's campaigns to date.

Rodriguez has also backed his offensive numbers with an edge in baserunning and durability. He's averaged a slightly higher stolen base success rate (80.2 percent to 79 percent) and more stolen bases (21.9 per full year to Jeter's 21.5) while grounding into one less double play (136 to 137) over the years. He's been just a shade more resilient than Jeter, too, averaging 153 games per season to Jeter's 151.

Of course, Derek Jeter's a strong offensive force in his own right. He's been very productive, compiling more than 2,000 career hits by age 32, so he's also on track for Hall of Fame-quality statistics. He is darn good at playing baseball, but A-Rod's far better.

Still, Rodriguez's day-in, day-out, year-in, year-out accomplishments aren't all that impressive to some. They'll point out when A-Rod hasn't come through when the game was supposedly on the line on this day or that day or some other time. That's simply not fair to Rodriquez.

It doesn't makes sense to pick and choose among certain isolated, short-term situations in evaluating a ballplayer, because in any one game or series, a terrific player can look terrible while a terrible player can look terrific. That's baseball. Respected talent evaluators know as much, which is why they look past flukes to the ways matters even themselves out over the long run. They put their faith in season-long and career-long stats in judging a player's performance, and when they see someone like Alex Rodriguez leading the league in everything from home runs to hits and total bases to batting average, they know he's going to help a team win more ball games.

The long term tells the truth and the short term doesn't necessarily reflect true abilities, and to see how that's so, check out the playoff hitting for both Rodriguez and Jeter.

In the most vital games of the year, A-Rod's had several good series and a couple not-so-good series. The former includes the 1997 ALDS against the Orioles, the 2000 ALCS against the Yankees, 2004 ALDS against Twins, and (most of) the 2004 ALCS against the Red Sox—in those 17 games, he averaged an incredible .647 slugging average to go along with a .412 on-base percentage (1.059 OPS). However, in another couple series, the 2000 ALDS against the White Sox and the 2005 ALDS against the Angels, things turned out much differently. In the latter games, A-Rod averaged a considerably more modest, if not pitiful, .254 slugging and .345 OBP (.599 OPS).

Rodriguez has had his ups and downs in October, but so has his rival.

Sometimes, Jeter's risen to the occasion. For instance, he's batted over .400 in seven good series, including the 1996 ALDS against the Orioles and the 2000 World Series against the Mets, when he averaged an impressive 1.000-plus in OPS. However, he's also sunk to the occasion by hitting less than .250 or less in another eight series, including the 1998 ALDS against the Rangers (.384 OPS), 2000 ALDS against the Athletics (.529), and 2001 ALCS against the Mariners (.318). Jeter's been both on and off come October, and sometimes at almost the exact same time, like the 2001 World Series when he came up with a late-inning home run off Byung-Hyun Kim but otherwise batted a dismal .148 over seven games.

Jeter's had the most playoff at-bats in Major League history (462), so he's had more than a few opportunities to compile good playoff memories and totals, but, like A-Rod, he's had both streaks and slumps along the way. There's nothing particularly unusual about that. Babe Ruth, Joe DiMaggio, Yogi Berra, and Mickey Mantle all had bad play-off series at one time or another (#36), but they were nonetheless recognized as big-spot performers in making up for the stumbles in the long term.

The most important thing is doing well overall, and this is where Rodriguez stands out—if A-Rod hit in the regular season with the same OPS (.927) number he had in his six postseason series (31 games) through 2005, he'd have finished ahead of the regular-season performances of Frank Robinson, Duke Snider, Al Simmons, Mike Schmidt, and more than a dozen other Hall of Famers.

Rodriguez's playoff hitting had a decided edge over nearly everyone, and everyone included Jeter. Actually, both A-Rod's OBP (.393 to DJ's .379) and slugging percentage (.534 to .463) were far better in October. That may be one reason, among others, that a confidential *Sports Illustrated* poll of 470 Major Leaguers once called out a certain "Captain Clutch" as the most overrated player in the game.

Anyway, in summary:

1. Through 2005, Alex Rodriguez had been a far better hitter than Derek Jeter in regular season games, and that means he's been far more likely to carry a team into the playoffs.

2. Alex Rodriguez has been a far better hitter than Derek Jeter in playoff games, and that means he's far been more likely to carry a team to a championship.
3. Because of 1. and 2., Alex Rodriguez has been a better clutch hitter than Derek Jeter.

IS ALEX RODRIGUEZ REALLY ON TRACK TO BECOME THE LEADING POWER HITTER OF ALL TIME?

40 Alex Rodriguez is so much better than Derek Jeter, and everyone else, that his ultimate peer group will be among the Pastime's all-time sluggers.

If you assume he's played exactly half of a 20-year career by 2005, then A-Rod will eventually surpass Hank Aaron's Major League records for lifetime home runs (by more than 100 home runs), in RBI (by more than 150), and total bases (by nearly 300 bases). Given Rodriguez's career rate through 2005, he'll bypass 755 career home runs, 2,297 RBI, and 6,856 total bases sometime in 2013.

With Rodriguez's renowned work ethic and durability, there's little reason to believe he'll slow down much in the future, but even if he does or if Yankee Stadium robs him of some righty power, he'll still do just fine. Let's say he downshifts from his production level of 42-plus home runs, 120-plus RBI, and 350-plus total bases per full year. Let's say Alex the Great slacks off all the way down to a mere 33 homers, 108 RBI, and 328 bases per annum through age 40—he'll still finish at No. 1 in the all-time categories as they now stand.

Barry Bonds' chase for the career home run record has made a lot of headlines for a long time. He may take the record. Until Alex Rodriguez catches him.

JETER & A-ROD—WHO'S THE BETTER LEADER?

41 No one can claim that Derek Jeter is anywhere close to Alex Rodriguez as a power hitter. In their 10 full years they've played in the American League, Jeter has fallen far, far behind in everything from slugging percentage (.461 to A-Rod's .577) and home runs (169 to 429) to total bases (2,845 to 3,576).

Quality numbers are all fine and good, The Derek Jeter Fan Club might argue, but they don't reveal their favorite's full value. While Rodriguez may produce more offense, Jeter produces more leadership for the Yankees. The *New York Times* called him the Bombers' "maximum leader."

Jeter = Leader. Everybody knows that. Everybody says so. Everybody's wrong.

After all, hitting is leadership, isn't it? Hitting . . . leads . . . to winning, and for that reason, a hitter named Alex Rodriguez was the Yankees' real leader over his first two years in pinstripes.

In 2004 and 2005, #13 led teammates in the all-important slugging and on-base percentage stats, along with offensive categories ranging from batting average and total bases to runs scored and stolen bases. Among other things, he hit 48 home runs in the process of winning the American League MVP award in 2005, becoming the first right-handed Yankee to hit more than 40 since Joe DiMaggio, nearly 60 years before. A-Rod finished a mere eight RBI short of Gary Sheffield in run production for 2004–05, despite Sheff's advantage in hitting with far more runners in scoring position.

Most important of all, Rodriguez's production carried the Yankees to 95 and 101 regular season wins. With the their winning the AL East by three games and a tiebreaker in those two years, the team's de facto offensive MVP was, more than anyone else, the one who slugged them into the playoffs.

Jeter? Jeter had excellent seasons in comparison to Major Leaguers who are not Alex Rodriguez. Unfortunately, his most remarkable contribution to the Yankees' recent fortunes was both incredibly selfish and disastrous.

When A-Rod was traded from the Texas Rangers before the 2004 season, the Yanks were faced with the necessity of moving one of two lifelong shortstops out of position. Either Rodriguez or Jeter would have to make a wholesale transition in replacing Aaron Boone at third base. The only question was who.

On the surface, there was no choice at all—Jeter, the inferior fielder, had to make way. Through the 2003 season, he had a noticeably lower fielding percentage than Rodriguez (.974 to .979) but, more importantly, far less range—Jeter's putouts and assists per game exceeded the league average just once in the eight previous seasons, even as A-Rod beat the AL average every single year. While Jeter significantly underperformed on defense in the typical year (a lowly 3.99 range factor vs. the AL average of 4.15), Rodriguez was his usual superstar self with the glove (4.47 vs. the same 4.15 average).

In fairness, it should be said that Jeter has made a few spectacular fielding plays, none more spectacular than the "flip play" in the 2001 ALDS against the Athletics or the diving catch into the stands in a July 2004 game against the Red Sox, but a handful of highlights didn't begin to make up for his deficiencies over 162-game seasons. DJ's day-to-day numbers confirmed what most observers already knew—he took too long to react to batted balls, got too many bad jumps, wasn't sure-handed enough, hesitated in throws to first base, and covered second base too slowly in the pivot.

Clearly, with Rodriguez coming on board in '04, Jeter's correct choice was obvious. He had to follow Mickey Mantle's precedent and shift away from his original shortstop position. The leader had to lead his way over to third base for the good of the organization.

Unfortunately, as the numbers shouted one thing, Derek Jeter, apparently, whispered something completely different. Either through backdoor needling or stony silence, the incumbent made it clear he didn't want to move in favor of the new arrival, and, for all intents and purposes, that settled things. With Jeter's all-important ego soothed, the Yankees' stuck with a rotten status quo in the most crucial defensive position in the infield. The team fielded one of the worst shortstops in the league over one of the best, but no one heard a discouraging word.

Talk about politics over performance. Talk about diva behavior.

And yet . . .

JETER & A-ROD— WHO HAS BETTER INTANGIBLES?

42 And yet the Derek Jeter Appreciation Society still stands by its man. Regardless of his relative shortcomings in offensive punch and his "me first" hold on shortstop, Jeter's believed to express leadership qualities in other more subtle ways. He has magic. Or, as it's more often expressed, "intangibles."

According to the standard theory, Jeter's exhibited more leadership than Winston Churchill, more chemistry than a Nobel Prize winner, more rah-rah spirit than a Dallas Cowboys cheerleader, and more vision than an optometrist. He's been singled out for valentines from Tim Kurkjian ("he has a nice face, a rugged face, a handsome face") and Tim McCarver (who once extolled Jeter's "calm eyes"). John Kruk thinks he's a winner.

Rodriguez, according to the magic/"intangibles" theory, is the Muggle to Jeter's Harry Potter. Word is, he doesn't have attitude, aura, or grit and guts, or poise and pride. Giddy broadcasters don't develop man-crushes on him. A-Rod apparently doesn't know how to win, or, perhaps, forgot at some point.

Back in the real world, though, the "intangibles"/magic theory is about as trustworthy as a $3 bill.

Derek Jeter is, by all accounts, an upstanding individual, a valued employee, and a fine American, but there's no reason to believe those qualities help him win anything but sacks of fan mail and rounds of cheers. Jeter's highly paid, All Star teammates are successful exactly because they don't need the captain's charm, and the struggling few who do need a pep talk—Carl Pavano, Jeff Weaver, Raul Mondesi, and Rondell White, among others—tend to wash out regardless of #2's motivational powers. The many free agent busts of the Derek Jeter Era have always resembled the stiffs Rodriguez couldn't redeem while playing with the Rangers.

There have been recent times when the Yankees have needed leadership, to be certain, but, unfortunately, the Prince of New York was AWOL. For instance, when an certain rival—let's call him "Alex Rodriguez"—was targeted by the Red Sox's pot shots during spring training 2005 and angry boo-birds in the summer of 2006, Jeter didn't lead his way from a highly-lucrative, milquetoast public image by taking a public stand. He certainly didn't dispel rumors of a long-standing resentment toward a certain MVP's accomplishments. No, on those days, Jeter only led himself into his usual arsenal of inoffensive platitudes. It was up to his "Mr. Torre" to take all the slings and arrows.

Off-field personality and work ethic do count in leadership, of course, but it's unclear why Rodriguez isn't considered Jeter's equal as a clubhouse presence. There have been no tantrums, no controversies, and no arrests, ever. When A-Rod's attacked, he says it's part of the game. He's seemingly oblivious to his superior performance. He's deferential to a fault ("Derek makes this team go. What happens out there begins with him"). Some insiders say they find Rodriguez more approachable than the nominal captain, and they've seen him put in at least as much sweat through 100 percent hustle and year-round workouts.

The only knock on A-Rod's lead, it seems, is in the way he sometimes cares too much. Regardless of all the individual awards and the set-for-life contract, he's not completely above it all or bulletproof, not in Jeteresque fashion. A superstar's numbers coexist with an ordinary guy's sensitivity, so he can drive too hard to prove himself against the fans' expectations. If and when Alex Rodriguez overcomes that very human situation, he may lead the Yankees to even greater heights.

WHY CAN'T RODRIGUEZ CATCH A BREAK?

43 Someone who's earned more than a quarter-billion dollars playing the game he loves will never be a prime recipient of public sympathy, but it's impossible to ignore the effect of bad luck and bad decisions on Alex Rodriguez's reputation. There are reasons he's always had to play Mondale to Derek Jeter's Reagan:

Jeter grew up with two loving parents in middle-class Kalamazoo. Rodriguez grew up with a single mom in the impoverished Dominican Republic.

Jeter always rooted for the Yankees. Rodriguez was a Met fan.

Jeter was drafted by guess-who. Rodriguez was drafted by the Seattle Mariners.

Jeter won Rookie of the Year in 1996. Rodriguez wasn't eligible for ROY.

Jeter was assigned the last of the Yankees' coveted single digits. Rodriguez got unlucky #13.

Jeter came up with a talent-rich roster featuring a young Mariano Rivera, Bernie Williams, and Jorge Posada, and he's always gotten vicarious credit for their accomplishments. Rodriguez signed with an organization featuring Chan Ho Park, Mark Clark, and Rick Helling, and he's always gotten vicarious blame for their failures.

175

Jeter won four championship rings in first five seasons. Alex Rodriguez is Don Mattingly.

Jeter's a bachelor who once dated Mariah Carey. Rodriguez is married and his wife, while gorgeous, has never hit the Top 10.

Jeter's never had a minute of worry over his 10-year, $189 million contract. Rodriguez's never stopped getting grief over his big deal.

Jeter succeeded icons like Lou Gehrig and Thurman Munson as Yankee captain in 2003. Rodriguez succeeded no one in being named Rangers captain in '03. Then he was traded.

Jeter never had to deal with trade headaches. When the Rangers couldn't figure out how to deal him to Boston, Red Sox fans blamed A-Rod.

Derek's new scent ("Driven") featured "chilled grapefruit, clean oak moss, and spice." No one wants to smell Alex.

Finally, Derek Jeter's crafted the most bland, media-ready image in sports. Alex Rodriguez—"he tries too hard to be perfect."

WHAT MOMENTS HAVE YANKEE HATERS LOVED MOST?

44 & 45 When some gaze on to the New York Yankees' realm, they see the greatness defined by 26 World Championships and 39 American League pennants, a parade of all-time greats, a tireless ownership, and a contented nation of millions. It's baseball heaven.

Then again, others look over at the Bronx Bombers and see an unlovable Goliath featuring an overgrown award collection, a string of overpublicized mercenaries, a born blowhard, and a bunch of entitlement-minded bandwagon jumpers. Damn Yankees.

So be it. Legions of fans can be matched by armies of haters, and for the latter group, some of the best bad times have included:

* Jack Chesbro's wild pitch lets in the winning run for Boston in the last day of the season, clinching the American League pennant for the Pilgrims. (October 1904)
* George Stalling goes public with well-founded suspicions that first baseman Hal Chase has been throwing games for gamblers. Strangely enough, team owners

decide to fire Stallings and replace him with Chase. Not-so-strangely, Chase takes the Yanks from second to sixth place as player-manager in the next season. (September 1910)

* Babe Ruth, felled with severe cramps and a fever, undergoes the abdominal surgery that will limit him to the worst season of his career. "The Bellyache Heard Round the World" may have been an intestinal abscess caused by too many hot dogs and sodas. Or, maybe, gonorrhea caused by too many hookers. (March 1925)

* Murderer's Row gets killed in four games in a row, including a three-game sweep by Cleveland. (August 1927)

* Future Lew Burdette is shipped off from the Bronx after 1⅓ career innings pitched. (August 1951)

* Burdette returns to the Bronx as a member of the pennant-winning Braves. After an unnamed Yankee official declares Milwaukee to be "a bush town," the Braves beat the Yankees in a seven-game World Series. MVP Burdette goes 3–0 with a 0.67 ERA. (October 1957)

* The Pittsburgh Pirates, out-scored by 55 to 27 and out-hit by 91 to 60 in the World Series, nonetheless out-win the Yankees by four to three. Mickey Mantle bursts into tears on the flight back home. (October 1960)

* Casey Stengel is fired by the Yankees for being 70 years old. (October 1960)

* Casey Stengel is hired by the Mets despite being 71 years old. In the last years of his life, he'll sign all autographs with the inscription "Casey Stengel, NY Mets, 1966 HoF." (September 1961)

* The Bombers complete a season that saw them go from 99-63/first place to 77-85/last place within two short years. (September 1966)

* Denny McClain grooves Mickey Mantle's 535th and second-to-last Major League home run. Years later, McLain is sentenced to eight years in federal prison. (September 1968)

* During a battle for first place in the AL East, Red Sox catcher Carlton Fisk beats up both shortstop Gene Michael and catcher Thurman Munson during a brawl at home plate. Boston wins in the bottom of the ninth inning, 3–2. (August 1973)

* Graig Nettles' broken bat produces a single and six hidden superballs. Nettles proclaims his innocence ("some Yankees fan in Chicago gave it to me and said it would bring me good luck"), but the men in blue toss him. (September 1974)

* Centerfielder Bobby Bonds invites his 11-year-old son in on batting practice, only to have manager Billy Martin run the scamp off the field. In 2006, Barry Bonds breaks Babe Ruth's home run record. (June 1975)

* Rookie Mark Fidrych of the Tigers baffles the first-place Yankees in a nationally televised *Monday Night*

Baseball game, 5–1. A near-sellout crowd in Detroit goes bonkers, calling out their hero for a deafening postgame curtain call. (June 1976)

* A bored Reggie Jackson jogs after Jim Rice's check-swing hit in the sixth inning of a crucial Red Sox-Yankees series at Fenway. Martin immediately pulls Jax from right field, despite the fact he'd already had two hits in the game. When the volatile slugger approaches the volatile manager, it takes half the team to keep them from exchanging punches. (June 1977)

* The Standard Brands Confectionary Company launches their new "Reggie!" candy bar by giving away 72,000 free samples on Opening Day. Its namesake hits a first-inning, three-run home run off Wilbur Wood of the White Sox, prompting stadium fans to give thousands of orange-and-blue squares right back. Chicago manager Bob Lemon laments, "People starving all over the world and 30 billion calories are laying on the field." (April 1978)

* A "tired and emotional" Martin, referring to former friends Jackson and George Steinbrenner, says "One's a born liar and the other's convicted." He "decides" to "resign" a couple days later. (July 1978)

* Goose Gossage and Cliff Johnson engage in a naked shoving match in the clubhouse showers. Gossage gets three months on the disabled list and Johnson gets a one-way ticket to Cleveland. (April 1979)

* A new decade dawns, one that would see a reverse youth movement featuring the dispatch of Willie McGee, Fred McGriff, Jose Rijo, Doug Drabek, Jay Buhner, and Al Leiter.

Meanwhile, the Yankees begin a 10-year spending binge for the free agent services of Dave Collins, Steve Kemp, Bob Shirley, Dale Murray, Joe Cowley, Roy Smalley, and Ed Whitson.

And Marty Bystrom, Claudell Washington, Steve Trout, and Jack Clark.

And John Candelaria, Steve Sax, Dave LaPoint, Rick Rhoden, Pascual Perez, and Mel Hall. (January 1980)

* After the Yankees lose three straight one-run World Series games in LA, Steinbrenner breaks his hand. The injury is caused by a fistfight with two phantom Dodger fans. Or, maybe, a punch against an elevator wall. (October 1981)

* After New York declines to resign him, Jackson returns to the Bronx as a member of the visiting California Angels. He receives a standing ovation, hits a game-winning homer off Ron Guidry, and receives a raucous round of REG-GIE! REG-GIE!'s. (April 1982)

* The 1982 season concludes after featuring three managers, five pitching coaches, three hitting coaches, and a record 47 ballplayers. (September 1982)

* The Yankees win "The Pine Tar Game" after George Brett's game-winning home run bat is disallowed by

AL umpire Tim McClellan. Brett is very, very unhappy. (July 1983)

* The Yankees lose "The Pine Tar Game" after George Brett's game-winning home run bat is allowed by AL President Lee MacPhail. Brett is very, very happy. (July 1983)

* Outfielder Dave Winfield causes an international incident when he kills a seagull with a warm up toss during a road game against the Toronto Blue Jays. Otherwise well-mannered Canadians are enraged by Winfield's mock "memorial" salute to the dead bird. Our neighbors to the north respond by hurling obscenities and dispatching the Ontario Provincial Police to book Winfield for cruelty to animals (the charges were later dropped). (August 1983)

* Beloved icon/manager Yogi Berra is unceremoniously dumped 16 games into the season. (April 1985)

* The Blue Jays win the AL East by two games. A rueful George Steinbrenner reflects on the Jackson/Winfield era by stating "I got rid of Mr. October and got Mr. May." (September 1985)

* Martin and pitcher Ed Whitson share an early-morning drink at a Baltimore bar, the kind that leaves a 57-year-old manager with a broken arm and a starter with bruised ribs. Both are gone within a few months. (September 1985)

* After the owner swears he'll never sell the team during his lifetime, *Saturday Night Live* begins running the "George Steinbrenner Health Watch" as a public

service. A despondent Phil Hartman reports that The Boss is currently feeling fine. (October 1989)

* Due to three errors in an inning, Andy Hawkins loses an eight-inning no-hitter to the White Sox by a score of 4-0. It's the Majors' first no-hit loss in 26 years. (July 1990)

* Stump Merrill and Bucky Dent lead the troops to a 67-95 record. The Bombers finish 15th in Major League attendance. (September 1990)

* Yankee fan Billy Crystal premieres *City Slickers*. He wears a Met cap throughout the movie. (June 1991)

* After starter Jack McDowell gives up nine earned runs in 4⅔ innings, the home crowd gives him a Bronx cheer on his way off the field. McDowell responds with a one-finger salute, taking care to turn in a 360 degree circle so everyone can take it in. (July 1995)

* Renegade Yankee executive George Costanza smears strawberries on Ruth's vintage jersey, streaks through the infield, and drags a World Series trophy through the stadium parking lot while yelling "Attention, front-office morons! Your triumphs mean nothing. You all stink. You can sit on it and rotate!" Costanza's later traded to Tyson Chicken. (October 1995)

* The front office fines debut author David Wells $100,000 for his claim that he suffered a "skull-rattling hangover" during his perfect game in 1998. Literary critics also slam the *Perfect I'm Not!* tome for its uninspired, derivative prose. (March 2003)

* The Yankees go up 3 to 0 against Boston in the 2004 American League Championship Series, but the Red Sox, faced with four straight do-or-die games, do. After the biggest winners in playoff history suffer the worst collapse in playoff history, thousands put away the "1918!" and "I'm Your Daddy" signs. (October 2004)

* Newly signed free agent Randy Johnson introduces himself to his new home through a heated exchange with a local TV cameraman. Johnson snaps "Don't get in my face and don't talk back to me!" His new friend replies, "Welcome to New York!" (January 2005)

WHAT ARE THE YANKEE HATERS' FAVORITE MOVIES?

46
The lineup for a Yankee hater's film festival:

Damn Yankees. A distraught Senators fan sells his soul to the devil in exchange for the American League pennant. Joe Hardy gets out of the deal but defeats the Yankees anyway. (1958)

The Bad News Bears. Scrappy, lovable Little Leaguers are tormented by the bullying and poor sportsmanship of their Yankee rivals. The Bears lose the big ball game but gain perspective—they tell the Yanks they can shove their trophy. (1976)

The Natural. A 19-year-old Roy Hobbs bets cash money he can strike out a thinly veiled version of a loud, strutting Babe Ruth ("The Whammer") on three pitches. Hobbs collects. (1984)

Brewster's Millions. Newly flush Minor League pitcher Monty Brewster pays seven figures to arrange a very special exhibition game. The Hackensack Bulls beat the New York Yankees. (1985)

Naked Gun. Reggie Jackson is brainwashed to act as an assassin against Her Royal Majesty Queen Elizabeth II. Thankfully, the daring of Italian tenor Enrico Pallazo defeats the former Yankee. (1988)

Major League. Jake Taylor, Wild Thing Vaughn, and the scrappy, lovable underdogs on the Cleveland Indians face surly Clue Haywood and company in the big game. There's a happy ending as the Yankees are defeated. (1989)

For Love of the Game. Billy Chapel, Gus Sinski, and the scrappy, lovable underdogs on the Detroit Tigers face mercenary Davis Birch and company in the big game. There's a happy ending as the Yankees are defeated. (1999)

Fever Pitch. Jason Varitek, Trot Nixon, and the scrappy, lovable underdogs on the Boston Red Sox face their No. 1 rivals in the big game. There's a happy ending as the Yankees are defeated. (2005)

WHAT WERE THE COOLEST NICKNAMES OF ALL TIME?

47 Anyone who's ever read the driver's license of a Manhattan cabbie knows that given names aren't always the best, most snappy names to be had. Sometimes inventive little nicknames do the trick instead, and some of the coolest ones in New York baseball have included:

BALLPLAYERS

Christy **"The Christian Gentleman"** Mathewson. Matty would have been a minister if he hadn't made it in the National Pastime. His alternative nickname, **"Big Six,"** referred either to his 6' height or an oversized fire truck from the early 1900s.

"Iron" Joe McGinnity. One of the most durable pitchers of all time, but the moniker originated from his one-time stint as a foundry worker.

Frank **"Home Run"** Baker. Retired with only 96 homers but did hit a couple in back-to-back games during the 1911 World Series.

Lou **"The Iron Horse"** Gehrig. Derived from an Old West phrase for a locomotive. Sportswriter Jim Murray called Gehrig **"Gibraltar in Spikes"**

"Dixie" **"The People's Cherce"** Walker. Always spelled (and pronounced) with a mid-century Brooklyn accent. Given name: Fred.

"King Carl" Hubbell. As in ERA royalty. Alternative nickname: **"The Meal Ticket"**

Dick **"Rowdy Richard"** Bartell. A Giants infielder who led the league in double plays and fistfights. "They hated him with a cold fury in Brooklyn."

Joe **"The Yankee Clipper"** DiMaggio. After a 19th-century sailing ship renowned for its grace and speed. Less imaginative alternative: **"Joltin' Joe"**

Tommy **"Old Reliable"** Henrich. Bestowed by Mel Allen after a train that always ran on time. In the words of one contemporary reporter: "He was without peer as a player and a gentleman."

Charlie **"King Kong"** Keller. Was unusually big and strong. And hairy, to be honest.

"Pistol" Pete Reiser. Had a habit of colliding into outfield walls, which was nearly as dangerous as playing with guns.

Phil **"Scooter"** Rizzuto. Used all of 5'6", 160 lbs. to win the 1950 MVP award. "Billy Hitchcock told me, 'you're not running, you're scooting.'"

Johnny **"The Big Cat"** Mize. Surprisingly nimble for a big man, but only stole 28 career bases.

Allie **"SuperChief"** Reynolds. Born in Oklahoma with a one-quarter Creek heritage.

"Whitey" **"The Chairman of the Board"** Ford. Another Allen invention—he liked how "board" rhymed with "Ford." An alternative nickname, "Slick," either referred his habit of "whiskey slick" drinking or spitball tossing. Given name: Edward

Enos **"Country"** Slaughter. Hailed from backwoods North Carolina before he arrived in the big city.

"Bullet" Bob Turley. Threw very, very fast.

"Marvelous" Marv Throneberry. Hit 16 home runs in 366 at-bats for the '62 Mets, which wasn't exactly marvelous, but wasn't terrible, either.

Jim **"Bulldog"** Bouton. After he wrote *Ball Four*, Pete Rose took to calling him "Shakespeare."

"Tom Terrific" Seaver. A completely fitting tag (#32). Alternative nickname: **"The Franchise"**

"Rusty" **"Le Grand Orange"** Staub. First heard while he starred in Montreal, Quebec. Given name: Daniel.

"Sudden" Sam McDowell. See **"Bullet Bob"** Turley.

Don **"Donnie Baseball"** Mattingly. By far the most popular Yankee of his era.

Hensley **"Bam Bam"** Meulens. Didn't exactly live up to the name—15 career home runs.

David **"Boomer"** Wells. Tended to talk a lot without saying much. Roger Clemens referred to him as "Eli," "cause if 'e talkin, 'e lyin'."

Roger **"Rocket"** Clemens. Raised in NASA's home town and threw pretty darn hard, too.

Hideki **"Godzilla"** Matsui. Back home, he hit enough home runs to destroy the Tokyo skyline.

Randy **"The Big Unit"** Johnson. Probably a reference to his, ummm, height. At 6'10", he's one of the tallest pitchers in MLB history.

MANAGERS

John **"Little Napoleon"** McGraw. Kind of redundant, isn't it? Opponents also called him "Muggsy," though not to his face.

"Prince Hal" Chase. In actuality, a cheating, gambling lout (#44).

Frank **"The Peerless Leader"** Chance. May well be the most flattering nickname of all time. Sometimes abbreviated as "The PL" (seriously).

Wilbert **"Uncle Robbie"** Robinson. The Dodgers loved their genial, roly-poly skipper so much that they changed their name to the "Robins" from 1914 to 1931. Brooklynites called his wife "Aunt Mary."

Miller **"The Mighty Mite"** Huggins. One of the smallest ballplayers of his time or any time. Managed Babe Ruth, one of the biggest ballplayers of his time or any time.

"Memphis Bill" Terry.

Casey **"The Ole' Perfessor"** Stengel. Like many academics, often referred to fact records to support his conclusions ("You could look it up.").

Ralph **"The Major"** Houk. Served as a U.S. Marine officer in World War II, winning the Silver Star for bravery in combat.

BALL CLUBS

The teams who collected the most cool nicknames in one clubhouse:

The '51 Giants, featuring a lineup with **The Brat, The Say Hey Kid,** and **Spider** along with a staff featuring **The Barber** and **Bambi**—managed by **Leo the Lip.**

Also known as Eddie Stanky, Willie Mays, and John Jorgenson, along with Sal Maglie and George Bamberger and manager Leo Durocher.

The '55 Dodgers, featuring a lineup with **Campy, Skoonj, Pee Wee, The Duke of Flatbush, Junior, Zim, Rube,** and **Dixie** along with a staff featuring **The Mad Monk, Newk** and **Oisk.**

Also known as Roy Campanella, Carl Furillo, Harold Reese, Edwin Snider, Jim Gilliam, Don Zimmer, Albert Walker, and Homer Howell, along with Russ Meyer, Don Newcombe, and Carl Erskine.

The '78 Yankees, featuring a lineup with **Sweet Lou, Mick the Quick, Mr. October, Bucky,** and **Chicken** along with a staff featuring **Sparky, Goose, Gator, Dirt,** and **Catfish.** Managed by **Billy the Kid** and coached by **Yogi.**

Also known as Lou Piniella, Mickey Rivers, Reggie Jackson, Russell Dent, and Fred Stanley, along with Albert Lyle, Rich Gossage, Ron Guidry, Dick Tidrow, and Jim Hunter and Billy Martin and Lawrence Berra.

The '86 Mets, featuring a lineup with **Mex, The Kid, Maz, Straw, Nails, Mookie, World, Teuf,** and **HoJo** along with a staff featuring **El Sid** and **Dr. K.**

Also known as Keith Hernandez, Gary Carter, Lee Mazzilli, Darryl Strawberry, Lenny Dykstra, William (!) Wilson, Kevin Mitchell, Tim Teufel, and Howard Johnson, along with Sid Fernandez and Dwight Gooden.

HIS MOM CALLED HIM "ELWIN"

Players whose names became nicknames:

Dazzy **"Clarence"** Vance

Muddy **"Herold"** Ruel

Lefty **"Francis"** O'Doul

Babe **"George"** Ruth

Babe **"Floyd"** Herman

Lefty **"Vernon"** Gomez

Schoolboy **"Lynwood"** Rowe

Spud **"Spurgeon"** Chandler

Preacher **"Elwin"** Roe

Ducky **"Joe"** Medwick

Bucky **"Stanley"** Harris

Whitey **"Caroll"** Lockman

Dusty **"James"** Rhodes

Moose **"William"** Skowron

Choo Choo **"Clarence"** Coleman

Tug **"Frank"** McGraw

Doc **"George"** Medich

WHAT WERE THE COLDEST NICKNAMES OF ALL TIME?

48

Fred **"Bonehead"** Merkle. See #8.

"Fat" Freddie Fitzsimmons. Rotund.

Johnny **"Grandma"** Murphy. Complained all the time, just like his teammate's grandmother.

Eddie **"The Junkman"** Lopat. Overcame rag-arm velocity with superb off-speed guile and guesswork.

Harry **"Suitcase"** Simpson. Played for six teams in eight years in the Majors, including the 1957–58 Yankees.

BASEBALL MULTICULTURALISM

Emil **"Irish"** Meusel—German

Keith **"Mex"** Hernandez—Spanish

"El Sid" Fernandez—Hawaiian

"Black" Jack McDowell—White-American

WILL THE YANKEES' NEW BALLPARK DEMOLISH TRADITION?

49 Nothing in the National Pastime can compare to Yankee Stadium.

161st Street and River Avenue is the most historical destination for the most historical franchise in the most historical game. The infield dirt is the infield dirt where Joe D. hit safely though 56 straight games in the Summer of '41. The grass is the grass where #7 was immortalized during Mickey Mantle Day in the Summer of '69. The outfield wall is the outfield wall bounded by Chris Chambliss' pennant-winning home run in the Autumn of '76.

Yankee Stadium holds too many good memories to count. It's the grandest, most prestigious ballpark in America. Good lord, it's the very Cathedral of Baseball. For many, the thought of demolishing it . . . that's down there with a decision to sell the Statue of Liberty for scrap metal or converting Gracie Mansion into storage space. It just couldn't and shouldn't be done.

But, oh, it could be done. The only remaining debate is over the "should" part.

Team ownership, the city, and state officially sealed its fate in 2005, announcing they were going to replace The House that Ruth Built in time for Opening Day 2009. And, to judge from the plans, they should have done it long ago.

The first thing to love about the new Stadium is its resemblance to the old Stadium. The club isn't moving across the continent but across the street, shifting from the current location to the present-day site of Macombs Dam Park. The new ball yard will be called Yankee Stadium, and the same field dimensions and look will prevail, as will the signature logo and pinstripes. The shrine's monuments and plaques and assorted keepsakes will still be around. The exterior walls of the old Stadium will have to go, but the playing field itself will live on as public parkland.

In some ways, the brand-spanking new Yankee Stadium will be even more traditional than the present building. For instance, it'll bypass changes from the massive Stadium overhaul of 1973–75 to replicate the original exterior. The famed latticework frieze will ring the entire roof again, too, for the first time in more than 30 years. The architects of the renowned HOK firm have pledged that the new model will stay true to dozens of other details from the original ballpark, some of which haven't seen the light of day for generations. Far from demolishing the oldest, most revered Stadium features, they'll be reintroducing them. The future will go back to the past.

While the new Yankee Stadium smoothes the path to a new address in key respects, it does break with tradition in other ways. And thank goodness for that.

An honest assessment of the present Yankee Stadium has to include plenty of characteristics worth losing. The 1910's style traffic access on the Major Deegan and Grand Concourse means today's commute is a nightmare, and antiquated facilities force fans to wait in line for concessions and urgent bathroom visits. And then there are the narrow walkways, tight aisles, and upper decks that are as steep as they are distant. They may as well be in Staten Island.

The new ballpark will demolish all of that. By 2009, fans will benefit from vastly improved facilities, ones that will include noticeably more accessible transportation, plentiful parking, convenient bathrooms, upgraded food stations, wider concourses, roomier seating, and more comfy seat alignments. The seating dimensions will be smaller and the scoreboard will be bigger. Fans will be paying higher prices in the new Stadium, to be sure, but then again, they'll be getting more for the money, too. What's taken so long?

The new ballpark's most meaningful departure from the not-so-good-old-days will be in its surroundings. Today's Stadium can look like a fortress, holding the outside world out and the inside in. Tomorrow's Stadium, though, will inject far more of the Bronx into the Bronx Bombers.

If all goes as planned, the team will inject a record $800 million team investment into new hotels, a museum, leased office space, park lands (including new ball fields), and a multiuse track facility, all in return for government money in an improved waterfront, new ferry pier, a Metro-North train station, and extended subway platform. It's a huge win for the Bronx, which is why so many local residents are cheering on the new Stadium proposal.

More importantly, the plans will allow the borough and ballpark to be integrated into an interconnected community for the first time. Ordinary urban streets will become an active, vendor-friendly promenades running from the new access points to the turnstiles. The Bronx County Courthouse parking lot will become a terraced pedestrian park known as Lou Gehrig Plaza. The Grand Concourse area will be more of a, umm, grand place to hang out by opening day 2009, with a look and feel resembling Chicago's cozy Wrigleyville or Boston's carnival-like Yawkey Way.

In short, the new Yankee Stadium promises to usher in a new era. Gone will be the days when the team bluffs a move to Jersey or the world sees the Bronx as a side ghetto. Arriving will be a time when 3–4 million happy fans per year are welcomed into a completely reborn neighborhood. Again, what's taken so long?

That's not the entire debate, needless to say. Despite the continuities in the new Yankee Stadium, its improvements, and transition into the Bronx, some still can't get past the sentiment tied to the progress. They want to hold on to the tradition, to hold on to the same old infield dirt and grass and outfield walls. They want to keep the same old building in the same old place doing the same old thing.

In another town, that notion might fly. Not in New York.

The very first New Yorkers came to build a new world in America and city residents are still building new worlds. For nearly four centuries, old-line technologies, thoughts, customs, rituals, and prejudices have arrived to our shores and streets to be swept aside by the new and improved. The shelf-life of its status quo has always been ticked off in New York minutes, and the Yankee organization is a perfect example of that impermanence. There have never been enough wins or championships or packed houses over the last 83 years. There never will be. Why would they turn down a once-in-a-century shot at bringing the whole thing forward once again?

The oldest, dearest New York tradition of all says, "Past times were great, but the future can be even better." And the new Yankee Stadium will carry on that one just fine.

IS KING GEORGE A TYRANT?

50 People say some pretty mean things about George Steinbrenner. And they're all true.

They say King George has racked up countless firings, rehirings, and firings over the years. He's constantly harassed, hollered, and heckled his employees to do better. He's been a *Seinfeld* character come to life, full of bluster, bellowing, and bullying. Everyone knew about his habit of treating even the brightest, most hardworking employees like a bag of used-up baseballs.

That one's undeniable.

The Steinbrenner-haters say his "winning is essential" slogan sucked the fun out of the game. High-strung, high-pressure ways contributed to a less than light and carefree atmosphere in Yankeeland, so 100-win seasons were no big deal, playoff spots were only necessary, and pennants were stepping stones. Nothing less than World Championships were enough to make the resident megalomaniac happy and even those represented relief more than joy.

Sounds about right.

The critics have also declared that George M. Steinbrenner III has been terminally greedy in his willingness to outspend for new free agents. He invented mad shopping sprees before Jennifer Lopez bought her first handbag, which means that Yankee rosters have always had more than their fair share free-agents-for-hire. Too often, New York's version of baseball competition has had as much to do with dollars and cents as strikes and balls.

Again . . . guilty, guilty, guilty.

There are reasons for all the loose "Evil Empire" talk around the Bronx Bombers. Depending on their views about taxes and *Star Wars*, opponents have ranked George Steinbrenner's Yankees up there with the IRS and Darth Vader among the top three villains of all time. It's a given.

But here's the strange thing about Steinbrenner—he's never been all bad. He's never been that bad at all.

You want to talk about the owner's hard-nosed striving? Well, despite all the millions in the bank and all the hardware in the display case, Steinbrenner's remained obsessed with working, working, and working to provide fans the best possible product, and he rightly expects as much from those around him. By now all Yankee employees, from the president to the ushers, know the deal—they get to be part of an incredible franchise only if they give incredible effort. Fair enough.

As for Steinbrenner's nothing-is-good-enough style, you can check the results on that one, too. It so happens he's built no less than seven 100-game winners, 16 playoff teams, 10 pennant winners, and six World Champions since he arrived in 1973. The franchise's stratospheric record of achievement may have had something to do with Steinbrenner's sky-high expectations.

Say what you will about King George's moneybags, too, but it's not exactly a bad thing when the biggest market in baseball has enough All Stars to fill a small galaxy. Plenty of baseball fans would kill for an owner with an inclination to spend on his teams' preeminence rather than his mansions' upkeep. Besides that, it's not fair to give the Yankees' credit card all the credit for the Yanks' winning ways—the Mets have just as many potential resources and fans, maybe more, but only Steinbrenner has demonstrated both the guts to spend and the brains to win.

All of that good has to be taken into account on Steinbrenner's ledger. Even at his worst, when he was mean, egomaniacal, and greedy . . . he was a motivator, striver, and business force.

Oh, and one more thing—most of King George's negative image is about as outdated as 1970's bell-bottoms and 1980's break dancing. Consider how The Boss has acted like a Florida semiretiree in the 1990's and new millennium:

The Old George once fired 16 General Managers in 25 years and 17 managers over 17 seasons. One time, Steinbrenner reportedly fired someone for delivering his lunch sandwich late, meaning Yankee leaders had the approximate job security of live-grenade jugglers.

The New George has employed the same General Manager, Brian Cashman, for nine years and, going into 2006, Joe Torre will be in his 11th year in pinstripes. Steinbrenner hasn't fired either one, despite the fact they've gone over five years (and nearly $1 billion in payroll) since their last title. The Yankee brain trust now has the approximate job security of Supreme Court justices.

The Old George generated headlines through screaming matches and bitter feuds. His favorite manager, Billy Martin, was at least as well-known for his fistfights as for his hit and runs. Steinbrenner frequently went out of his way to publicly insult players like Ken Clay, Doyle Alexander, Ken Clay, Jim Beattie, Dave Winfield, Sparky Lyle, and the entire 1981 Yankee playoff roster, to name a few. Once, he signed free agent Dave Winfield, then turned around and conspired against him. He was Oscar the Grouch without the charm or manners.

The New George is far too mellow to whisper many media comments. His favorite manager, Joe Torre, is as well-known for his hugs as for his hit and runs. Steinbrenner often goes out of his way to publicly praise "warriors" like Paul O'Neill, David Cone, and Roger Clemens. Once, he criticized Derek Jeter, then turned around and filmed a Visa commercial with him. He's Mr. Rogers without the edge.

The Old George tossed away homegrown prospects like Fred McGriff, Willie McGee, and Jay Buhner. The Yankees went through 13 straight years without playoff appearances, and fans got up to chant "Steinbrenner sucks!" Tears of rage.

The New George holds on to farm hands like Mariano Rivera, Jorge Posada, Derek Jeter, and Bernie Williams. The Yankees have enjoyed 11 straight playoff years, and fans get up to chant "Thank you, George!" Tears of joy.

Now, that's no tyrant. For a long while, King George has been more like a teddy bear.

WHY HAVEN'T THE METS EVER HAD A NO-HITTER?

51
Strange facts about the Mets and no-hitters:

* The New York Met franchise played 6,988 regular season games from 1962 to 2005, but no one's ever pitched a no-hitter for them. Not once.

* They're basically all alone in their lack of no-hitters. Every other franchise that's been around since '62 has had at least five of 'em. A team that came into the Majors in the same year as the Mets, the Houston Astros, has had 10 no-hitters. Among all Major League franchises, 12 have had at least 10 no-hitters.

Among the three other Major League teams that haven't had a no-hitter, one is seven years younger than the Mets (San Diego), another is 31 years younger (Colorado), and the other is 36 years younger (Tampa Bay).

∗ The odds say that the Mets should have had at least one by now.

No-hitters aren't all that rare. In the modern era, they've come along at a rate of slightly under two per season, every season, and there've been as many as six in a single campaign. There were 37 in the 1990's. On June 29, 1990, two were thrown on the same day. Since the Mets' first opening day, 61 no-hitters have been thrown in the National League alone.

∗ No-hitters aren't all that hard to pull off. They've been accomplished while their authors have walked as many as nine batters. Nolan Ryan walked 26 batsmen over the course of his seven career no-hitters.

∗ Pitchers really don't have to be any good to throw no-hitters. More than a dozen have thrown no-hitters despite sub-.500 career records. Some of the no-hit pitchers since 1962: Tommy Greene, Ed Halicki, Ray Washburn, George Culver, Ken Johnson, Bud Smith, and Don Nottebart. Guys like Virgil Trucks and Steve Busby have thrown two no-hitters in their careers.

Bobo Holloman tossed a no-no in his first Major League start, for the Browns in 1953, despite going 3–7 in his one and only year in the bigs. Ed Head (that was his real name)

203

threw one, and he didn't last past 27 Major League games. Dick Fowler threw a no-hitter for his only win of 1945. Bobo, Ed, and Dick were not good baseball players.

✱ No-hitters aren't all that hard for teams to pull off, either. During an interleague game in 2003, for instance, the Astros used six pitchers to combine for a no-hitter. On multiple other occasions, teams have used three pitchers. Ball clubs have maintained no-hitters while giving up as many as three errors.

✱ The Mets haven't thrown a no-hitter despite playing in the National League, where the absence of a designated hitter typically leads to .5 fewer hits per game. By the way, American League clubs have thrown 51 no-hitters since 1962.

✱ The Mets haven't thrown a no-hitter despite playing in Shea Stadium, one of the two or three most pitcher-friendly ballparks in the Majors. Through 2005, its park factor has favored hitters only three times in 42 seasons.

✱ Met pitching staffs have been good enough to have had a no-hitter by now. They've finished among the top three National League teams in hits per nine innings pitched in no less than 14 seasons.

✱ Met stars have definitely been good enough to have had a no-hitter by now. They've finished among National League leaders in hits per nine innings pitched on 25 different occasions. They've also won five ERA titles, led the league in strikeouts nine times, won four Cy Young awards, and have been recognized with Cy Young votes in 23 seasons. There have been more than half a dozen years when a Met (Tom Seaver, Dwight Gooden, David Cone) could claim to be the best pitcher in the league.

* Seven former Mets have thrown a total of 13 no-hitters after leaving Flushing. Ryan became the most accomplished no-hit pitcher of all time, starting two years after he was traded by the Mets in 1971. Two former Mets, Gooden and Cone, threw no-hitters for New York, only they were wearing Yankee uniforms at the time.

* Met pitchers have thrown one-hitters in 27 games. Tom Seaver, Gary Gentry, Jon Matlack, Gooden, and Steve Trachsel have all had multiple one-hitters.

Once, in July 1969, Seaver came within two outs of a no-hitter, only to have it broken up by one of Jim Qualls' 31 career hits. Another time, in September 1984, Gooden came up short due to a questionable scoring call on an infield dribbler.

The numbers say that the Mets have been around long enough to have had many, many no-hitters by now. They aren't that rare. They aren't that hard to pull off, either on an individual basis or team basis. The Mets play in the more pitcher-friendly league and in one of the most pitcher-friendly ballparks. They've fielded the kind of elite staffs and superstars to toss a dozen.

There's no rational reason at all why the Mets haven't pulled off a no-hitter by now, and the absence grows more amazin' by the day. If anything confirms the role of screwy bad luck in baseball, this is it.

ARE THE RED SOX THE NEW YORK YANKEES OF MASSACHUSETTS?

52 With apologies to the great state of Minnesota, they're the American League's real twins. The Boston Red Sox and New York Yankees entered the world in the same year, 1901, and they've looked and acted alike ever since.

Like many siblings, the two charter members of the AL can be seen hanging out in similar locales and wearing similar clothes. The Sox and Yanks play their games in two of the three oldest ballparks in the Majors, the ones easily distinguished by signature outfield dimensions in left (Fenway's Green Monster wall) and right (Yankee Stadium's blue porch). Their players still wear classic uniforms dating back to their great-grandfathers' heyday, the ones based on the red-white-and-blues and pinstripes.

If the resemblance between the two starts off with appearances, it continues in economics. They practically invented big markets—the Stockings have had a monopoly on the richest region of the country (five states, along with half of Connecticut, in all) while the neighboring Yankees are at home in the USA's most populated city. No wonder the I-95 teams are at or near the top of the Majors in every-thing from local cable ratings to gross revenues and over-all franchise values.

With such a huge pool of available fans and dollars, it's no surprise that both the Red Sox and Yankees have been baseball's big spenders for decades now. It all started more than 40 years before free agency came along in the 1970's, when Tom Yawkey's BoSox bought off smaller-mar-ket teams to field stars like Joe Cronin, Jimmie Foxx, and Lefty Grove. The Yankees weren't as interested in paying out, but then again, George Steinbrenner's been doing his best to make up for lost time over the last 30 years or so.

Nowadays the two have adopted much the same spend-ing habits. Guess which two teams have traditionally ranked at or near the top in free agent contracts, year-in, year-out? Yup. The Sox and Yanks rank number one and two in player spending for the new millennium, and were two of the three franchises generous enough to be subject to the luxury tax last year. In 2000 and 2004, they bankrolled the two most expensive world champions in sports history.

The cost of such free spending is a mercenary hue, and the Red Sox and Yanks have seen more than that, too. When they faced off in the American League Championship Series in 2004, the BoSox had exactly one homegrown player making it into the starting lineup and pitching rota-tion (Trot Nixon), while the Bombers had only three of 13 (Bernie Williams, Derek Jeter, and Jorge Posada). When they aren't tangling on the field, their competition involves bidding on superstars-for-hire from Jose Contreras to Alex Rodriguez and Curt Schilling.

The family resemblance between the Red Sox and Yankees goes all the way to the top. Quick—which of the two is led by a ferociously competitive, hard-nosed motivator and guided by a brainy, wunderkind General Manager? Trick question, guys. Larry Lucchino equals George Steinbrenner, just like Theo Epstein (youngest GM in history) spells Brian Cashman (third youngest).

But the resemblances go further. Ball clubs are about winning, and no Major League teams have done that like the Red Sox and Yankees.

Consider the Red Sox's winning ways from 1967 through 2005. They've had 33 years with a .500 or better regular season record and 11 playoff squads. Those are the most winning seasons in the Major Leagues in those 38 years, and as for playoff appearances, they're third only to Oakland and . . . the New York Yankees in the AL. If "winning" is defined as some combination of consistent respectability and frequent playoffs, the Red Sox and Yanks have been the most winning regular season performers in the Majors for more than two generations now.

Identical twins have also been known to enjoy each other's company, and the Red Sox and Yankees are no exception. They've finished 1–2 in the American League or AL East standings a record 18 times, including nine times in the 11 years from 1995 to 2005. No two teams in MLB have ever been paired so often or for so long.

A Nation and an Empire wouldn't mean anything without fans, of course, and the Red Sox and Yanks are alike in that one, too. Their homes have vastly different seating capacities—Fenway's tight, 34,000-seat bandbox doesn't begin to compare to the Stadium's 57,000 plus seats—but they've long been accustomed to sellouts. Guess which two 2004 franchises led the Majors in capacity sold and overall ticket sales?

Further, no teams' followers put the "fan" into "fanatic" like Boston and New York. They're the ones who routinely sell out Spring Training games in minutes, then bid remainders up to rock-concert levels on eBay. They're the ones breaking those attendance records despite some of the highest ticket prices in the game (Fenway's #1, but the Stadium isn't far behind). Stray Bostonians and New Yorkers have also boosted their favorites' road attendance up to third and fourth in the Majors (per venue capacity).

Oh, but some say, none of that matters. Forget the franchises' near-identical origins. And looks. And markets. And spending. And regular season winning. And popularity. And long-standing standings. We're told that the Boston Red Sox and New York Yankees are vastly different because they've had vastly different playoff fates.

Well, the facts are lopsided on that one. In all those 1–2 standing years, the Yanks have beat the Sox out for the top spot 15 out of 18 times. They've won 26 World Championships to the Sox' six, and 39 pennants to the Red Sox' 11. They kicked Boston down in the pennant race back in 1949, 1978 . . . .Suffice it to say that autumn in New York is often a very happy time, while the Red Sox followers have had some scary Halloweens.

But that's all beside the point now.

After all, the unforgettable Sox/Yanks showdown in the 2004 American League Championship Series . . .

Finally . . .

Changed . . .

Everything.

For once, it was the Sox who came through in crunch time. It was the Yankees who choked. It was the Sox who brought home the World Series trophy and killed the '1918' signs along with the 100 percent phony, media-fueled Curse of the Bambino (#4).

That October's results should, by rights, bring about a revolution in public image. No longer can anyone pretend that the Red Sox represent the scrappiest little underdog in New England. Now, with their fat championship rings gleaming in the spotlight, baseball has to call the Boston Red Sox what they've been all along—a historic, big-market, high-rolling, hard-driving, big-winning overdog.

The New York Yankees of Massachusetts.

DO THE YANKEES AND RED SOX HATE EACH OTHER?

53 The facts are crystal clear, in that the Sox and Yanks share near-identical origins, looks, markets, spending habits, regular season accomplishments, popularity, and publicity (#52). After more than 1,900 games and one century, no American League ball clubs have played each other as often as Boston and New York.

Just name two other baseball teams with that kind of fused character. Heck, name two more similar teams in any sport. The Red Sox and Yankees are family.

But all those ties are hardly mentioned nowadays. Familiarity is said to breed contempt, and the Sox-Yanks are supposedly to be no different. The standard line from the mainstream media says these two are to Major League animosity what China is to people.

We've heard it all before. Bostonians detest those who've kicked them around so often and for so long. The Sox supposedly seethe at the sight of pinstripes. For their part, New Yorkers are highly offended when the neighbors try to steal all the attention rightfully belonging to the Bronx. Yank fans supposedly cringe at all the woe-is-me whining from up north. On either side, loose talk has been made about a bunch of crybabies and greed-heads. We're told that the Red Sox and Yankees hate each other.

Don't believe it. They may be a bit dysfunctional, but the Red Sox and Yankees are still family, and they don't hate each other, not even a little.

Genuine hate is about unfairness and exclusion. In baseball, negativity helped maintain the color line for decades and froze feudal economics into place for even longer. In the outside world, it's led to all kinds of strife based on whatever it is that can divide people, be it race, religion, politics, culture. If you hate someone, you always want them diminished and gone, maybe permanently.

The Red Sox-Yankees rivalry is completely removed from that kind of mindset, all down the line. They're the pros in the highly professionalized game of the new millennium.

The opposing ballplayers are certainly more sweet than bitter. Former free agents like Johnny Damon and David Wells are the best of friends with guys in the other locker room, and good luck trying to find a Red Sox star to put down classy Joe Torre, Derek Jeter, and Hideki Matsui, or find an unkind Yankee comment about the even-tempered, hustling Jason Varitek and David Ortiz. The biggest insult of recent years was the Sox's refusal to put first-year player Alex Rodriguez in the pantheon with the "real Yankees."

A-Rod was devastated.

Things have been so calm and peaceful between Arod and the Sox for so long that the controversy-hungry media has gotten desperate. In 2004, for example, Varitek got steamed enough to shove Rodriguez. The two-second tussle was covered like it was an on-field manslaughter. Curt Schilling has occasionally mentioned he wants to win and shut up the New Yorker jeers. Columnists were shocked, absolutely shocked. It was almost enough to make a baseball fan forget the love-fest between the two sides during the Sox's World Series ring ceremony in April 2005 (#54).

And do the Red Sox and Yankees' employers detest each other? No way.

Owners like Larry Lucchino and George Steinbrenner are some of the most aggressive competitors the Major Leagues have ever seen, without a doubt. Like the players, they're intensely interested in winning. Neither is above mouthing off about an "Evil Empire" or "sick" comments in stray moments of anger.

But, even there, competitive fire shouldn't be mistaken for something else. Red Sox/Yankees games generate off-the-charts attendance, revenues, and media attention from March into October. The owners have (literally) millions of reasons to love their rivals—when the Sox see the **Y A N K E E S T A D I U M** sign or the Yankees roll into Fenway, they're greeted by a chorus of ka-chinging cash registers. "Hatred" should always be so profitable and chummy.

Finally, the fans. Don't you believe that Red Sox and Yankee fans hate each other.

For decade after decade and generation after generation, each side has used the other as the ultimate measuring stick, the one they'd most like to defeat. How else are the Red Sox to prove their faith or the Yankees to display their excellence? A Red Sox win simply means more when the Yankees are losing, and vice versa. It's like defeating your best friend in pickup basketball, or beating out your brother-in-law for the bowling league. (In fact, that seems like an excellent analogy, since so many Red Sox and Yankee fans are mixed up in the same neighborhoods, workplaces, and families.) Scratch the surface, though, and you'll find a true competitor's respect for the other guy's effort.

Taking on the Marlins or Redbirds in the World Series after an epic ALCS battle against The Other Side . . . well, OK. It's the anti to the climax. Nothing's the same as the Red Sox-Yankees clashes, which may be one reason why the rivalry sometimes bores other fans silly.

Of course, there have always been those who have taken the back-and-forth ragging too far—that's inevitable in a sports story involving crowds of thousands and fan bases of millions. Thankfully, though, those jerks have frequently been in the minority of good-hearted fans and/or in the custody of strong-armed security guards.

In actuality, the dusty old jokes about the Sox-Yankees animosity only live on for simplicity's sake. "I hate those (fill in the blanks)" is easier to pronounce than the more accurate phrase, which boils down to "I fear you guys so much that I would give up a minor organ just to beat up on you one more time." In sports, it's important to vent. "You've got great players, but I think ours are even better" doesn't hack it. A loud round of "Yankees suck," on the other hand, isn't quite inaccurate, but more punchy.

Still, don't let any of that side talk fool you. These separated-at-birth franchises, the ones with all the respectful players, partnered owners, and passionate baseball fans, they would-n't have it any other way. Yeah, the Sox and Yanks have been known to get carried away. But, hey, family's like that.

WHAT WERE THE MOST EMOTIONAL MOMENTS IN YANKEE HISTORY?

54, 55, & 56

Rooting for the Yankees isn't like rooting for U.S. Steel.

At their very best, the Bronx Bombers haven't been a faceless, impersonal corporation at all, but a set of warm, vivid characters and occasions. For all the many runs scored and the many games won, some of the Yankees' off-field moments may have been just as emotional and memorable:

* "Some ballyard," Babe Ruth declares on Yankee Stadium's first opening day. "I'd give a year of my life if I could hit a home run." To the delight of a capacity crowd, he does just that, swatting the first official homer in Stadium history during the Yanks' 4–1 victory over the Red Sox. (April 1923)

* After Cub fans spend the previous few days showering him with jeers, tossing lemons, and spitting on his wife, a "fat, washed up" Ruth slams the 15th and final World Series homer of his storied career. Several witnesses insist the Bambino called the shot. (October 1932)

* While pitching in the National League, former ace Waite Hoyt is taunted by the Chicago Cubs. He responds, "If you guys don't shut up, I'll put on my old Yankee uniform and scare you to death." (Summer 1933)

* Playing with excruciating pain from a broken toe, Lou Gehrig doesn't take one day off to rest or shield his league-leading hitting stats. He wins the Triple Crown anyway. (September 1934)

* Longtime owner Jacob Ruppert, on his deathbed, asks his World Series-winning manager for one last visit. When Charlie McCarthy says, "Colonel, you're the champion again," the weakened Ruppert responds, "Fine, fine. Do it again next year." (November 1938)

* With a capacity crowd in attendance, the Yankees' captain is honored on "Lou Gehrig Day." Former teammates from the 1927 Yankees come from across the country to

provide praise and gifts between games of a double header against the Washington Senators.

Gehrig, visibly trembling from the nerve disease that had just ended his career, is reluctant to address the assembly and grandstands. He's finally persuaded, however, and declares that, for all the love he's received from friends, family, and fans, "I consider myself the luckiest man on the face of the earth." As the captain walks away, he's embraced by Ruth and showered with tearful applause.

When Lou Gehrig passes away less than two years later, just before his 38th birthday, there are no eulogies; the pastor of Christ Episcopal Church simply states, "You all knew him." (July 1939)

* With the Cleveland Indians' Ken Keltner playing him deep at third base, Joe DiMaggio refuses to extend his 56-game hitting streak by bunting for what he calls a "cheap hit." He goes 0 for 3, but begins a new 16-game hitting streak the next day. (July 1941)

* As Tommy Henrich steps up to the plate in the final home game of the season, it's announced that the at-bat will be his last for the duration of World War II. Tigers pitcher Dizzy Trout steps off the rubber and the Yankee Stadium crowd gives a dewey-eyed Henrich a tremendous, rolling cheer. (September 1942)

* A dying Babe Ruth attends ceremonies honoring the 25th anniversary of Yankee Stadium and the retirement of his #3 jersey. In the last public appearance of his life, Ruth

declares, "The only real game in the world, I think, is baseball." (June 1948)

✴ After the Bambino's death, hundreds of thousands New Yorkers pay their respects at St. Patrick's Cathedral and Yankee Stadium. George and Claire Ruth's graves in Hawthorne, Westchester County, are less than two miles from Lou and Eleanor Gehrig's final resting places in Valhalla. (August 1948)

✴ Casey Stengel is hired as the team's 10th skipper, leading several column writers to dismiss him as a "clown." At his first press conference, Stengel answers:

I didn't get the job through friendship. The Yankees represent an investment of millions of dollars. They don't hand out jobs like this just because they like your company. I know I can make people laugh and some of you think I'm a damn fool, [but] I got the job because the people here think I can produce for them.

Stengel's Yankees go on to win 10 pennants and seven World Series in the next 12 years. (October 1948)

✴ "Joe DiMaggio Day" is held in the Bronx. The man of the hour declares:

When I was in San Francisco, Lefty O'Doul told me, "Joe, don't let the big city scare you. New York is the friendliest town in the world." This day proves it. I want to thank my fans, my friends, my manager, Casey Stengel, and my teammates, the gamest, fightingest bunch of guys that ever lived. And I want to thank the good Lord for making me a Yankee.

218

That last line is still inscribed in the Stadium's clubhouse runway. (October 1949)

✳ Ogden Nash's *"Lineup for Yesterday"* poem is published. One section reads:

G is for Gehrig.

The Pride of the Stadium;

His record pure gold,

His courage, pure radium.

(Winter 1949)

✳ A new coach, angered by an umpire's call, begins tossing bats from the dugout onto the field. DiMaggio tells him to stop, saying, "On this team, when we get mad, we don't throw things—we hit home runs." (Summer 1951)

✳ DiMaggio retires from baseball at the age of 36, despite a standing offer to play another year for $100,000. He tells friends he wants to go before age and injuries make him "an ordinary player." (December 1951)

✳ Ernest Hemingway's last major work of fiction, *The Old Man and the Sea*, is published. "I must have confidence and I must be worthy of the great DiMaggio who does all things perfectly even with the pain of the bone spur in his heel," the struggling title character thinks. "I would like to take the great DiMaggio fishing. They say his father was a fisherman. Maybe he was as poor as we are and would understand." (Summer 1952)

✳ His Holiness Paul VI, visiting Yankee Stadium during the first-ever papal visit to the United States, holds Mass and blesses 80,000 faithful. A plaque honoring the visit is later placed in Monument Park. (October 1965)

* Paul Simon, who grew up in Forest Hills, releases "Mrs. Robinson," a song that includes the lines, "Where have you gone, Joe DiMaggio? / A nation turns its lonely eyes to you."

A few months later, when Simon runs into DiMaggio at a restaurant, he's asked what the song means. Simon says it's about lost heroism. DiMaggio thanks him for the compliment, but says he prefers Simon & Garfunkel's "Bookends" ("Time it was and what a time it was / A time of innocence / A time of confidences"). (Summer 1967)

* Meatloaf's "Paradise by the Dashboard Light," featuring Phil Rizzuto's narration, is released as the first single from Bat out of Hell. The album wins a Grammy and eventually sells 34 million copies, making Scooter the best-selling shortstop of all time. (Summer 1977)

* Following Thurman Munson's death in a plane crash, Yankee teammates and fans observe a moment of silence at Yankee Stadium, followed by a thunderous, eight-minute ovation for the late captain. Three days later, hours after delivering his friend's eulogy, Bobby Murcer drives in five runs to spark a 5–4 win over Baltimore. (August 1979)

* A recently freed Nelson Mandela visits Yankee Stadium during his tour of America. "You know who I am," the South African leader says, "I am a Yankee." The crowd roars back, "Amandla," the Zulu word for power. (July 1990)

* Newspapers report that George Steinbrenner had given confidential contributions to dozens of needy students, athletes, firefighters, indigent ballplayers, and youth groups over the years. Joe Torre and Derek Jeter, among others, set up their own charitable foundations later in the 1990's, distinguishing the Yankees among the most generous philanthropists in sports. (Early 1990s)

* Shortly after checking into a rehabilitation facility, Mickey Mantle pens a *Sports Illustrated* article ("My Life in a Bottle") apologizing for years of alcoholism. Despite failing health, he spends his last days promoting substance abuse counseling and organ donation while advising "This is a role model—don't be like me."

In Bob Costas' eulogy, it's said, "In the last year, Mickey Mantle, always so hard on himself, finally came to accept and appreciate the distinction between a role model and a hero. The first, he often was not. The second, he always will be." (Spring/Summer 1995)

* Cal Ripken plays in his 2,131st consecutive game, breaking Lou Gehrig's all time record for durability. As Ripken addresses a Camden Yards crowd that includes Joe DiMaggio, he says:

Tonight I stand here overwhelmed that my name is linked with the great and courageous Lou Gehrig. I know that as he's looking down on tonight's activities, he isn't concerned with someone playing more games than he did. Instead, he's viewing tonight as just another example of what's right about the great American game. Whether you're name is Gehrig or Ripken, DiMaggio or Robinson, or some youngster who picks up his bat or puts on his glove, you are challenged by the game of baseball to do your very best, day in and day out. And that's all I've ever tried to do. (September 1995)

✱ Joe Torre seeks his first World Championship after 32 years in the Major Leagues even as his older brother, Frank, is hospitalized with heart disease at Columbia-Presbyterian Hospital. In October, the underdog Yankees win the World Series around the same time Frank Torre undergoes a successful heart transplant. In the following years, a fully recovered Frank will watch Joe win another three titles as Yankee manager. (September/October 1996)

✱The *New York Times* publishes a Paul Simon editorial about the recently deceased DiMaggio. "We mourn the loss of his grace and dignity, his fierce sense of privacy, his fidelity to the memory of his wife, and the power of his silence," Simon writes. (March 1999)

✱ After years of apologies from George Steinbrenner, Yogi Berra returns to Yankee Stadium for the first time since being fired as manager in 1985. Newspaper headlines read **"IT'S OVER"** when the Hall of Famer arrives for the home opener, but an even more memorable return occurs on "Yogi Berra Day" with Berra and Don Larsen looking on from the owner's suite, David Cone throws the 13th perfect game in modern Major League history. (July 1999)

✱ Even as team staples Paul O'Neill, Scott Brosius, and Luis Sojo mourn the deaths of their fathers, the Yankees tie a Major League record by winning their eighth straight World Series game. (October 1999)

✱ Yankee Stadium holds a "Prayer for America" interfaith service for the more than 2,800 New Yorkers who perished in the September 11th attacks on the World Trade Center. The ceremony, which includes representatives from all major creeds, ends with The Boys and Girls Choir of Harlem singing "God Be with You 'Til We Meet Again." (September 2001)

✱ At the Fenway Park home opener, the Red Sox unveil a World Championship banner and distribute World Series rings. Respectful Yankees watch the ceremonies from the visitors' dugout, even tipping their caps to Hall of Famer Johnny Pesky. Mariano Rivera takes a playful bow at pregame introductions and concedes, "After 86 years, I think they deserve to win one." (April 2005)

ARE THE METS SECOND PLACE IN NEW YORK?

It's Rum . . . and Coke.

Salt . . . and Pepper.

Tom . . . and Jerry.

Some are destined to a perpetual second place in the world, which is exactly why no one orders Coke and Rums, requests Pepper and Salt, or watches Jerry and Tom.

New York baseball can look much the same. For outsiders, it's easy to think the town's always been about the Yankees . . . and Mets.

It's understandable. Beyond the Yanks' vast advantage in superstar payrolls are their advantages in a glittering ballpark, winning chronicles, and glamour. The Yankees are the ones who play in The House that Ruth Built. They're the franchise that won 15 World Championships before Don Zimmer was a rookie. They're the ones with a starry tradition that's included The Iron Horse, The Yankee Clipper, The Mick, and Donnie Baseball, among many, many others. Their fans are the ones crying along in the *Pride of the Yankees* speech, chuckling at the Yogi quotes, and puzzling over the Phil Rizzuto broadcasts.

The Mets shouldn't have been competitive with that kind of attraction, but, very often, they've been more than competitive. The fact is, for much of their shared history, it's the Mets who've left the Yankees in second place as a gate attraction.

The Mets' attendance advantage started early, around the time they were born as an expansion team in 1962.

Even in their first couple of years, when Casey Stengel's new ball club thudded into last-place finishes, their annual attendance wasn't very far behind the dynastic Yankees, drawing 900,000 (1962) and a very respectable 1.1 million (1963) to the Yankees' 1.5 million and 1.3 million. Once the Mets moved from the old Polo Grounds to a new Shea Stadium in 1964, their popularity took off—they bested the Yankees' gate on an annual basis, without fail, until 1975. After being outdrawn by 800,000 in 1962–63, the Amazin's outdrew the Yanks by over 9.1 million paying customers in 1964–75.

What spurred the Mets' edge over the Yankees?

Well, after the Bronx's dynasty collapsed in '65, some of the Metsies' atrocious early finishes didn't particularly stand out in comparison. Losing may not have been altogether lovable, but Flushing didn't know anything else, and Met status apparently wasn't quite as ugly as the sight of the once-mighty Yanks laid low.

Several other advantages pulled the Mets ahead in popularity. Certainly, the novelty of a new ballpark helped in '64, when their 1.7 million in attendance first beat out the pennant-winning Yankees. For three full years, 1973 to

1975, Yankee Stadium was closed for renovations, so Bomber fans may have been reluctant to take in their team's ball games at Shea. Always, there was a lot to be said for Flushing's easier transportation access and lower ticket prices.

The single most significant asset in the Mets' favor, though, was the aura they created through their miraculous, championship-winning year of 1969. With New York and America living in a season of moonwalks, Woodstock concerts, and counter-cultures, the Mets' shocking victory (#34) tapped into the upside-down upheavals of the times.

It was the '69 title that catapulted the Mets from their accustomed status as New York's fan favorites on up to overwhelming fan favorites. In the Year of the Miracle, the Mets doubled the Yankees attendance (2.2 million to 1.1), followed up with an all-time city attendance record with 2.7 million in 1970, then outdrew the Yanks by an average of half a million customers per year for years afterwards. The afterglow from '69 didn't subside until 1976, when a last-place club fell behind the resurgent Yankees' pennant winners.

The 1976 to 1983 period was the first time the Yankees overcame the Mets' attendance advantage. The Yankees, no doubt, won back many turned-off fans by taking four pennants and two World Series from 1976 to 1981, even as the Mets reverted to a 1960's-like futility on the field. In addition, Yankee Stadium's reopening in '76 helped at the gate.

The Mets turned it all around, however, when they started winning again. From 1984 to 1990, the franchise fielded seven straight winning seasons, two division winners, and the World Series winner of 1986, even as the Yankees went downhill from good (1985's 97–65) to worse (1990's 67–95). The Amazin's success on the field was matched at the gate, as they, once again, outdrew the Yankees, year-in, year-out. In 1985, the Mets surpassed their 1970 mark to set a new attendance record in the Big Apple, and in the nine years from 1984 to 1992 Shea's turnstiles welcomed 4.1 more fans than Yankee Stadium's turnstiles. For most of the 1980's, they owned the town.

Empires rise only to fall, though, and the Mets' run in good standings and good attendance was over by 1993. In that year and every year through 2005, the Yankees took over as both the better team and better box-office attraction, most often by 400,000–500,000 fans per year, but sometimes (2004, 2005) by a million fans or more.

It might be demoralizing for Mets watchers, seeing the Yankees' nearly unprecedented string of success since '95, but it shouldn't obscure the way that the Amazins have repeatedly proven themselves as the town's No. 1 team. If and when they match their rivals in the standings, they'll be back on top. Once again, New Yorkers will be talking about the Mets . . . and Yankees.

GRIDIRONS

WAS THE 1958 GIANTS-COLTS CHAMPIONSHIP "THE GREATEST GAME EVER PLAYED"?

58 True story.

Once, I was driving along with a friend who was, appropriately enough, a big car buff. He was, as always, talking about the latest makes and models and engines and such, so I asked him what he considered to be the best all-around car for the money.

"BMW," he said.

I asked why.

He paused for just a moment, then said, "It's the ultimate driving machine." At the time, BMW's advertising line described "The ultimate driving machine."

The response always struck me as intriguing. Here was a guy who could rattle off dozens of expert reasons why particular cars were better than other particular cars, but when asked a spontaneous question about across-the-board performance, he retreated back into a simple, pat marketing slogan.

I can't be certain, but I think he answered that way for a reason. An extensive knowledge of possible answers can be kind of debilitating in its complexity. No one wants to sit around wracking their brains for the most complete, accurate possible answer to a general question, so, when asked about a big issue, most people (including my pal) give simple, incomplete answers that seem to encapsulate their thoughts well enough.

Anyway, that story comes to mind when I hear someone refer to the 1958 NFL championship game between the Giants and Baltimore Colts as "The greatest game ever played." It may be a simple, quick answer, but it's not necessarily the best answer.

To be fair, the game was pretty diverting.

The Giants started things off with a Pat Summerall field goal, but the Colts scored two touchdowns to take a 14–3 lead in the second quarter. Baltimore drove down to the three-yard line in the third quarter, but the Giants put up a great goal line stand, then charged back with a 95-yard touchdown drive of their own. New York gained a 17–14 lead when Charlie Conerly connected to running back Frank Gifford for another touchdown, but Baltimore answered with a series of Johnny Unitas-to-Raymond Berry passes with less than two minutes on the clock. They hit a field goal with 19 seconds left and, with the game tied at 17–17, the squads went into overtime. The Giants couldn't score on their first possession, but the Colts did, ending the game with a Don Ameche one-yard run and 23–17 final.

That's a pretty good afternoon's entertainment, no doubt, full of big plays on offense and defense alike. Unfortunately, labeling the '58 championship as the "greatest game ever played" means ignoring several important facts.

As it turned out, mistakes, rather than stellar performances, played a large part in the final outcome of the game. While today's average NFL contest features three turnovers, this one featured no less than eight fumbles (six were lost to opponents). Two of them, by Gifford in the second quarter, led to Colts touchdowns. There were so many miscues that the referees got in the act—eyewitnesses reported that Unitas and Berry only got a chance for their last-minute rally because the refs blew the spot for the ball during a prolonged injury time-out.

In addition, the bungle-filled game wasn't very balanced, either. Ameche was the lead runner with 65 yards, but Conerly and Unitas otherwise dominated through passing. Players on both sides (Art Donovan of the Colts and Gifford of the Giants) said their teams had given better all-around efforts earlier in the season.

So why was a good-but-not-so-great contest labeled as "the greatest"? Some of it may go back to the novelty value in the first (and to date, only) sudden death finale in a championship game, or the historical reputations of Unitas, Berry, Gifford, and the dozen other Hall of Famers involved as players or coaches.

Mostly, though, NFL Commissioner Bert Bell and others adopted the label because of the game's impact on the business of football. It attracted a new level of attention in the biggest market in the game (the Giants sold out their home schedule for the first time in the following season). Even more importantly, Colts-Giants gained the NFL's first big, coast-to-coast television ratings, thereby announcing the league's arrival as the nationwide broadcasting phenomenon we see today. Commentators began to look for a momentous description for that turning point and eventually settled on "The Greatest Game Ever Played." It was a good ad line.

For some, undoubtedly, the back-and-forth drama and stellar personnel of the Giants-Colts game may have made for a singular experience. It's not necessarily a wrong answer, but it may be too pat. BMWs are great cars, but they may not be the "ultimate driving machines."

DID THE GIANTS MAKE THE RIGHT CALL IN PASSING OVER LANDRY AND LOMBARDI?

59 & 60

Tom Landry.

Vince Lombardi.

Allie Sherman.

One of these names isn't like the other two.

Tom Landry will forever be known as one of the greatest coaches in football history. All he did was put up 20 straight winning years with the Dallas Cowboys from 1966 to 1985, a completely unapproachable run that included two Super Bowl victories, five conference championships, and 13 NFC East Division titles. He retired with no less than 270 regular season wins, and his 20 career playoff wins are the most ever.

Vince Lombardi didn't do too badly for himself, either. He had nine winning seasons in nine years as Green Bay's head coach from 1959 to 1967, compiling a 105–35–6 (.750) record en route to five NFL championships and six division titles. His Packer teams went 9-1 (.900) in the playoffs, including an unprecedented three straight wins in championship games. The NFL named Lombardi "Man of the Decade" for the

1960's, ESPN named him "Coach of the Century," and the Super Bowl had him as namesake for its annual trophy. Like Landry, Lombardi waltzed into the Hall of Fame on the first ballot.

Allie Sherman, sadly, has never been in the same discussion. His Giants only enjoyed three winning seasons in eight campaigns from 1961 to 1968. Sherman's teams did make it into championship games three straight times, but lost all three. He'll only waltz into Canton if he has an admission ticket.

As different as their later paths might have been, though, the three coaches once shared something unique and important—they were the prime candidates to succeed Jim Lee Howell as head coach of the New York Giants back in the late 1950's. Lombardi and Landry, famously, served as New York's offensive and defensive coordinators under Howell. Sherman only took the top job in 1961 after Lombardi left for Green Bay in '59 and Landry departed for Dallas in '60.

Looking back, the Giants apparently made a huge mistake in passing over Landry and Lombardi, but you could call that a classic second-guess. You could argue that, at the time, the team made the right call.

In Tom Landry's case, it wasn't quite accurate to say that the Giants "passed him over" at all. He'd long been a respected figure within the organization, first coming aboard as hustling cornerback in 1950. Landry compiled an impressive 31 interceptions in 70 career games, and when he transitioned into a role as an assistant coach and then coordinator, he was equally impressive. His 1954–59 defenses, featuring an innovative set of linebacker audibles, blitzes and slanting down linemen, were ranked second, third, fourth, fourth, first, and first in the 12-team NFL.

As respected as Landry was, though, geography issues effectively prevented him from taking over as a head coach in New York. Born and raised back in Texas, he never left for long, returning to the Lone Star State year after year for off-season jobs in oil field supplies and real estate. In his autobiography, Landry stated that he always wanted to raise his growing children back home, regardless of the Giants' opening.

To be sure, the Giants could have tried harder to keep their star coordinator in the fold. Rather than providing a strong recommendation to Tex Schramm and the expansion franchise in Dallas, the ownership could have made a full-on effort to change Landry's mind with a steady barrage of flattery and cash. To judge from the man's Bible-Belt upbringing and down-home ties, though, it's highly doubtful that any amount of salesmanship could have made Tom Landry fit in secular, cosmopolitan New York.

Lombardi's possible future with the Giants had different, but even more serious, road blocks.

Lombardi, to be sure, was a hometown guy who was eager to make his name. He grew up in Sheepshead Bay, gained stardom in Fordham's "Seven Blocks of Granite" lines in the 1930s, and later stuck around town as a semi-pro player, law student, high school teacher, and assistant college coach. By all accounts, he was happy to return to the old neighborhood when he was first hired by the Giants in '54.

For all his deep, local connections, though, it was far from clear if Vince Lombardi was ready to become a big-time NFL coach in the late 1950's. From 1954 to 1957, his offenses were nothing special, finishing sixth, third, fifth, and seventh in the league despite featuring future Hall of Famers Frank Gifford and Rosie Brown and stars Kyle Rote and Alex Webster. In 1958, his last year as coordinator, the Giants finished nineth in NFL scoring, only scoring 30-plus points once on the season. It was Landry's defenses that carried the load that year—the Lombardi offense was the worst to win an Eastern Division title in 20 years.

His lackluster results aside, Lombardi also presented a problem in his highly erratic psyche. It may not be recalled in the hero worship around him today, but the living Vince Lombardi was a notoriously moody individual, one who frequently went from warm caring to volcanic fury at the blink of an eye (Landry would describe him as a "borderline manic depressive"). He was an insensitive egomaniac, too, who didn't get along with his fellow coaches and frequently inflicted foul-mouthed tirades on reporters. He was downright abusive to his wife and children. One player later summed up Lombardi's snarling approach to the world by saying, "He treats us all alike. Like dogs."

There may have been excellent reasons why Notre Dame, Fordham, and every team in the NFL rejected him as a head coaching candidate until he was 46 years old—Vince Lombardi was an extremely difficult, even troubled, man, and the Giants would have had every right to believe he'd crack under the increased pressure that went along with a head coaching job.

History tells us Lombardi's domineering ways did succeed with the Packers' situation in Green Bay, but it's worth asking—could they have worked in the Giants' drastically different situation?

Over there, the coach had a tiny group of docile, company-town reporters acting as unofficial stenographers. Here, he would have had a horde of curious reporters ready to question his every move. Over there, he was starting with the nil expectations that came with a 1–10–1 record in the previous season. Here, he would have had to deal with a fan base accustomed to Howell's string of winning seasons. Over there, he assumed de facto dictatorship by pushing around the Packers' discredited, rubber-stamp community board. Here, he would have dealt with the hands-on Mara family.

There are plenty of reasons to believe that the problematic Lombardi, like the unwilling Landry, just didn't have what it took to succeed as a Giants head coach.

Conversely, Allie Sherman seemed like an almost ideal candidate for the job.

Sherman had gained a reputation as a boy genius of sorts by the time he came in as New York's offensive coordinator in 1959. He was the first to bring the T-formation from college to the pros and was among the first to use televisions, computers, and scientific tools to break down game plans. In his first year, using many of Lombardi's old players, he took a ninth-ranked offense to a second place by generating 38 more points in 14 games (the total went from 246 to 284, a 15 percent increase). From 1961 to 1963, his offenses never ranked lower than No. 2 in the NFL.

Still, things didn't work out for Sherman. His high-powered Giant offenses may have reached the NFL championship game three straight times, but he never did craft the defenses to take the team over the top. History's verdict would have been kinder if he delivered at least one title, but the fact is, he didn't. Allie Sherman once beat out Tom Landry and Vince Lombardi but, ultimately, he lost.

SUPER BOWL III—WHO WAS THE REAL MVP?

61 The day after, a *Daily News* headline read: "B'Way Joe Jolts Colts, 16–7."

The front page was the first, but not the last, version of the standard storyline on Super Bowl III, one that had a big star and his underdog team coming through to win the big game. The headlines probably hit the presses the moment it looked like Namath's pregame "guarantee" might come through (#78).

For starters, B'Way Joe didn't jolt anybody in particular on the afternoon of January 12th, 1969. Namath had an alright day, nothing more, completing 17 passes in 28 attempts while throwing for a skimpy 208 yards and losing 11 net yards on two sacks. After 40 years, Namath remains the only QB to take the Super Bowl MVP trophy without tossing a touchdown pass. His offense scored 16 points, the second-least winning total in Super Bowl history, and he's the only quarterback ever to be rewarded for scoring less than 23 points. If you go by the numbers, Joe Namath was probably the least valuable "Most Valuable Player" of all time.

With Namath failing to deliver points and big plays in Super Bowl III, the Jets had plenty of other MVP candidates on the field. They had place kicker Jim Turner, for instance, whose

239

three kicks made the difference in the scoring. They also had wide receiver George Sauer, who picked up 133 receiving yards, most of them coming after he converted short, safe pass routes into tough upfield gains.

The single most worthy recipient of all, though, may have been Matt Snell. The fullback set up Turner's kicks by carrying the ball 30 times for 121 yards (4.0 yards per carry) and scored the Jets' only TD during the second quarter, the culmination of a drive that saw him gain 80 yards on six carries. Even more importantly, Snell's steady yardage gave New York an edge in total offensive plays (74 to the Colts' 64) and time of possession (the Jets ended up with a 36:25 to 23:35 advantage). While Namath was busy handing off (the ball), Ewbank and the Jets had Snell putting away (the game). Evidently, the coach had his own view on the team's authentic MVP.

SUPER BOWL III—DID THE JETS REALLY WIN THE GAME?

62 If Joe Namath's big star moment was mostly myth, so is the idea that the Jets "won" Super Bowl III through their own accomplishments. New York delivered a solid, workmanlike effort, to be sure, but the story of the game wasn't the Jets' positives but the Colts' many negatives.

After Super Sunday, tight end John Mackey admitted that "we believed that all we had to do was show up," and they sure acted like it—they started planning their victory party five days beforehand and worked out "winner" shares at their Super Sunday breakfast.

The game that followed was a tragicomedy of errors for the semiprepared team. Journeyman quarterback Earl Morrall (playing for his seventh team in 14 seasons) had a career year for the Colts in the 1968–69 regular season, but he picked the worst possible time to come back down to earth, going 6 for 17 for 71 yards and three interceptions. His replacement was a hobbled, way-past-his-prime Johnny Unitas, who completed 11 of 24 pass attempts while tossing an additional interception.

Throughout the action, Baltimore displayed an uncanny ability to get closer and closer to a score, only to toss it away time after time. Morrall's first interception, for instance, came with the Colts at the Jets' 25-yard line early in the second quarter. He was picked off in the end zone. The second pick came later in the quarter, after the Colts had driven down to New York's 16-yard line. Morrall was intercepted at the 2-yard line. Just before the half, the Colts made it back into Jets territory (the 42-yard line) yet again, but the QB was intercepted in the end zone yet again. Instead of coming away with a sure 21 or so points in the quarter, they came away with nothing.

Now, some Jets fans can spin those facts into a positive, claiming that the Colts' back-breaking mistakes weren't bona fide mistakes at all, but byproducts of the Jets' pressure. It's true, in a limited sense. New York did gain an early lead, construct good drives, and stick with Ewbank's sound, chew-up-the-clock plan. They were competent. They didn't push the "self-destruct" button.

Apart from that minimum, though, the Jets' performance didn't affect much of anything on the Colts' side. No one forced the football to bounce off tight end Tom Mitchell and into the hands of Jets cornerback Randy Beverly. No one forced Morrall to overlook a wide-open Jimmy Orr in the end zone while throwing an interception into the grateful arms of Jets safety Jim Hudson. Most of the Colts' incompletions were the product of inaccuracy rather than the New York rush (the Jets finished with zero sacks). Certainly, no one forced Baltimore kicker Lou Michaels to miss an easy 27-yard field goal.

The Colts did all that to themselves. It was suicide by interception and incompletion, a bungling effort that wiped out the Colts' advantages in gains per offensive play (5.1 to the Jets' 4.6) and rushing yardage (143 vs. 142).

Technically, New York did win Super Bowl III, and the final score indicated as much. With some competence and a lot of luck, they found themselves in a situation where not-bad was good enough. Still, you can argue that the Jets didn't do all that much to take the championship. The Colts gave it to them.

DID JOE NAMATH DESERVE TO MAKE IT INTO THE HALL OF FAME?

63 If ever there was a player who seemed destined for fame and the Pro Football Hall of Fame, it was a young man named Joe Namath. There was no one like him.

Namath started off as a multitalented sports star back home in Beaver Falls, Pennsylvania, a spectacular talent who set off a nationwide recruiting frenzy in his senior year in high school. The University of Alabama was the lucky suitor, and, sure enough, Namath set school quarterbacking records en route to the 1964 college championship. The Crimson Tide's head coach, the great Bear Bryant, later called Namath the best athlete he'd ever seen. On campus, he was the toast of Tuscaloosa. His nickname was "Babe"—as in Babe Ruth.

Once his bright college years passed, things only got better for 'Bama's All-American. The NFL drafted Namath, but he passed them over to sign a record-breaking contract with the New York Jets of the new American Football League. Within a couple of years the club, playing in brand-new Shea Stadium, was transformed into a winner, so Namath led the most popular football team in the biggest city in the United States. At that point "Broadway Joe" was one of the most eligible bachelors around (#70), a headline-in-waiting and poster boy for his franchise, his league, and his sport.

Life was very sweet even before Namath achieved the seemingly impossible. When the Jets, Namath's Jets, reached Super Bowl III in January 1969, Namath guaranteed a victory (#79) and, incredibly enough, the team won, becoming the biggest underdog ever to take a pro football championship. Those were heady days indeed, a time when Vince Lombardi called Namath "almost the perfect passer."

If being a Hall of Famer is all about raw talent, glamour, publicity, and a very memorable title, Namath was an undeniable candidate before he turned 26 years old. Then again . . . some might say being a Hall of Famer isn't about any of those things. Some say it's about on-field greatness and that, in those terms, Namath was anything but undeniable. Actually, in terms of performance, Joe Namath was a very deniable candidate for the Hall of Fame.

Namath's early reputation, admittedly, had some substance to it. He won AFL Rookie of the Year honors in 1965 with 2,220 passing yards and 18 touchdowns in 13 games. It was a promising start, one he followed up with a 1966 campaign for 3,379 yards and 19 touchdowns, then an astounding 4,007 yards in 1967. In an era when 3,000 passing yards was considered a landmark, Namath set a then-record for yardage.

Unfortunately for Joe and the Jets, all those gaudy numbers weren't nearly as spectacular as they appeared at first glance. The reason was turnovers.

It turned out that Namath never did get the hang of a quarterback's #1 job, the part about not throwing the ball to the guys on the other side. He threw more touchdowns than interceptions in only two of his 12 seasons in the league, once in his rookie season and once again in 1969. Over time, it was a couple of years of the Good, many years of the Bad (for example, 26 TD's/28 INT's in 1967, 15 TD's/17 INT's in 1968), and a few years for the Ugly (19 TD's for 27 mistakes in 1966, 15 touchdowns for 28 oop's in 1975). Namath finished with a horrendous 220 picks for his career.

Namath's mistake-prone ways were compounded by a general inaccuracy with the ball. As it turns out, when Namath wasn't tossing the ball over to the other opposition, he wasn't throwing it to anyone in particular—he put up a terrible 50.2 percent completion percentage over the years, a number that would cost most starting quarterbacks their jobs in the modern era.

Just how bad were Namath's numbers? Consider that, at the time of his induction into the Hall in 1985, the man's QB rating was 52nd out of 67 eligible NFL passers. By the end of 1997, his rating placed him as a God-awful 95th out of 112, ranking him behind guys like Wade Wilson, Bubby Brister, Lynn Dickey, and Eric Hipple.

Forget the all-time best—Namath's career TD/INT ratio and completion percentage didn't even make the top 10 list among Jet passers!

That's enough to put some tarnish on the Hall of Fame bust, but it only gets even worse from there. As bad as Namath's interception and incompletion stats were, there's reason to believe that Namath was *far worse* than his raw numbers indicated. Namath ruined his knee back during his Crimson Tide days (the Jets didn't have a clue until after he'd signed), so his scatter-arm was compounded by painfully slow legs. After five knee operations in pro ball, a once-great young athlete was so immobile that sportswriter Paul Zimmerman called him a "million dollar statue."

Don Shula and others tried to pass off Namath's lack of mobility as some kind of off-hand virtue ("He'll stay in the pocket until the last possible second"), but it only led to disastrous results. Without the ability to maneuver away from defensive pressure or take yardage on a scramble, defenders had carte blanche to tee off on Namath on all passing situations. Namath's frequent injuries forced his coaches to rely on second-stringers in dozens of games, but that may have been a blessing in disguise, because Off-Broadway Joe probably killed as many Jet drives through immobility as he did through his frequent interceptions and incompletions.

Oh, but some might say, numbers aren't the be-all-and-end-all, particularly in a team-oriented game like football. The Jets did begin winning when Broadway Joe came on to the stage, so he may have lent them glitz and swagger. Namath's most important gift may have floated above mere stats—it may have shown up in the way he found "a way to win."

Not quite.

Let the record show that Namath teams only found a way to win in three of 12 seasons (1967, 1968, 1969). Most often, what the Jets found was a way to lose, compiling an atrocious 74–90–4 mark from 1965 to 1976. The Namath-era Jets made the playoffs exactly twice (1968 and 1969), and their dear leader retired with a career playoff record of 2–1.

Finally, Namath's cheerleaders can always argue that their guy belongs in the Hall because he did pull off a huge win during his one successful season, the one capped off by Super Bowl III. That win, along with Namath's famous "guarantee" and so-called "MVP" performance, all deserve some important context (#79, 61), but, as far as it goes, it's true, Namath's team did take it all.

Once.

And it's not that big of a deal, at least as far as the Hall of Fame is concerned. If a single ring is a credential for the Hall, then Brad Johnson, Trent Dilfer, Mark Rypien, Jeff Hostetler, and Doug Williams can expect very good news from Canton sometime soon. They can't, though, because no one's willing to ignore their mediocre-or-worse careers outside the Super Bowl. The same reasoning should apply to all, including the one-time media darling of the swinging sixties.

The funny thing is, Joe Namath has always been unique. It's impossible to find another player with the same kind of raw athletic potential and celebrity attached to his image. It's impossible to find another player with a lofty reputation so unaffected by real-world results and common sense, either. There's still no one like him.

WHO WAS THE MOST HATED NEW YORK FOOTBALL PLAYER OF ALL TIME?

 AN OPEN LETTER FROM MARK GASTINEAU

Dear Football Fans of New York,

I've heard the rumors.

Less than 20 years after my retirement, some people are already suggesting that maybe someone else was the most hated player in the history of New York football. Oh, how quickly they forget.

For instance, some are whispering Sam Huff from the 1950's-era Giants was more hated for playing dirty with late hits, illegal tackles, and eye-gouging, and such. Give me a break. You want to hate someone based on their bad sportsmanship? Well, I wasn't bad, I was the worst. The worst of the worst. There are reasons why the Mark Gastineau Fan Club meets in a phone booth.

Don't you remember my signature "sack dance" from the early 1980's? I'd take down an opposing quarterback behind the line of scrimmage, then proceed to wave my arms, pump my legs, and shake my fists as if I'd single-handedly won the Super Bowl. On every sack! It was beautiful.

You couldn't invent a more disrespectful stunt, and boy, you should have seen how our opponents responded. I guess one of my proudest days came during a Jets-Rams game at Shea in 1983. Jackie Slater, one of the classiest and most respected (yuck!) players in the game, got so upset that he shoved me from behind in mid-spasm. It sparked a bench-clearing brawl involving 37 players, and ponder that one for a moment—when was the last time you saw a bench-clearing brawl in the NFL? I mean, they said it was impossible to make violent, furious football players even more violent and furious.

No way. Everything was possible with a selfish, hated player named Mark Gastineau.

Just the thought of my "dance" was enough to energize our opponents, and when they started wailing on our entire defensive line, boy, you should have heard some of the curses. "Shut up and play ball," my teammates would scream and beg. I would have, too, if I didn't have an unbeatable commitment to being hated by all sides.

That brings me to my next point. A lot of players have been hated by their opponents, but I'm proudest of the bad feeling I inspired in my own locker room. You have to remember, I was careful to expand my "me-first" attitude far, far beyond my notorious dancing.

Here's one example—I rarely even faked an interest in stopping running backs and inside tackling. Why? Because that helped the team without padding my stats. No thanks. Also, I was usually free to run wild for the QB only because Joe Klecko was drawing double teams right next to me, but I'd never give him a word of credit. To me, it was "Joe who?"

Look, no one can doubt there were certain moments that could only be "Gastineau moments." I'd always show up late for meetings, but the coaching staff was afraid of my sulky attitude, so it couldn't single me out for punishment. They'd end up punishing the whole team for my prima donna act. Another time, I took advantage of the Jets' casual dress code by wearing some of my ugly, torn-up jeans. Of course that ruined it for everyone—soon enough they changed the rule to coat-and-tie!

I still chuckle at that one.

I had a natural talent for inspiring people, I won't deny it, but it ticks me off when people forget the work ethic behind the hatred. It took time to shave my chest and oil myself up for the publicity photos I handed out to the media. It took money to have a girlfriend's name tattooed to my butt. It took effort to wear a mink coat for my saunters around the locker room. None of it just happened.

One time, I'll never forget, I tore my Rolls through the training facility's parking lot with squealing tires. A rehabbing Freeman McNeil turned his neck to check out the sound, reinjured himself, and was out of commission for weeks. Some say that was luck. I say, "Luck is the residue of design.'"

What, I hear you say? "Mark Gastineau, you're another Lawrence Taylor. People may not have rejected your habits, but they also respected your skills on the field."

Oh, how wrong you are.

Sure, I was great player in my time—five straight Pro Bowls from 1981 to 1985, including then-records with a 20-sack year in '81 and a 22-sack year in '84. Still, the numbers just don't indicate the ways I helped the Jets lose games.

For instance, there was the time in the 1986 divisional playoffs against Cleveland, when my two unsportsmanlike conduct penalties cost us 30 total yards in the last four minutes. We lost a 10-point lead and, eventually, the game. Also, there was that other time I took Ken O'Brien over to Studio 54 in '83, then got us both arrested in a brawl. That caper ended up costing O'Brien his starting job in the next season.

Last but not least, there was the time I betrayed my teammates by crossing their picket line during the '87 strike. Now, Keyshawn Johnson may have popped off to reporters from time to time, but was he ever pelted with eggs as an infuriated mob screamed curses and threatened his life? If the security guards didn't stop them that day, I'll tell you, those chumps would have had my head on a spike! That one day, alone, should have been enough to establish *you-know-who as the worst clubhouse cancer of all time.*

I think I've put together a hate-able resume that speaks for itself, but you don't have to believe me. After all, I am a notorious liar. Just look at the evidence:

1. *I averaged nearly 20 sacks per year in the early 1980s **without ever being voted team MVP**. The writers once named me NFL Defensive Player of the Year without my teammates acknowledging me! That's hard to do, guys.*

2. *I left such a stink around Hempstead and the Stadiums that the Jets still won't retire #99. Beloved Joe Klecko—77.5 career sacks, retired number. Be-hated Mark Gastineau— 107.5 career sacks, no retired number.*

I don't want to ramble here, but I've barely scratched the surface. I was hated for taking steroids. For dropping out in the middle of a 1988 season, one whole day after I promised to stick around for the playoff run. For a post-retirement career that's included multiple divorces, arrests for drug possession and domestic assault, parole violations, income tax evasion, allegations of fixed boxing matches, and the obligatory lawsuits.

I could go on and on, but I think you get the idea. I was the complete package. I, Mark Gastineau, was the most hated football player in New York. Fans, give the devil his due.

Sincerely,
−Mark Gastineau

BILL PARCELLS OR BILL BELICHICK—WHO'S THE BETTER COACH?

65 People say that Bill Parcells is a born bully. He constantly berates, humiliates, insults, and threatens his players. He always keeps his assistants submissive and silent. He shouts down, manipulates, and stonewalls reporters.

Funny thing is, that's the word from those who *like* the guy.

All can be forgiven when a guy wins football games, though, and that's where Parcells gets a free pass from many fans and commentators. For all the downside, the guy has built an enviable reputation as a Hall of Fame–quality mastermind over the years. He's the most successful head coach the Giants *and* the Jets have ever seen.

At first glance, Parcells more than earned that reputation during his stints as head coach with the Giants, Patriots, Jets, and Cowboys. He's taken two Super Bowls with the Giants, an AFC championship game with the Patriots, and divisional playoff game with the Jets. In 18 years of coaching, he's guided all four franchises into the playoffs, putting together a 11–7 postseason record along the way.

That's a pretty gaudy track record, all right, but it's not exactly case closed on Bill Parcells as some kind of sideline genius.

Coaching football, like playing the game, involves a highly specialized team effort, and that's been especially true since Parcells started off as a boss in 1983. Head coaches are the natural recipients of the cheers and jeers, of course, but insiders know they're always dependent on good assistants to navigate the ever-more complex modern game. Brainy, tireless coordinators, who contribute everything from scouting and instruction to play-calling and game strategy, have been known to work wonders to make higher-ups look good, at least for a while.

Parcells himself has readily acknowledged that he hasn't been a one-man gang. He, and many others, have gone on record to proclaim that Bill Belichick's defensive schemes played a vital role for him with the Giants and Patriots to the Jets. In Super Bowl XXV, to take but one shining example, the coordinator's innovative 2–3–6 alignment sparked New York's upset win over Buffalo's high-powered offense.

Belichick undoubtedly contributed to Parcells' successes, but no one knows just how much. More than likely, it was a lot.

For a sense of Parcells' reliance on his defensive coordinator, consider Big Bill's record with Belichick at his side:

Team	Years	Won/Loss	Win %	Winning Seasons
Giants	1983–90	85–52–1	.620	6 in 8
Patriots	1996	11–5	.687	1 in 1
Jets	1997–99	29–19	.604	2 in 3

Working together, the two Bills combined for a 125–76–1 record, a .622 winning percentage, and nine winning seasons in 12 years. They produced seven playoff teams and won five divisions, three conference titles, and two championships. All in all, some superb credentials.

Unfortunately for Parcells, Belichick eventually moved on to become a head coach in his own right, and once his junior partner was off, so were Parcells' numbers:

Team	Years	Won/Loss	Win %	Winning Seasons
Patriots	1993–-95	21–27	.438	1 in 3
Cowboys	2003–05	25-23	.521	2 in 3

Through 2005, Parcells' Belichick-free teams have racked up a 46-50 record, a .465 winning percentage, and three winning seasons in six years. They qualified for the playoffs just twice, losing in the first round both times.

Hard to believe, isn't it? The solo Bill Parcells put together a losing record and zero playoff wins. That's no one's definition of greatness. That's no one's definition of goodness, even.

Even as Parcells transformed from Vince Lombardi to Vince Tobin while off on his own, the same can't be said for Belichick. After a rough few years with the Browns, he's thrived as the Patriots' head coach. Consider not-so-Little Bill's overall marks:

Team	Years	Won/Loss	Win %	Winning Seasons
Browns	1991–95	36–44	.450	1 in 5
Patriots	2000–05	63–33	.656	5 in 6

It works out to a sparkling 99–77, .563 winning percentage. Belichick's put up five losing seasons in 11 career years, but that's easily forgiven because he's guided five teams to the playoffs and won three division titles, three conference games, and three Super Bowls. At 11–2, he boasts the best playoff record in the history of the NFL. Yup, he's been even better than Walsh, Don Shula, and Joe Gibbs. And a certain Jersey-born bully.

As lopsided playoff results have indicated Belichick's superior coaching skills, the long term trend in regular season wins will only emphasize the point. After their first five years in the NFL, neither Belichick (36–44, .450) nor Parcells (42–36, .538) had particularly impressive winning percentages, but in the years since they settled in, Belichick's far surpassed his old boss—he's gone 60–33 (.645) to Parcells' 121–87 (.582). Belichick was still 64 career wins behind Parcells' total of 163 at the end of the 2005 season, but, given the fact that Belichick is 12 years younger, he's likely to surpass his old boss in both career wins and winning percentage well before he retires.

Of course, Parcells' apologists have their explanation for all the above. Maybe Parcells had had one bad year—six times over. Maybe Belichick's been propped up by some secret coordinator / mastermind of his own during the last few years. Maybe Belichick stole Parcells' lucky rabbit's foot on his way out the door. Maybe pigs will fly in next year's passing game.

There are a lot of excuses and maybes, but here are some facts and certainties:

1. Parcells was wildly successful when Belichick was around.
2. Parcells' talent for winning ball games suddenly vanished when his favorite coordinator disappeared.
3. Belichick's successes have only grown in the years since a certain fat guy got out of the way.

Bill Parcells has gotten away with some pretty ugly behavior over the years, but it might be time for reality to finally catch up to an oversized ego and overinflated reputation. The facts say he wasn't the best coach of his time. The facts say he wasn't even the best coach on his own staff.

WAS KEYSHAWN JOHNSON RIGHT ABOUT WAYNE CHREBET?

66 All along, Wayne Chrebet was the good guy, and Keyshawn Johnson was the bad guy.

Chrebet, a native of Garfield, NJ, was the 5'10" scrapper who managed to make the Hofstra University football team as a walk-on. He was the one who went undrafted by the NFL, only to return to the Hofstra practice fields for a free agent tryout with the New York Jets. Chrebet was the humble, salt-of-the-earth sort who made it on to the NFL roster, stuck with the team, and didn't make waves with outrageous comments. When he was through with his 11-year career in 2005, the *New York Times'* Dave Anderson called him "one of the noblest Jets in franchise history."

Chrebet was always the good guy, and Johnson was always the bad guy. A reform school graduate from out in

LA, Johnson was a strapping 6'4" specimen who established himself as an all-state high school player before being recruited into the USC football factory. He was the one taken #1 overall in the NFL draft before swaggering over to the Jets. And he was a loud, crass guy who made all sorts of waves by publishing an autobiography called *Just Give Me the Damn Ball!* Even kindly Dave Anderson thought he was an a--hole.

Johnson was most especially the bad guy when he described his teammate and fellow wide receiver, Chrebet, as the Jets' "mascot." It was typical "Me-Shawn," of course, and the comment was roundly criticized when it wasn't written off as more of the same bluster. But Johnson was right. If Chrebet wasn't exactly the team poodle, he wasn't a bona fide NFL receiver, either.

The numbers say that Chrebet's 1995–2005 career was, at best, not good. Certainly, Chrebet was never among the top dozen or so wide receivers in the league—he put up a single 1,000+ yard receiving season (in 1998) and made a single appearance on the top-10 leader boards for receptions, receiving yards, and receiving touchdowns (he finished 2002 tied for fifth in receiving TD's). He never came close to a Pro Bowl selection, either. Fantasy football's official rankings had Chrebet averaging a lowly #53 among the NFL's wide receivers in an average year.

Chrebet was mostly a non-factor as a Jet flanker, averaging a mere 3.82 receptions per regular season game and, on the relatively few occasions he did catch the ball, Chrebet was mostly limited to dink-and-dunk short-possessions, averaging only 12.7 yards per reception/48.5 yards per game. He finished his career ranked 18th in Jets history in yards per catch, and if you guessed he didn't find his way into the end zone very often . . . bingo. Hofstra's pride averaged just .27 touchdowns per regular game over the course of his career, good for a pitiful 14.1 catch/touchdown ratio that ranks behind 13 other Jet receivers.

Chrebet's buddies in the press corps once dubbed him "Mr. Third Down" for his supposed ability to convert in clutch spots. Given those drive-killing numbers, it would have been more appropriate to call him "Mr. Fourth Down."

The funny thing is that Chrebet's stats, crummy as they are, probably make him look far better than he deserves. Remember, Chrebet played with some pretty good Jet quarterbacks from 1995 to 2005 (Boomer Esiason, Vinny Testaverde, Chad Pennington), all of them working on a short yardage, West Coast-style passing game. Chrebet also played opposite first- and second-option receivers like Johnson, Laveranues Coles, and Santana Moss, meaning he never, ever drew shutdown cornerbacks or double coverage, either. In addition, Chrebet played the majority of his career alongside an incredibly consistent run-producer in Curtis Martin, who took even more heat off the Jets' passing game.

The fact that Chrebet—playing with more-than-competent quarterbacks, in favorable offensive schemes, alongside legitimate weapons, and a Hall of Fame running back—still couldn't rank among the top 50 receivers of his day . . . that's downright sad.

Yet, through it all, Chrebet was anything but downcast. After all, his sorry production didn't prevent him from collecting paychecks week after week, year after year, millions after millions. He stuck around long enough to catch 580 balls, actually, behind only Don Maynard on the Jets' all-time list. By the time he retired, he'd played an extraordinary 152 games, placing him among the top five players in the franchise's 45-year history.

Believe it or not, Chrebet was actually among the most senior position players in the entire League by the time he finally hung it up in '05. In playing 11 straight seasons with the same squad, he was joined by a handful of superstars like Brett Favre, Jerome Bettis, and Tim Brown. There you had a handful of sure-fire Hall of Famers . . . plus Wayne Chrebet.

How did Chrebet manage to produce so few results for so incredibly long?

It may go back to the beginning. He was always the good guy, the scrappy, undersized local who walked on from a nothing college program and kept his mouth shut. He was white. He was Wayne Chrebet. He was never the bad guy, the troubled and talented hired gun who demanded big-time stardom. He wasn't black. He wasn't Keyshawn Johnson.

One way or the other, Chrebet was never held to the same performance standards that applied to others. When Johnson called him a mascot, he was right.

WHAT WAS THE BIGGEST DISASTER IN THE JETS' MOVE TO GIANTS STADIUM?

67 It's hard to pick a single reason why the Jets made a huge, historic, horrific mistake when they evacuated Shea for the Giants Stadium in 1984. There are just so many reasons to choose from.

It may have been the way the move forced the great majority of the Jet fan base into hours of extra travel time. Instead of taking quick and easy mass transit into Flushing, Queens, tens of thousands were suddenly introduced to the pleasures of gas-guzzling, exhaust-filled crawls into the New Jersey swamps. Thank goodness for annual ticket price hikes—they distracted thousands of commuters from the grrrrrrrridlocked commutes and clogged game-day parking lots.

Or, maybe, it was the "forget-you" signal sent when the Jets followed the Nets across the Hudson River and into the suburbs. Or their cute persistence in labeling themselves as a "New York" team—as if some kind of mass geographical amnesia could make fans forget the vamoose outside the city limits and state line.

Or, perhaps, the move to East Rutherford was most memorable in the way that it neatly sliced the organization into two pieces, with the majority of team personnel living and working on Long Island only to commute over to the city and suburbs for travel and games.

Then again, maybe it's best to forget all those factors—they only concern fan convenience, civic pride, and common sense, and that may be too much to ask for. The biggest disaster in the Jets' move into Giants Stadium was the way it relegated them into permanent second-class citizenship.

It might be hard to recall nowadays, when the New York Jets were actually playing in New York, they had their own, understated way of doing things. It just wasn't that they occasionally won while the Giants stunk (though that definitely helped), it was in the way they came out of a new kind of football tradition in the 1960's. The Giants' decades of conservative family ownership, even their "G-Men"/"Big Blue" nicknames, always seemed to align them with the button-down government or IBM-style big business. Shea Stadium's Jets came to represent an attractive alternative to the establishment, a young franchise in a young stadium, from a young league, boasting young talents.

At the same time, Gang Green's home in Flushing lent a much-needed anchor. Shea was in the mode of concrete donut architecture, and it was surrounded by chop shops, OK, but it was a place fans could call their own. It was the real estate where the new Mets and Jets both won titles in '69, the turf where fans could remember Riggins rambling and Walker running and the Sack Exchange stuffing. It put the "home" in "home games."

By moving out of Shea and into Giants Stadium in '84, the Jets left that all behind, and for what?

The Jersey Jets transformed themselves into a Rodney Dangerfield franchise, the only one in American sports forced to play games under someone else's name, markers, and logos. (Sorry, no amount of temporary green tarps or official references to "the Meadowlands" could cover up that ugly reality). They became outsiders in their own building. They became the Giants' junior varsity.

Make no mistake, there was a message in seeing the Jets play in Giants Stadium. Just imagine the firestorm if the Mets claimed Yankee Stadium as their own or the Islanders pretended they were taking home ice in Madison Square Garden. Better yet, imagine the lordly Giants swallowing their pride to play in . . . Jets Stadium.

For all their self-sabotage to their reputation, though, you could argue that the very worst mistake in the Jersey move was the way it dogged Gang Green's long-term winning potential.

By plopping themselves down in Bergen County, the heart of Giants country, the Jets inevitably picked up thousands of ticket holders who viewed them as a second-choice team, as nothing more than a means to see some NFL football while their real favorites were sold out. Predictably, the Jersey Jets soon established one of the highest no-show rates in football, and with frenzied, massive fan reactions tipping the balance of so many football games, the Jets' relatively thin crowds contributed to one of the worst home records in the NFL, too. Overall, the Jets' move away from Shea Stadium set off a vicious cycle, where second-rate fan perceptions have contributed to second-rate crowds and then second-rate performances, over and over again.

Recently the Jets and Giants have been making noises about building a brand-spanking-new, jointly owned facility. If it works out, the place may finally overcome Gang Green's familiar woes. The fans should hope for as much, because the Jets have been grounded long enough in the Meadowlands.

IS THE HEISMAN TROPHY WORTH WINNING?

68 Among Heisman Trophy winners, the future always seems so bright.

Recognition as the most outstanding college football player in the country invariably follows blessings in physical talents and winning teams, the kind that come with packed football stadiums, adoring fans, national television exposures, all the perks of celebrity. By the time a fresh-faced young man arrives to accept his prize in New York's Downtown Athletic Club, his present can look like bright blue skies.

Unfortunately, his future can feel like a hit from an unblocked linebacker.

Of the 70 Heisman Trophy winners from 1935 to 2005, exactly seven have made the NFL Hall of Fame, but even that dismal stat may give too much credit—most of the 90 percent who didn't make it to pro greatness didn't even make it to pro mediocrity.

The roll call of past Trophy winners has included dozens who didn't amount to anything as real-world, pro football players. For every Paul Hornung ('56) making it to the Hall of Fame, there was a Terry Baker ('62) and John Huarte ('64), who couldn't make it to a starting team. For every

Alan Ameche ('54) winning multiple All-Pro honors, there were always guys like Billy Vessels ('52) and Dick Kazmaier ('51), who couldn't even win a roster spot. All along, the likes of Steve Spurrier ('66), Gary Beban ('67), and Pat Sullivan ('71) proved that varsity glory didn't guarantee one good year in the NFL.

The Heisman has always had a dismal record in forecasting college players' true abilities and potential, and the reason is fairly fundamental—it's never made much sense to hand out an individual award for an inherently team-oriented sport like football.

The nature of the sport doesn't provide reliable statistics or visibility to the very best players among linemen and defensive backfielders, for one thing, effectively eliminating three-quarters of the most outstanding college players in the country from consideration as the most outstanding college player in the country. In 71 years, exactly three defensive players (Larry Kelley '36, Leon Hart '49, and Charles Woodson '97) have been handed little Heisman statues.

It's no secret that glamorous skill players (quarterback, wide receiver, running back) are the only viable Heisman candidates, but even in that tiny group, it makes little sense to single out individuals. With their constant, crucial interdependence on any one play, it's always difficult to tell if a football team is winning because of a particular player's performance, or if a player's being carried by a suburb roster instead. For example, a rifle-armed quarterback can put up great numbers by overcoming mediocre teammates, but a workman QB can look just as good due to above-average contributions from his offensive line, receivers, and runners. It's hard to tell, even for expert evaluators.

The problem in isolating football players' performance is especially dire when it comes to the college game. While the NFL levels out competition through drafts and salary caps, the NCAA still allows certain programs vast advantages in talent recruiting, pro-level coaching, and creampuff schedules. There's even more room for programs to benefit from the best of the best support, in other words, so there's more room for statistics to be inflated far beyond what program players earn through their own merits.

Those structural problems have always been there in the Heisman, but in recent years, the artificiality of the process has sunk to new lows. Coaches have gotten wise to the fact that highly-touted award candidates produce more media attention, which translates to more money for the school program, which translates to more money in the coaches' pockets. As a result, they've gone out of their way to boost star quarterbacks and running backs, showcasing them in the offensive schemes and padding their reputations through blow-out scores. Lately, the coaches have been goaded on by glory-hungry school boosters, who've put together multimillion dollar marketing campaigns for their alma maters' candidates, too.

By now the Heisman selection process has degenerated to the point where it's more or less ruled by TV exposure and paid PR buzz, and the proof of its broken system can be seen in its results. Consider the 25 Trophy winners from 1979 to 2003, and what they produced in pro ball:

	Number	Players
Incomplete / Injury	1	Bo Jackson ('85)
Never Played	3	Charlie Ward ('93)
		Eric Crouch ('01)
		Jason White ('03)
Busts	8	Andre Ware ('89)
		Ty Detmer ('90)
		Desmond Howard ('91)
		Gino Toretta ('92)
		Rashaan Salaam ('94)
		Danny Wuerffel ('96)
		Ron Dayne ('99)
		Chris Weinke ('00)
Good	6	Charles White ('79)
		George Rogers ('80)
		Ricky Williams ('98)
		Doug Flutie ('84)
		Mike Rozier ('85)
		Carson Palmer ('02)

Very Good	4	Hershel Walker ('82)
		Vinny Testaverde ('87)
		Eddie George ('95)
		Woodson ('97)
Hall of Famers	3	Marcus Allen ('81)
		Tim Brown ('87)
		Barry Sanders ('88)

Over the last 25 years, Heisman Trophy winners have enjoyed a less than one-in-three shot at an above-average NFL career. No one knows what the football future will hold for Matt Leinart ('04) and Reggie Bush ('05), but more likely than not, it'll be a leap from college stardom into pro mediocrity. Or worse.

At this point, there's little to no mystery involved in the Heisman, little respectability to tear down. Knowledgeable fans know it's a fool's errand to award individuals in the ultimate team game. Few insiders believe winners are selected on talent and potential rather than self-serving, money-grubbing public relations. NFL talent evaluators and draft experts, certainly, ignore the confused, alternative-reality process that showers honors on the terrible Andre Ware and Gino Toretta while ignoring the terrific Emmitt Smith and Warren Sapp.

The only remaining mystery is in the Trophy's continued relevance. If the Downtown Athletic Club doesn't junk its little statue, it should completely overhaul its confused selection process. Then, and only then, will the Heisman Trophy be worth winning.

WAS WELLINGTON MARA A TRUE FOOTBALL FAN?

69 & 70

It's tempting to say that old Wellington Mara was as popular as Santa Claus, but that wouldn't be accurate. Among the NFL's power brokers and their sycophants, Mara was bigger than Santa. Even Jolly St. Nick didn't have the wise, amiable reputation Mara garnered over the years.

When he passed away in 2005, it was said that 89-year-old Giants owner was a brilliant boss. (Harry Carson: "He knew good football and good football players.") He was a benevolent Founding Father of the National Football League. (The *Boston Globe*: "A savior of the game.") He was a Players' Pal (The *New York Times* described his "air of paternal benevolence"). He was a Fans' Friend, too, mostly because he was such a big football fan in his own right. (Mike Lupica: "There was never anyone who loved a team like this.")

Not to speak ill of the late Mr. Mara, but it was all fiction. You might as well believe in Santa Claus:

MYTH #1. MARA THE BRILLIANT BOSS

The old fellow, famously, started off as a very young fellow, serving as a 9-year-old ball boy during the Giants' inaugural season of 1925. In the 1930's, Mara helped scout college players for his father, Tim Mara, and, starting in the 1950's, took pictures of offensive and defensive alignments during game time.

Apart from scouting assists and camera work, though, Mara's contribution to the Giants' on-field success was minimal. Contrary to some suggestions, it was Tim Mara who ran the teams' day-to-day operations throughout their 1950s glory days, the one who drafted players like Frank Gifford, Kyle Rote, Sam Huff, and Jim Katcavage while trading for players like Andy Robustelli and Dick Modzelewski. His 42-year-old son was an innocent bystander.

The senior Mara never did turn over control before dying in 1959, and that may have been a very wise decision on his part. Wellington Mara's inherited champions continued rolling from 1961 to 1963, but the front office proved utterly incapable of replacing its aging stars. By 1964, the wheels came off with a 2–10–2 season and the Giants stayed in the cellar for most of the next two decades, seeing 17 non-winning seasons from 1964 to 1983. Under the ole' King-Midas-in-reverse, the team's perennial winners became perennial losers.

New York's fortunes didn't begin to turn around until George Young came aboard as General Manager in 1979, and even that hiring couldn't be credited to Mara—the decision was made at the behest of Commissioner Pete Rozelle, who was embarrassed that a flagship franchise had been turned into a league joke.

After the Young hiring, the elderly Mara didn't even try to make football-related decisions and rarely deigned to talk to reporters. He mostly confined himself to lingering at practices and glad-handing, with one notable exception coming right before the January 2001 championship game. When reporters claimed that the streaky Giants were paper contenders, a brave Mara promised that the Giants would be "the worst team ever to win the Super Bowl."

They were man-handled by Baltimore, 34–7.

MYTH #2. MARA THE HIGH-MINDED FOUNDING FATHER

By virtue of his surviving birth and dad's will, Mara inherited his way into senior NFL management status in 1959. He was indeed one of the founding father's of the modern league. Unfortunately.

Mara and his early 1960's contemporaries created sports socialism, a system whereby most all of the league's revenues (including all-important TV packages) were pooled into a share-and-share-alike system. Once Rozelle lobbied Congress for a convenient little antitrust exemption and bought off the American Football League through a merger, owners effectively eliminated direct financial competition among themselves.

273

Strangely enough, the millionaires' brazen collusion is still portrayed as an innovative, high-minded leap into the future. It was anything but. The NFL didn't do anything but create an internal monopoly, rigging its market to tramp down profit-killing competition while driving up profit-inflating charges. Rich white men have been setting up similar cartels since the dawn of time, because they know the set-up's lock in rewards regardless of their performance or their customers' wishes. All the insiders won, including the big-market Mara—the guaranteed money ensured that the Giants' decades-long losing streak wouldn't hurt his bottom line, for instance.

Mara founded an upside-down, un-American scheme in which winning didn't matter. But it gets worse.

The fixed system continues on to this day. In a free market, the God-awful, incompetent owners among the Lions, Bengals, Saints, and Cardinals would have been forced to sell out long, long ago. In the world of socialist NFL-onomics, the rich have only gotten richer, regardless how many losers they produce for the fans.

The Bottom Line: If the United States had founding fathers like Wellington Mara, a lot more people would be living in Canada right now.

MYTH #3. MARA THE PLAYERS' PAL

Mara's first contribution to the NFL's profit-churning machine wasn't his last.

Once Mara and his fellow plutocrats eliminated competition among themselves, they sought to eliminate resistance from the players' union, mostly by provoking management/labor showdowns throughout the 1970's and 1980's. Mara, a member of several key committees, was among the hardest of the hardliners, and after the strikes of 1982 and 1987, they succeeded in bringing the union to heel.

The NFLPA's Gene Upshaw still tries to put a brave face on his feeble status, portraying the union's long-familiar surrender as a wondrous, touchy-feely business "partnership" with the lords of the game. Back on planet earth, the Mara rules have proved completely catastrophic for the hired help.

Modern pro players don't have protection from massive pay cuts, don't have arbitration rights, don't have meaningful protection from arbitrary management fines, and don't have full free agency. The moment they're too crippled to be useful, broken-down veterans are kicked out to the nearest street curb. Though NFL owners collect almost twice the annual revenues of Major League owners, their players make about half the average annual salary of baseball players, and the gap's even larger than that among the sport's most elite stars.

Mara's NFL has always treated player livelihoods like tackling dummies. But it gets worse.

Modern medicine should have cut down the rate and severity of football injuries in the new millennium, but more and more players are getting more and more hurt as time goes on. Today, incredibly, an estimated 90 percent of all those who play for four years or more suffer from some form of lifelong disability. That's more than eight times the damage from baseball, and includes everything from cracked bones, bruised organs, and debilitating arthritis to concussion syndrome, heart disease, and partial paralysis. Players like Johnny Unitas and Earl Campbell have spent most of their adult lives too handicapped to walk or hold their infant children.

The NFL's response to the injury epidemic? Nothing. Under-the-thumb players are all too disposable, you see. The league's never instituted blood testing to crack down on steroid-fueled hits, never enforced weight curbs on monster linemen, never reformed the playing rules to tramp down on the mayhem. Today, pro football players have the shortest, most painful careers in the four major sports, but retire to find the stingiest, most litigious pension plans around.

The Bottom Line: Mara, the ultimate company man, didn't just allow the modern NFL's player-hating system—he built it. With a friend like him, football players didn't need friends.

MYTH #4. MARA THE FOOTBALL FAN

For all his racketeering and union-busting, Mara's indirect influence on the fans' game may have been even worse.

Contrary to popular belief, most young athletes are pretty cagey in choosing their future line of work, and the very best of the best two-sport stars take one good look at the NFL's relatively low salaries, unprotected contracts, injury carnage, and complete disregard for player health . . . and a great many decide to take their chances in baseball. Not all of them can make it—players like Josh Booty, Chris Weinke, Ricky Williams, Chad Hutchinson, Drew Henson have all flunked out of the Minor Leagues in recent years—but those who have any realistic shot at baseball do their best to avoid football. They want to end up like Dave Winfield, Willie Wilson, Kirk Gibson, Alex Rodriguez, and Joe Mauer, all of whom turned down possible football stardom in favor of the relative riches, protection, and safety to be found in the National Pastime.

Mara's system ensured that fans will never see many great young talents on the gridiron. But it gets worse.

Mara's hard-line negotiations helped produce a system using across-the-board, hard salary caps, one that's forced executives to release some of the most popular, productive players in the game on an annual basis. Fans have completely given up on teams' maintaining any kind of stable personnel from year-to-year, which is why colorful unit nicknames (The Steel Curtain, The Doomsday Defense, The Sack Exchange, The Hogs) have become extinct. Modern units don't stick around long enough to be recognized, let alone nicknamed.

Under the Mara rules, the fans have lost any sense of team identity. But it gets worse.

With massive turnover forcing NFL coaching staffs to rebuild from scratch on an almost annual basis, players can't learn complex game plans the way they used to (that's especially true when it comes to the crucial, closely coordinated teamwork on the offensive and defensive lines). Every team basically operates like a first-year expansion team and, as a result, the quality of play has dropped off on a league-wide basis. It's not particularly easy to see, since the same problem affects all 32 teams, but Mara's brand of socialism has definitely hurt playing fundamentals throughout football.

The NFL's many apologists justify the system's gaping flaws by insisting that it produces more competitive balance, at least in comparison to baseball. Funny, though, several studies have shown that old talking point's off the point—in recent years the Major Leagues have had a greater diversity in champions, more conference/league champions, and playoff teams.

The Bottom Line: Would a true football fan discourage young players, destroy team identities, and downgrade the quality of the game? Wellington Mara did.

MYTH #5. MARA THE FANS' FRIEND

Mara was often portrayed as a holdover from an earlier, simpler time, when a team owner was more a man-on-the-street than a ruthless, profit-minded tycoon. He was a warm-hearted sportsman in the owner's luxury box, that was who he was.

(Oh, what a wonderful world it would be if men on the street could inherit dad's playthings and multimillions, instead of working for a living. But, hey, let's go with the story.)

Well, Wellington Mara may have had warm feelings toward the Giants' legions, but they surely didn't stop him from squeezing them with the highest ticket prices in the NFL. That would be the same NFL which already featured the highest ticket prices in the four major sports. Fan friendship didn't stop Mara from moving the Giants, either. They had perpetual sellouts in Yankee Stadium's 60,000-plus seating throughout the 1960's, but "the conscience of the league" wanted even more cash, so he finagled a tax-subsidized, custom-built stadium in the early 1970's.

In other words, Wellington Mara was responsible for making the affordable New York Giants of yesteryear into the expensive New Jersey Giants of today. But it gets worse.

Mara's little evacuation was a first in the "let's-abandon-our-hometown" movement that swept football in the 1980's and 1990's. Soon enough, team owners/escape artists like Bob ("Good Bye Baltimore") Irsay, Bud ("See Ya Houston") Adams, and Art ("Screw Cleveland") Modell were betraying their fan bases, too, and they weren't just moving across the river, either. By the turn of the millennium, ever-more lavish public handouts and wandering franchises ruled football.

The Bottom Line: Here's some free advice: if your friend charges you robber-baron prices, abandons your hometown, and hangs out with a bunch of rich extortionists, get a new friend.

And that was the reality behind the reputation. Wellington Mara didn't know the first thing about winning football, knew all too much about socialist sports rackets, screwed over football players, then helped ruin the fans' game.

Like Santa, Mara was popular, but that's all he was. There was nothing to his rep.

COURTS

BROADWAY JOE VS. CLYDE— WHO WAS THE MOST STYLISH STAR IN NEW YORK SPORTS HISTORY?

71 & 72 Back in the day, Joe Namath was far more than a rich Jets quarterback, just like Walt Frazier was far more than the Knicks' best-ever point guard.

Namath and Frazier also established themselves as icons of style for the late 1960's and early 1970's, showing how far famed athletes could go as handsome, self-assured exemplars of all-around stardom. Men about town, they had a knack for showing up at the hottest nightclubs, the swankest restaurants, and the flashiest parties in New York City. They were among the first athletes to show up in the society pages almost as often as the sports section. Before, jocks could be well-known. Afterwards, they could be celebrities.

Still, while both Joe Namath and Walt "Clyde" Frazier will always be associated with style, one wasn't nearly as stylish as the other. A certain star's cool had it all:

BROADWAY JOE   CLYDE

The Tag

"Broadway Joe" grew up in Beaver Falls, PA, and played ball in Queens. Howard Cosell came up with an alternative "Joe Willie" nickname for some reason, but, as usual, Cosell wasn't telling it like it was—Namath's birth certificate reads "Joseph William."

The Knicks' trainer dubbed Frazier "Clyde" after the gun-toating, bank-robbing title character in 1967's *Bonnie and Clyde*. He said that the rookie reminded him of Clyde Barrow (Warren Beatty) in the way he always wore a fedora with a certain panache.

This may have been the coolest nickname anyone's ever had.

The Threads

Namath usually sported long hair and thick sideburns to go along with the standard wide lapels and bell-bottoms. He once wore a full-length fur coat on the sidelines, which was supposed to be a big deal for some reason.

Walt Frazier may have been the most incredible fashion plate in New York history, let alone sports. He had lambchop sideburns and wore ensembles that included rich, dark topcoats, butterfly collars, black leather pants, alligator boots, silk scarves, Superfly sunglasses, gold watch fobs, a big, brass CLYDE belt buckle, and, naturally, those wide-brims. Combine all of it with graceful, lightning-fast moves on the court, and Clyde Frazier was the father of basketball as an expression of street style.

283

BROADWAY JOE	CLYDE

The Ride

When he signed his first pro contract in 1965, Namath received a Jetgreen convertible as part of the signing bonus.

In the early 1970's Frazier could be found tooling around in a white Rolls Royce with "WCF" plates.

The Pad

Namath's bachelor penthouse at 300 East 76th Street featured a white llama rug.

Frazier's Manhattan digs had a round bed with ceiling mirrors.

The Ladies

Namath, who was frequently photographed with various models and starlets, once said "I like my Johnnie Walker Red and my women blonde."

In 2003, during a drunken sideline interview, he told ESPN's Suzy Kolber that he wanted to kiss her. Twice.

Frazier, who grew up in the south, believed that gentlemen don't kiss and tell. He's never discussed the beauties who saw the round bed and ceiling mirrors.

Clyde once shook hands with Ms. Kolber.

Keepin' Cool

When NFL Commissioner Pete Rozelle ordered him to divest from a nightclub associated with mobsters, Namath "retired" for a few weeks, then caved during a tearful press conference. The next week's *Sports Illustrated* cover: NAMATH WEEPS

Clyde Frazier wouldn't cry if he was trapped in an onion factory for a week.

Bein' Real

Some believed a young Namath wore off-beat "white" cleats in college, but he didn't—his standard black shoes were wrapped in thick support tape for his frail knees. The Jets, eager for a hip marketing image, soon began to special-order whites for him. (And no one ever explained what was so rebellious about wearing white shoes in the first place. Pat Boone and Lawrence Welk wore white shoes).

Frazier never felt the need to go along with some phony-baloney branding gimmick.

Gettin' Paid

Namath lent his name to a failed fast-food chain, shaved his legs in a pantyhose commercial, and cut off his Fu Manchu for $15,000. In 2005 he shilled for a billion-dollar, white-elephant stadium proposal on the West Side. He was a sellout.

Frazier was one of the first NBA stars to sign a major shoe contract, popularizing the snazzy suede Pumas that can still be seen today. Later in life, he lost a gravity-defying Afro and endorsed all-too-useful Just for Men hair products.

285

BROADWAY JOE   CLYDE

Showbiz

Namath couldn't resist a live camera, no matter how cheesy the production. He will forever be responsible for movies like *C.C. and
Company*, *Norwood*, and *The Last
Rebel* and guest-starring in vast
wasteland fare like *Love Boat,Fantasy
Island*, and *The A Team*. To his credit,
though, Namath once did a memorable cameo with Bobby Brady.

Clyde once starred in a movie
called *Aaron Loves Angela*, but he
mostly stuck to lighting up
Broadway with his game. He
sometimes played the banjo for
kids.

Literary Career

Namath was the "author" of *I Can't
Wait 'Til Tomorrow (Cause I Get
Better Looking Every Day)*. And you
thought *Just Give Me the Damn Ball!*
was the worst book written in the
English language.

#10 wrote *Clyde: The Walt Frazier
Story*, which wasn't bad. It had
stories of struggles to overcome
the odds while enjoying basketball and life.

Loquaciousness

Namath was included in the *Monday Night Football* booth for a year, along with fellow good-guy O.J. Simpson, then did *NFL on NBC* broadcasts for a while in the late 1980's. Blame it on the strange western-Pennsylvania-by-way-of-deep-South accent, but he wasn't any good.

Frazier could have rested on his laurels as a resident MSG hero, but he became one of the most celebrated color commentators in basketball by developing thesaurus-intensive descriptions all his own. "Clyde-isms" are improv poems with a constant barrage of rhyming phrases along with creative alliteration ("thrillin' and chillin,' dishin' and wishin'").

Only Frazier himself has been indescribable.

WAS PATRICK EWING TO BLAME FOR THE KNICKS' TITLE DRAUGHT?

73 Conversations about the Knicks' Patrick Ewing tend to be start off great.

But they always reach a big "but."

As a Georgetown underclassman, the 7-foot Ewing was one of the most dominant players in NCAA history, leading the Hoyas to three national championship games in three years. After he was selected by the Knicks as the first overall pick in the 1985 draft, he more than lived up to his promise as an incredibly prolific scorer, rebounder, and shot-blocker.

When Willis Reed called Patrick Ewing the greatest Knick of all time, he must have been thinking of the man who owns team records in every major offensive and defensive category in team history. Or Ewing's incredible average of 80 games played per season from 1987–88 to 1996–97. Or the way he gained honors as a Rookie of the Year, 11-time All Star, and one of the "50 Greatest NBA Players of All Time."

Best of all, Ewing was the proven clutch performer who averaged 20.6 points and 10.4 rebounds per game over an

135 career playoff games. He was the major reason in the Knicks emergence from the mid-1980's wilderness and into the longest sustained success they've ever had—13 straight playoff appearances from 1987–88 to 1999–2000, including three Atlantic Division titles, four appearances in the Eastern Conference Finals, and two Conference titles. Ewing also led teams to an NCAA championship and two Olympic gold medals (one in college and one with the 1992 "Dream Team"). He was great.

But.

Pat Ewing never did overcome the holes in his game. Too often, he clogged the middle of the court, took iffy jumpers instead of forcing his way into sure dunks, and didn't readily pass off from double-teams. His relatively slow reflexes, smallish hands, and predictable post moves contributed to a too-high 3.5 turnover rate per 40 minutes.

Worst of all, Ewing didn't come through in the clutch. His 20.6 postseason average was more than two points less than his regular season numbers, and he always seemed to come up small in elimination games. He was a major reason why the Knicks are still waiting for the true test of a winner: an NBA championship. He wasn't great.

The greatness/"but" thing tends to comes up again and again with Patrick Ewing, and it is a bit confusing. In the final analysis, though, it's up to the pro-Ewing crowd to clear the big man of responsibility for New York's many playoff failures in the 1990's. They can't do it. There are too many "buts."

For instance, Ewing apologists tend to lump him in with Hall of Famers like Karl Malone or Charles Barkley—1990's-era stars who didn't win because they lacked the teammates to counter the best support players in Chicago and Houston. They argue that you can't blame Patrick Ewing for the fact that Charles Oakley, Derek Harper, and Greg Anthony didn't answer the Bulls' Scottie Pippen or the Rockets' Clyde Drexler.

But . . . it's not fair to judge Ewing's supporting cast independently. Part of the beauty of basketball is the way a star can make those around him better, and as the Knicks' featured offensive weapon, it was up to Ewing to get creative off the dribble and get others involved in the flow. Hakeem Olajuwan did that for the Rockets by constantly adjusting to opponents' defenses and creating shots on the perimeter. Ewing didn't do that for the Knicks. He didn't have effective teammates mostly because he didn't do enough to help make his teammates effective.

By 1999, the Knicks' inability to play crisp full-court ball inspired something called "the Ewing theory," a notion that a squad can get better once its nominal star goes down. The proof came in the way that New York played a more fluid, fast-paced game once their starting center went out for the first round of the '98 playoffs against the Heat and the majority of the '99 Easter Conference Finals against the Pacers. New York won both.

In Ewing's defense, supporters also point to the times when he lifted the team to new heights. He did come through with a bullying 44-point, 13-rebound effort in Game 4 of the '90 playoffs against the Celtics, an 18-point, 17-rebound game against Chicago in the 1994 Eastern Finals, and a 25-point, 11-rebound effort in Game 3 of the '97 Semis. He overcame painful injuries in leading the Knicks to wins in Game 6 of the '92 Eastern Finals against the Bulls and Game 5 of the '99 series against Miami, too.

Those were there, it's true, but. . . .

What about all the many times Ewing let the team down? The two most egregious examples came in the closing minutes in Game 7 of the '95 Semi Finals against the Pacers, when A) he went for a finger-roll instead of a slam dunk, B) missed, and C) lost the game. In the '99 Eastern Finals against Indiana, he missed six straight shots in the moment of truth.

On other occasions, Ewing failed because he didn't even try. A Michael Jordan or an Olajuwan would have allowed CBA castoff John Starks to go 2-for-18 in Game 7 of the NBA Finals or Charles Smith to miss four straight shots in a Game 5 of the Eastern Finals . . . if their families were being held hostage at the time. Otherwise, they would have demanded the ball for themselves. They were leaders. They took responsibility for the game. Ewing wasn't. He didn't.

There are other reasons why Ewing—the highest-paid, highest-profile player on those playoff losers—has to get the blame for the draught. He was dominated by Olajuwan in the playoffs, which may have been excusable, but he was also owned by Bill Cartwright, which wasn't. And who can forget the Easter Conference Semis in '97? The Knicks had Miami beat, 3–1, but PJ Brown ignited a brawl in Game 5, conveniently resulting in the suspension of Ewing and friends. As they sat and stewed during Games 6 and 7, the Heat stole the series out from under them. Unforgivable.

All that happened on Patrick Ewing's title-less watch. He was a great player.

But.

He was the one with the responsibility.

MICHAEL JORDAN & PAT RILEY—WHO WAS PUBLIC ENEMY NO.1 IN THE GARDEN?

74 & 75 One was born in 1963. The other was born in 1945. One was black. The other was white. One wore tank tops and worked the court. The other wore Armani and worked the sideline. One shaved his head. The other used the most famous hair gel in basketball.

Michael Jordan and Pat Riley were perpetually different, especially in their relationships to the 1990's Knicks.

Jordan was always the Knickerbocker nemesis. From the day he started as a guard with the Chicago Bulls in 1984, the ultimate competitor set out to dominate New York and anyone else who got in the way of his championships. He never, ever changed.

Riley shifted in relation to New York. He started the 1990's as coach of the Knicks' West Coast rival, left the game for a year, then signed on as head coach in 1992. He instituted the team's ugly but effective brand of ball, the one with a slow-up offense and physical defense, then led plodding, predictable squads to wins in seven playoff round wins in four years. Suddenly, in 1995—one year after going all the way to Game 7 of the Finals—Riley sent the Garden a fax announcing his resignation. He spent the rest of the decade behind the Miami Heat's bench, meeting up against his former employers in the playoffs in 1997, 1998, and 1999.

Jordan and Riley were two very different guys—one a bitter rival, the other a rival/friend/rival. Who was the Knicks' more hateable public enemy No.1?

Like most arguments, this one comes down to a definition of terms. If the worst possible enemy is the guy who always, always finds a way to win out, then there's no argument at all.

Jordan matched up against the Knicks in four playoff series from 1991 to 1996 . . . and he won four playoff series from 1991 to 1996. He was gracious enough to retire for a few years there, providing just enough daylight for New York to reach the Finals in '94 and '99, but otherwise, it was always the same. When he showed up at Madison Square Garden for a big game—regular season, postseason, didn't matter—he always seemed to find a way to win. He was never anything but the Grim Reaper in Nikes.

No one was in Jordan's league as a 1990s winner, including Riley. After he flew down south, he met up with his old team four straight times from 1997 to 2000 and won exactly once, and even that one series ('97) was tainted by the fallout from the infamous PJ Brown/Charlie Ward melee. Otherwise, New York's players, coach, and fans made the most of their shots at Riley revenge. After everyone had vented a tad, he was never quite as hateable again.

Still, that doesn't feel exactly right. Being public enemy No. 1 has to do with more than wins and losses—it has to do with the expectations that go along with the victories and defeats. You can't just judge MJ and Riles on their records, but according to their own standards.

With Jordan, you always knew what you could expect. Without fail, there was the #23, the tongue wag, the arm band, the fist pump. A game matching aerial heroics to uncanny pull-up shooting and stifling defense. A relentless commitment to applying a last-second dagger. Doing all the above with the kind of gentleness and remorse associated with a rampaging mako shark.

He was always Jordan. It was impossible for the Knicks to begrudge a more-than-worthy adversary on his own terms.

Riley, though? There was no getting a fix on him.

For years, he made enemies and alienated people as the Lakers' slickster coach. Then, suddenly, he was back home (Schenectady-born and raised), promising to bring some of the Lakers' old pixie dust to a new dynasty. Fans hated grab-and-hold playing style. Fans loved the raucous excitement he brought to 433 straight Garden sell outs. And then, suddenly, it was nothing but negativity. With no good-bye press conference—nothing—he bolted. He abandoned the city for a town outside the New York/Chicago/LA triumvirate, and for an expansion franchise with a stupid name.

Most of all, though, Knick fans hated the way Riley's talk didn't quite match up with Riley's results. He said Patrick Ewing was the big man to deliver a championship. Then he let little John Starks go wild with a 2-for-18 in Game 7 of the '94 Finals. He once said "there's winning and there's misery." Then he lost. The notorious fax declared that he "cared deeply" about his players. But not deeply enough to stick with a winner. He said it was about "team." Until it was about "me."

It was impossible for the Knicks Nation to respect Pat Riley in his own terms. In that way, he was the worst enemy of all.

IS ISIAH *COMPLETELY* RESPONSIBLE FOR THE KNICKS FIASCO?

76 SOURCE: THOMAS' CO-WORKERS, FINANCING UNDER INVESTIGATION IN KNICKS COLLAPSE

Peter Handrinos

4:36 EST

7th AVENUE & 31st STREET, NEW YORK, NY—Embattled New York Knicks president Isiah Thomas, already under investigation for his handling of the once-proud basketball franchise, recently suffered a new setback when an inside source revealed his coworkers and financier were being sought for questioning.

Thomas has been widely suspected of gross executive negligence and fraud virtually from the moment he took over the Knicks offices in late 2003. Horrified onlookers have testified that the storied organization has traded for players with the exact same skills (undersized shooting guards Stephon Marbury, Steve Francis, and Jamal Crawford), a confused youngster with heart issues (Eddie Curry), and big-money, small-performance backups (Malik Rose, Maurice Taylor).

As a result of the ill-considered transactions, the Knicks finished the 2005–06 season at 23–59, the worst mark in an

Eastern Conference that included a first-year expansion team. The dismal record was accompanied by an exploding $125 million-plus payroll, one roughly double that of the 2004–05 champion San Antonio Spurs. In sum, the 35-win team Thomas inherited three years ago has somehow become 12 losses worse and $37 million more expensive.

Thomas has given away numerous first round picks even as he's taken on long-term contracts, so it is not clear how Knick fans can hope for a turnaround within the next several years. As a result, recent studies have found the area around 2 Penn Plaza has become a listless patch of urban blight.

NEW CHARGES

A source, who would only be identified as a sports fan close to the widening investigation, has confirmed investigators' belief that Thomas has indeed acted as the main offender in the team collapse, but emphasizes a new theory placing his actions within an extensive network of fraudulent practices. New scrutiny is being placed on the unpopular president's players, coach, and team owner as well.

"The fact is, there's no way Thomas could have done this much damage as some kind of loose cannon. He had accomplices, a henchman, and a kingpin, and they have to be dealt with, too," the source said.

In that regard, numerous Garden witnesses have described a lazy group of career underachievers on the

Knicks roster. Recently fired head coach Larry Brown, who has been around the NBA for more than 30 years, confessed that "I never in my life thought I'd have to be in a position where I'm begging guys to play. . . . Somehow, you've got to find five guys that care enough to compete." Guard Quentin Richardson corroborated Brown's statement, saying "I played for the Clippers when we were bad. I ain't never been around nothing like this. I never lost games like this. And it seems like we don't care."

The team's players have also been indicted for their selfish ways. Point guards Marbury, Crawford, Nate Robinson, and Jalen Rose, in particular, have been identified as shoot-first types who won't hustle or show up on defense.

This story's inside source revealed that coach Brown himself can expect intensive questioning regarding his past role in the Knicks' reversals. Authorities want to know why Brown agreed to coach in a situation completely unsuited for his team-first style, why he repeatedly alienated his own players through widely quoted media criticism, and why he shuffled through more than 40 starting lineups in his one year behind the bench. They've noted that a 33-win team became a 23-win team in the year after Brown's arrival.

One of the most respected coaching talents in the game before the 2005–06 season, inside sources state that Brown may have been implicated in a covert scheme to intentionally destroy the Knicks from the inside, perhaps in an effort to have Thomas fired. Facts are still emerging on this aspect of the story. Brown was terminated one season and 331 days after signing a record-breaking $50 million coaching contract.

Brown has been accused of abandonment during previous stints in Carolina, Denver, Los Angeles, New Jersey, Kansas, San Antonio, Los Angeles again, Indiana, Philadelphia, and Detroit. During a press conference in July 2005, the Long Beach native described the Knicks position as the one "dream job" he'd been waiting for.

FINANCING QUESTIONS

Finally, it was revealed that franchise owner James Dolan may also be questioned for his role in the Knicks' "Enron-like" business practices.

Dolan, who has been seen in the company of cable television executives on several occasions, will most likely be interrogated on his approving contracts for a washed-up Glen Rice (four years, $36 million), underachieving, overweight Jerome James (five years, $30 million), non-factor Penny Hardaway ($13.6 million), and perpetually injured Allan Houston (six years, $100 million). Another line of questioning may involve the Thomas/Brown power struggle and the unprecedented ridicule it's attracted in the New York press.

"Writers are comparing Isiah Thomas to a concessionaire running through the aisles while throwing hot coffee directly into the faces of unsuspecting fans," said an inside investigation source, "One magazine wrote, 'Knicks fans don't want Isiah Thomas fired; they want him jailed.' That goes beyond incompetence. Way beyond. The questions are—what did Dolan know and when did he know it?"

In a possible attempt to establish a future insanity defense, Dolan has declared his absolute confidence in Thomas and his repeated statements that "the future is bright." This story's source noted that that the Knicks owner said much the same thing before firing Hall of Fame coach Lenny Wilkens and forcing out the highly respected Jeff Van Gundy.

A TURBULENT TENURE

Thomas, alias "the Baby-Faced Assassin" or "Zeke," has long been a familiar figure in the harsh corridors of NBA power. After a Hall of Fame career as a point guard for the Detroit Pistons from 1982 to 1994, he was hired as Executive Vice President of the expansion Toronto Raptors, only to depart the franchise under mysterious circumstances. A brief, disastrous stint as a television commentator followed, one most notable for what have been described as "predictable" commentaries and "clumsy, monotonic" deliveries.

A year and a half after Thomas assumed ownership of the Continental Basketball League in 1998, a decades-old player development organization went bankrupt amidst now-familiar allegations of managerial ineptitude and out-of-control spending. Finally, Thomas was hired as head coach of the Indiana Pacers from 2000 to 2003, but failed to make it past the first round of the playoffs with the NBA

Finals team he inherited. He was terminated by Pacer president Larry Bird shortly before his arrival in New York.

Earlier this year, the Knick President, 45, openly declared that if he met internet columnist/critic Bill Simmons on the street, "there would be a problem." He is currently being sued by a one-time Knicks vice president for sexual harassment arising from what the plaintiff described as "demeaning and repulsive behavior." Veteran player Sam Perkins once said of Thomas, "He talks congenial with you, but when he snaps he's like a thug with a sling blade. He snapped several times. You don't want to see it."

Mr. Thomas, who has declared himself innocent of any wrongdoing, would not return numerous calls for comment.

SHOULD THE NETS MOVE TO BROOKLYN?

77 In 1958, the Brooklyn Dodgers became the Los Angeles Dodgers.

That same year, the New York Giants recast themselves as the San Francisco Giants.

In 1976, New York's most popular football team relocated to East Rutherford, New Jersey.

In 1977, the New York Nets became the New Jersey Nets.

In 1984, the New York Jets started playing in Jersey, too.

Notice a pattern?

For some time now, it's been fashionable for franchises to ditch New York in favor of the greener pastures to be found across the Hudson River, whether they be in the Golden State or the Garden State. One way or the other, the Big Apple wasn't big enough to accommodate them. The sad trend has been going on for so long now that it seems irreversible.

It isn't.

There was no good reason in the world why multiple teams had to flee from the richest, most populated metropolis in the country and, under the terms of a pending development proposal, the Nets may prove as much. In recent years, ownership's made a lot of noise about moving away from the New Jersey Meadowlands complex and into the heart of Brooklyn, thus throwing all precedents out the window. For the first time since 1904, New York City would welcome someone else's team. Someone would come back home. Someone would build something. The ultimate city game would find a new home in the greatest city in the world.

There would be an incredibly positive message in the Nets' move back to New York state, and the plan looks even better in the way that it could prove to be a fresh start for the organization.

The Nets came of age in the 1970's within an American Basketball Association plagued by a second-rate reputation and second-rate facilities, and the franchise never really broke free of that tradition, especially since it moved from Long Island to New Jersey.

A move to Brooklyn would have the potential to turn that whole thing around. For once, a faceless suburban organization could establish ties to the most bohemian, hip borough in the city. It wouldn't be surrounded by parking lots and suburban sprawl, but lively residential neighborhoods and busy shopping areas. Fans wouldn't face down traffic gridlock, but access nearly a dozen rail and subway lines. They wouldn't gaze upon a generic piece of concrete, but a Rockefeller center-type hub designed by the world-renowned Frank Gehry.

Brooklyn would be nothing less than a franchise rebirth for the Nets that would give city basketball fans their first-ever choice between two potent rivals. The Knicks, along with the Boston Celtics, are the only two surviving franchises from the original NBA of 1950, so they'll always have a brighter history, but one move could set up the Nets' brighter future. What a face-off—Knicks and Nets/Manhattan and Brooklyn. The matchups would eventually stir intra-city passions that haven't been seen outside the Yankees/Mets interleague games.

Of course, owner Brett Ratner isn't all that concerned with building the New York sports market or even the Nets' future. He's a businessman who wants to make a business deal, and that's where the Nets' bright prospects grow awfully cloudy.

The Nets' relocation is a relatively small part of a plan to invest in an extensive borough transformation. Plans for a 20,000-seat arena go beyond basketball to possible profit-centers in concerts, ice skating rinks, commercial space, restaurants, retail shops, and mixed-income housing, among other things. There are massive, complex plans involving billions of dollars, millions of square feet in office space, thousands of apartments, hundreds of businesses, dozens of buildings, and several city blocks between Atlantic Avenue and Dean Street.

In a best-case scenario, Ratner's urban renewal project will take years to complete, and it's far from clear if a best-case will ever happen. Like previous proposals in the South Bronx and Harlem, Brooklyn's downtown revival project is going to come up against all kinds of resistance from a gaggle of self-appointed environmentalists, the not-in-my-backyard crowd, amateur architectural critics, free-lancing celebrities, and various other activists for the status quo. Politicians, naturally, will want their own piece of the pie before they sign off on the necessary infrastructure and tax breaks. Even if all that clears, the NBA may veto a new arena at Flatbush and Atlantic.

So, despite the positive message, team revival, and new growth involved, the Nets may never move over to Brooklyn. They definitely should, though.

#2 Separated out from New York's identity, street life, mass transportation, and glitzy Madison Square Garden, the modern-day Nets have set themselves up as a perpetual #2 franchise over in Jersey.

Consider, for instance, recent history. The Nets have enjoyed five straight winning seasons and two Eastern Conference championships through the conclusion of the 2005–06 campaign, even as the Knicks turned them over to the a punchline under President Isiah Thomas. Jason Kidd's New Jersey teams have gone 19-3 in head-to-head games against New York.

Despite all that on-court success, the Nets' recent playoff teams haven't come close to outdrawing the mighty Knicks in attendance or rating points. As a matter of fact, the Nets have *never* outdrawn their rivals in attendance or rating points. Not once in 30 years. It's no wonder that John Starks once said "The Knicks are just so entrenched in the New York area that fans will love them no matter what." He's justified in that arrogance—the Nets/Knicks have always been the most pathetic intermarket sports "rivalry" this side of the Lakers and Clippers.

The Nets have been completely set up to fail against their competition in the New York sports market, and they're all alone in that. There have been years—more than a few—when the Mets have been good enough to out-perform the Yankees in attendance. It's been the same for the Jets against the Giants. Ditto for the Islanders against the Rangers. Only the Nets have been stranded as perpetual also-ran's.

RINKS

WERE THE ISLANDERS THE MOST SUCCESSFUL EXPANSION TEAM OF ALL TIME?

78 Expansion teams are the youngsters of the sports world—newcomers coming on to the scene eager for the adventures to come in their big league futures. Sadly, though, it rarely works out very well. New franchises' first few years don't include as many adventures as they do defeats—a good many of them coming in a pretty humiliating and painful fashion. Every so often, an expansion club like the '62 Mets (40–120) or '76 Buccaneers (0–14) establishes itself among the most monumental losers of all time.

Young teams usually go through very rough childhoods, but the New York Islanders proved to be spectacular exceptions to a very old rule.

The Isles kicked off their NHL existence with an abysmal 12–60–6 record in the 1972–73 season, but quickly ascended to a 33–25–22 record in their third year and never looked back. In 1975, they won two playoff rounds, and in 1976, 1977, and 1978, they were eliminated from the postseason only after falling to the year's eventual Stanley Cup winner. By 1979–80, the Islanders would no longer be denied, as they won the first of four straight Stanley Cups from 1980 to 1983.

Without a doubt, the Islanders' early, tremendous success hasn't been duplicated in New York sports, and probably hasn't been repeated by any expansion team in any major sport. No one has ever been so good so quickly.

To see how that's true, consider the regular season and playoff records for those entering the Major Leagues, NFL, NBA, and NHL from the 1960's to the 1990's. Excluding franchises with established track records in the now-defunct AFL, ABA, and WHA leagues, that's 52 teams in all. Every comparison period is arbitrary in one way or another, but the best measure of success may be in the teams' first decade.

The Islanders put up eight winning seasons in their first 10, putting them ahead of every other expansion team out there. Their closest competitors are the Arizona Diamondbacks of baseball (they've had five winning seasons when they concluded their eighth campaign in 2005), the Miami Dolphins and Cincinnati Bengals of football (six winning seasons), the Milwaukee Bucks of basketball (six), and Atlanta/Calgary Flames of hockey (six).

By the way, the Islanders' three year ascent to a winning regular season was also lightning-fast compared to the majority of expansionites, which averaged six years to get above .500. Among the major sports, the Isles have only been surpassed by the Diamondbacks, Jacksonville Jaguars, and Carolina Panthers, all of which fielded winners in their second season.

Beyond their almost immediate respectability, the Islanders were probably the most successful playoff performers among the expansion franchises. Within their first 10 years, they'd already won two league championships, two conference championships, and four division championships. (They were also on track for an additional championship and a couple more conference championships in their 11th and 12th years).

The Islanders have some tough competition in this respect. No other hockey club has had more than a single conference championship in its first 10 years, and the D'Backs are the only baseball team to have as many as three divisions to go with a single league championship. However, the Milwaukee Bucks did have a single league championship, two conference championships, and five division championships. Even more impressive were the Miami Dolphins' two championships, three conference championships, and four division championships.

If Milwaukee can be set aside because a single more division can't make up for one less championship, Miami is tougher to discount. Still, even against Don Shula's squad, the dynastic Islanders of 1972-1982 probably come out ahead with a more impressive overall record.

New York was probably the best of the best because it was the only one to combine early, consistent excellence with spectacular playoff successes. The Dolphins had fewer winning seasons and, despite their perfect season in 1972, also had a just-slightly lower winning percentage in regular season games (59.9 percent to the Islanders' 60.0 percent). Finally, while the Dolphins did win an additional conference championship, the Isles were the more prolific postseason presence—they won 18 of their 22 playoff rounds (81.8 percent) from 1975 to 1982, while the Dolphins only required a 8–3 record (72.7 percent) in the NFL's far more abbreviated schedule.

The bottom line is—if you absolutely, positively had to count on an expansion team to win a regular season game or playoff round during its first decade, the New York Islanders were the team to take. No franchise has ever grown up faster or stronger.

NAMATH & MESSIER— WHO MADE THE GREATEST "GUARANTEE"?

79 & 80

You'd think history repeated itself if you didn't know any better.

January 9th, 1969: New York Jets leader Joe Namath, faced with a do-or-die playoff game, defies a hallowed sports tradition by out-and-out ensuring a win. "The Jets will win on Sunday, I guarantee it," says Broadway Joe. And the team does win.

Twenty five years pass. And then:

May 25th, 1994: New York Rangers leader Mark Messier, faced with a do-or-die playoff game, defies a hallowed sports tradition by out-and-out ensuring a win. "We know we have to win it. We can win it. And we are going to win it," says the Broadway Blue. And the team does win.

You'd think history repeated itself.
If you didn't know better.

Actually, you could argue that Namath's famous guarantee, while well-remembered, had nothing on Messier's declaration—not in stakes, not in its audacity, and not in its pay off, either.

To see how that's so, it's important to remember the circumstances for the quotes.

When Namath spoke out before the Super Bowl in January 1969, the Jets were in a truly dire situation. The American Football League had already been blown out of the first two Super Bowls by a combined score of 68 to 24. The Chiefs and Raiders never led in either game, and both teams had a superior record to the Super Bowl-bound Jets during the 1968–69 regular season. The Jets came into the championship game against the Colts as an 18-point underdog because they deserved to be a record 'dog— New York had scored 139 more points than they allowed on the season, while Baltimore's differential stood at 258.

All that put Namath in a spot where he didn't have anything to lose by popping off. If the Jets went out and got pounded, as expected, the quarterback would have hardly been blamed for the result. Like those Fred Williamson, Raymond Clayborn, Patrick Ewing, Lou Piniella, and others, the Namath "guarantee" would have been forgotten as so much empty blather. And Namath didn't put a reputation on the line, either—he hadn't won a thing before '69.

Messier, in contrast, had everything to lose in making his declaration before Game Six of the Eastern Conference

Finals. Three years earlier, Messier had forced a trade from Edmonton with the explicit promise of ending the Rangers' 50-plus years without a championship. New York was the favorite in the '94 Finals, having put up a superior regular season record (52–24–8 vs. 47–25–12), winning first place in the Patrick Division, and sweeping the regular season series with the Devils by 6–0.

By going down three games to two in the Jersey series, Messier was on the verge of breaking his promise, and the Rangers were on the verge of losing face to a hungry, upstart rival. In guaranteeing a win, Mess knew his words would be remembered. He really was putting hard-won reputations on the line.

The other thing is that the exact circumstances of the two quotes were a tad different, too.

When Joe Namath delivered his little promise, he was at a Touchdown Club dinner and, if he had a couple of drinks in him, it wouldn't have been the first time. By his own admission, Namath didn't walk into the room meaning to say anything special—he was only responding to Lou Michaels of the Colts, who'd been taunting him over the upcoming game. What was later depicted as some kind of stirring, bold declaration was, in reality, the result of some after-hours, tipsy trash-talk. "It was more anger and frustration than anything," Namath conceded after the fact.

Mark Messier was a world a way from a meet-'n-greet evening party when he delivered his guarantee. He spoke to the media before setting down to work at an afternoon practice. The captain was as sober as they come, and he delivered spontaneous outbursts about as often as he wore toupees. He made his headlines because he meant every word.

Finally, let's remember the follow-up to the two "guarantees."

Namath did help win Super Bowl III a few days after his stunt, but he may have been the least valuable Most Valuable Player in the 40-year history of the NFL championship (#61). His Jets benefited by their opponents' Keystone-Kops mistakes far more than any effort on their own part.

Messier? Messier was as good as his word.

The captain, playing on the enemy's home ice, rang up an unforgettable hat trick against Hall of Fame goalie Martin Brodeur in Game Six. With the series tied at 3–3, the Blueshirts proceeded to win only the second Game Seven playoff game in their 68-year history, then took the Stanley Cup in the subsequent Finals. The game-winner was scored by . . . you guessed it.

Joe Namath and Mark Messier did deliver the two most famous guarantees in New York sports, but that doesn't mean that they were anything alike. Only one of the two had a reputation to protect, the guts to put it on the line, and the talent to deliver. Mess didn't repeat history—he made it.

ARE THE NEW JERSEY DEVILS THE CLASSIEST TEAM IN NEW YORK?

81 When you think of New York class and quality, certain names come to mind. The Four Seasons and Le Cirque in are synonymous with fine dining. Tiffany's and Saks Fifth Avenue are the best of the best in shopping. The Ritz Carlton and Waldorf Astoria are among the greatest hotels in the world. There are architectural marvels of the Chrysler and Flatiron Buildings and the treasures of the Metropolitan Museum of Art and Guggenheim and the posh addresses of Park Avenue and Central Park West.

New York class is associated with many fine names, but it has rarely been connected to a team playing in a tiny Jersey suburb. That's a shame, though. Expectations and reputations aside, the classiest sports organization in greater New York may be New Jersey's own Devils.

It's been a long, long time since Wayne Gretzky called the Devils a "Mickey Mouse" franchise. Nowadays they're more like a Magic Kingdom:

THEY'RE WINNERS

They've boasted 16 straight winning seasons from 1989–90, to 2004-05 with 16 straight playoff appearances, five division championships, four division championships, and three league championships. None of New York's new millennium teams have won so much, so consistently, for so long.

The Yankees have more titles to show for their 1990's/2000's run, true, but the Devils have been winning even longer—despite a microbudget and four playoff rounds per year. It's worth noting that the Yankees went 8–5 in playoff rounds from 2000 to 2005. The Devils went 12–3.

THEY'RE TEAM-FIRST

Mike Milbury tried trading the Islanders to success; Glen Sather tried buying the Rangers another Stanley Cup. Jersey's got another concept.

In the 1990's the Devils pioneered a slow-down, neutral-zone trapping system that emphasized disciplined teamwork over solo heroics, then made it work because proven stars like Scott Stevens and Ken Daneyko sacrificed their numbers for the sake of the greater good. At the Meadowlands, big egos are checked at the door.

THEY'RE DIVERSE

Long before Omar Minaya signed the first of "Los Mets," New Jersey was the most international franchise going.

Back in 1989, just as the Iron Curtain started falling, the Devils started signing Soviet stars like Viacheslav Festisov and Sergei Starikov, thus helping to introduce a new wave of flashy Eastern European talents to hockey fans everywhere. The road away from the Cold War passed through the west-bound lanes of the George Washington Bridge.

THEY'RE LOYAL

Contrary to their infernal name, the Devils are very virtuous, especially with those who believe in the organization.

They stuck with mainstays like Stevens, Bobby Holik, Claude Lemieux, Scott Niedermayer, and Martin Brodeur from the early 1990's lean years and into multiple Cup celebrations, and still retain the majority of their homegrown stars. When trusty coach Pat Burns came down with cancer during the 2002–03 season, GM Lou Lamoriello lent his private and public support, telling him he had a job whenever he was healthy enough to return. When Daneyko went into alcohol rehab in 1997, they had his back, too.

THEY'RE SQUARES

The Devils didn't come on the scene until 1982, but their values are stuck in a 1950's time-warp. They don't believe in contract holdouts, out-of-control budgets, outrageous quotes, or facial hair. They do believe in first-class talent development, smart spending, clichés, and shaving. Isiah Thomas and the Knicks should take notes.

THEY'RE HUMBLE

It isn't all that hard to be humble when you play in front of small crowds, but the Devils have never let on-ice successes go to their heads. For instance, they didn't retire their first two jerseys—Stevens' #4 and Daneyko's #3—until the 2005–06 season. Stevens' ceremony came during Super Bowl weekend.

The Devils don't easily separate individuals from the whole, and their no-nonsense style flows from president/resident mastermind Lamoriello. The embodiment of low-key intensity, the multimillionaire can be found either putting in long hours at the front office or showing up at practice in the same old dress slacks.

THEY'RE TRUE TO THEMSELVES

The "New York" Giants and "New York" Jets play over by Exit 16W, too, but their very names scream denial. The Devils? They're the Garden State's own, no bones about it. To date, they're the first and only New Jersey champions in big-time sports.

A few years ago, a state politician tried to pressure them to adopt a "Swamp Dragons" nickname. They laughed it off. Now that's integrity.

The Devils may not automatically call to mind some of the finer name brands of greater New York. They work on the less fashionable side of the river. They're the third-most popular hockey club in the area. They don't play the most popular sport in America.

Give them this, though—they do things the right way. They do have class.

IS HOCKEY A MAJOR SPORT?

82 The sports world's sort of like a high school cafeteria.

Off to the side, you have multiple, close-knit cliques. There's the shady boxing crowd. The upscale tennis set. Throughout the dining hall you've got any number of others hanging out due to shared interests in golf or soccer, et cetera, all doing their own thing.

At the center of attention is the cool kids' table, where the Major Leagues, the National Football League, and National Basketball League can always be found. Their popularity, power, and money are unmatched, inspiring the admiration or envy of all around them.

The question is—where does the National Hockey League fit in the picture?

On the one hand, the league is a strong attendance draw, one that can expect to take in more than 20 million paying customers per season. That compares favorably to the NFL's 17 million-plus in combined regular season gate, and lags just behind the NBA's 21 million or so per year. In 2005–06, one season after a year-long labor lockout, hockey was still going strong, with franchises welcoming an average of 16,550 fans per game.

The NHL's drawing power is undeniable, and not just in Canada—during the most recent season, five of the 10 most popular teams in the league hailed from the United States. Of the top 20 teams, 14 came from the Land of the Free.

You'd think that would gain the NHL a secure place at the cool kids' table, no problem, and, in a way, it does. Its highlights gain air time on *Sports Center*, its recaps make it into newspapers' sports sections, and the locals' scores are always mentioned in talk radio updates. Along with baseball, football, and basketball, the game's included in habitual references to the "Big Four" team sports.

The problem in hockey's status is the way that it fails to register in just about anything but attendance and rote customs. Take the NHL's television ratings. You may need a microscope.

Hockey's numbers, in New York and throughout the US, have varied from miniscule to worse. During the last three years of its just-concluded contract with the NHL, for instance, ESPN drew regular season ratings of less than 0.5 (working out to about 500,000 fans per game). When ESPN dropped the sport from its schedule in 2004–05, the League was forced to skate over to the Outdoor Life

Network to stay on air. The move automatically chopped the NHL's potential audience from 90 million down to 63 million, but that was just as well, since it's now drawing 0.2 ratings (about 165,000 viewers) across the nation. In New York, the biggest playoff series in years, the Rangers-Devils tilt of spring 2006, drew a measly 1.4. As a point of comparison, early regular season games for the Yankees and Mets combined for a 10.6 number.

The Majors Leagues, NFL, and NBA don't have to share schedule slots with fourth-tier sports like rodeo riding, cycling, and skeet-shooting, but the NHL's tiny audiences give it no other choice. There have been some weekend afternoons when more people were watching the Arena Football League.

The ratings stats, as dismal as they are, only scratch the surface of hockey's puzzling absence in the sports scene. We're eagerly anticipating the arrival of a mass-market hockey book or movie, because it will be the very first mass-market hockey book or movie. Likewise for a break-out marketing figure younger than 45-year-old Wayne Gretzky. And the average American sports fan still doesn't grasp the basics of the game—good luck finding one who knows high sticks from twizzle sticks and blue lines from highway lines.

Hockey still hasn't reached beyond its hardcore fans, and no one knows why, exactly. Maybe the popular kids have already saturated the sports market. Well-publicized labor lockouts may have snuffed out the fans' good will. There may not be enough Americans or minority players to accompany its foreign-born stars (how do you pronounce Jagomir, anyway?). Maybe there aren't enough frozen lakes anywhere south of Minneapolis. No one knows.

For whatever reasons, Canada's favorite game, unlike maple syrup and quality bacon, has never translated to mass American sensibilities. Until it does, hockey will continue to be the most minor "major" sport around.

CENTER COURTS

CONNORS & MCENROE— WHO WAS THE WORSE BRAT?

83 & 84

Throughout their careers, Jimmy Connors and John McEnroe could do it all.

They provided some of the greatest performances tennis could offer.

Connors was one of the most aggressive ground strokers of all time, an expert backhand player who climbed to No.1 ranking by 1974, only his third year on the pro players' tour. He held top-three status for 12 straight years on his way to winning a record 105 singles titles, including eight Grand Slams. By all accounts, Jimmy Connors was a great on-court athlete for a great long while.

Like Connors, John McEnroe's game helped define tennis in the 1980's. Athleticism and deft precision keyed a spectacular five-year run from 1979 to 1984, one that garnered an astounding 77 titles, including seven Grand Slams. Like his longtime rival, young McEnroe played some of the best matches ever seen.

Versatile as they were, though, Connors and McEnroe had a knack for representing more than great tennis. They were all about the worst in the sport, too.

324

Their awful reputations were nothing professional, all personal. They were based in the ways Jimbo and Mac always played with an utter lack of respect or good manners, in their consistent, unavoidable vulgarity and temper fits. The two may very well have been the most stuck-up, obnoxious brats to make it to the very top of any major sport, a pair less suited for whites and rackets than diapers and rattles.

In careers full of controversy, the most enduring debate in Connors vs. McEnroe is on the identity of the worse role model, so let's settle it, once and for all. The following breaks down Jimbo and Mac's misbehavior into 12 key categories, using a scale where 0 represents no good manners whatsoever and -10 represents the worst possible psychodrama:

SPORTSMANSHIP

Jimbo—Used an array of tricks and tics to distract opponents (constantly bouncing balls before a serve, blowing on his hands, tugging at his shirtsleeves, rocking back and forth); would sometimes play to the crowd in order to break his opponent's concentration; often mocked his opponent's form while his head was turned; a friendless loner among tour players; wouldn't be caught dead acknowledging others' hard work. Grade: -10

Mac—Usually too introverted to notice opponents one way or the other; made an exception during a 1986 match against Brad Gilbert, when he shouted "You don't deserve to be on the same court as me! You are the worst! The f---in' worst!" Grade: -5

LOVE OF THE GAME

Jimbo—Played with an exuberant joy, at least when he happened to be winning; sometimes twisted his face into a smirk/sneer/smile. Grade: -2

Mac—Usually played with the kind of facial expression you'd wear if your teeth were being cleaned during an IRS audit; freely conceded that he didn't particularly enjoy playing tennis. Grade: -8

AUTHORITY ISSUES

Jimbo—Employed a patented repertoire of glares, scowls, frowns, and snark on officials; once gave a linesman the finger; once called an offending umpire "an abortion." Grade: -7

Mac—Memorably referred to various judges as "incompetent old fools," a "disgrace to mankind," and "the pits of the world"; at Wimbledon in 1985, claimed "I get screwed by umpires in this place"; too many official fines and reprimands to mention; one veteran linesman called McEnroe the most out-of-control athlete he'd come across in his 20-year career. Grade: -10

FAN RELATIONS

Jimbo—Would exchange banter with the crowd when things were going his way; would whine and cry about routine crowd noise when things weren't; sometimes cursed out offending fans; once told an older lady, "Shut up, broad." Grade: -8

Mac—Frequently ordered the crowd to shut up; once barked "I'm so disgusting you shouldn't watch. Everybody leave"; once spat in front of a woman who'd clapped after his double fault. Grade: -5

INTERNATIONAL RELATIONS

Jimbo—Mostly passed up Davis Cup in favor of pay-for-play tournaments, well after he'd already earned millions; skipped the French Open for most of his career; rarely bothered to show up for the Australian Open, either. Grade: -8

Mac—Helped win five Davis Cups in international competition, but somehow managed to convey the worst caricature of an ugly American along the way; once told a French crowd to "Shut your fat frog mouths"; referred to an Australian judge as "You fat turd"; once knocked over a soda can with his racket, thereby spilling sugar water all over the King of Sweden. Grade: -8

HUMILITY

Jimbo—Employed a motormouth promoter taken to quotes like, "When the history of tennis is written, this will be known as the Jimmy Connors era"; once showed up to a tournament saying that "There are going to be 127 losers and me"; his comment on the death of Elvis Presley: "What a shame, there are only a few of us kings left." Grade: -9

Mac—Plagued by insecurity in his early career, but eventually got over it; once wrote "I'm the greatest tennis player who ever lived"; his autobiography's hardcover edition had a picture of McEnroe mimicking a James Dean portrait. Grade: -8

LITIGIOUSNESS

Jimbo—Refused to join the newly-formed players' union, then sued Arthur Ashe for $10 million; filed another multi-million dollar lawsuit when Ashe called Connors' Davis Cup boycott "unpatriotic." Grade: -9

Mac—The son of a high-powered lawyer, but never sued anyone famous. Grade: 0

RESPECT FOR TRADITION

Jimbo—On one memorable occasion, skipped the ceremony honoring every living Wimbledon champion. While dozens of retired greats traveled thousands of miles to show up at All-England, Connors spent his time practicing on an adjoining backcourt. Grade: -10

Mac—Helped keep the faltering Davis Cup tradition going in the 1980's. Grade: 0

INAPPROPRIATE PUBLIC DISPLAYS OF AFFECTION

Jimbo—Displayed a serious exhibitionism problem throughout his career (rubbing his crotch with the ball, swinging his racket around as a quasi-phallic symbol, miming masturbation); grunted louder than necessary on big points; known to celebrate a key point with a primal scream and pelvic thrusts. Grade: -8

Mac—None. See "Love of the Game." Grade: 0

THE LADIES

Jimbo—A high-profile romance with fellow teen prodigy Chris Evert resulted in a very brief engagement and very long estrangement; Evert once saw then-fiancé Connors sitting next to an actress at Wimbledon, then lost her composure and the match; his shellacking of Evert's then-husband in the '82 U.S. Open led to strain in her marriage; "dated" Miss World; married a Playboy centerfold. Grade: -8

Mac—Wrote at length about love matches with model Stella Hall, assorted groupies, and "a famous actress"; came out against mixed tournament play, saying, "I'm not sure men can really know the women's game. I mean, how would they know how women are feeling at a certain time of the month?"; married the formerly famous Tatum

'Tantrum" O'Neal, because she "reminds me of myself."
Grade: -8

DIVA BEHAVIOR

Jimbo—Once canceled a hotel reservation when he couldn't
score 10 suites and 30 free tournament tickets; rude to bus-
boys. Grade: -8

Mac—Hung out back stage at Rolling Stones, Van Halen,
and Eagles concerts; has been known to name-drop his
friend "Jack" and mention Mr. Nicholson's advice. ("Johnny
Mac, don't ever change.") Grade: -6

SHOW BIZ

Jimbo—Made noises about quitting it all for Hollywood,
but didn't follow through; once sang on *The Howard Cosell
Show* in 1975, a tape that has since been burned and scat-
tered to the winds. Grade: -4

Mac—An aspiring rock musician who took guitar les-
sons from Eric Clapton, he once opened for the Stones; has
appeared on shows from *Saturday Night Live* to *Howard
Stern*; wrote a terrible book called *You Cannot Be Serious*,
which became an inexplicable success; hosted terrible
shows called *The Chair* and *McEnroe*, which became expli-
cable failures. Grade: -7

The final tally is Jimbo -91, Mac -65. Game, set, match,
Connors.

CHRIS & MARTINA— WHO WAS THE BETTER PLAYER?

85 Back and forth, back and forth.

Chris Evert and Martina Navratilova played 80 matches over the years, all of them defined by tennis' relentless demand that one shot be answered by another. Their rivalry was like that, too, with one argument for one player quickly finding a counterargument on the other side of the net. To weigh Chris vs. Martina, it may be best to break their qualities down into categories:

FIRST POINT: CONSISTENCY

Chris made it to a Grand Slam Finals in 15 of the 16 years from 1973 to 1988, and won at least one Slam per year for 13 straight years (1974 to 1986). Martina was darn close, making the Finals in 13 of 14 years (1978–91) and winning in 10 of 13 years, but she falls short here.

Evert, 15–0

SECOND POINT: PEAK PERFORMANCE

Chris' five best years were from 1974 to 1978, and they were some of the best years anyone's ever had—she put up a 325–21 overall record (.939 winning percentage) in tournament matches en route to 140 straight weeks with a No.1 ranking. She was at her very best in Grand Slam tournaments, making 13 Finals and winning eight of them (.615).

If Chris had some of the best years anyone's ever had, Martina had *the* best years anyone's ever had. At her five-year peak from 1982 to 1986, no one could touch her—she compiled a 427–14 mark (.968) and spent 156 straight weeks at No.1. Not only did she win more in her prime, she reached more Grand Slam finals (16) and won more of them (12-4, .750).

Even, 15–15

THIRD POINT: CLUTCH PERFORMANCE

Another skin-of-their-teeth margin here.

Chris was as poised a big game player as anyone, reaching a total of 34 Grand Slam Finals during her career, winning 18 of them (.529) and 32 percent of all Slam matches.

Martina didn't quite measure up to that standard. She reached 32 Grand Slam Finals, winning 18 (.562) and taking 27 percent of matches in Slams play. She had a higher winning percentage in the Finals, but that can't quite make up for her two fewer Finals appearances and lower overall winning percentage.

Evert, 30–15

FOURTH POINT: LONG-RUN EXCELLENCE

If there was a single most impressive facet in Chris' overall game, it was in her longevity in singles play. Before her

1989 retirement, she went 1,309-146 (good for a record-breaking winning percentage of .900) and compiled 154 overall titles, including those 18 Grand Slams. She held on to No.1 ranking for a total of 262 weeks.

Chris Evert's gaudy numbers blow away nearly everyone. Everyone except Martina Navratilova.

Martina's career saw more match wins (1,438, against 212 losses), more titles (167, the most ever), an equal number of Grand Slams, and far more weeks at the top (331 weeks total). Navratilova had a lower career winning percentage (.870), but her advantage in the other categories puts her over the top in this category.

Even, 30–30

FIFTH POINT: HEAD-TO-HEAD

Finally, the tie-breaker has to come through the Chris vs. Martina clashes over the years. With everything else being nearly equal, the superior player should have won more head-to-head matches.

You have to give it to Martina. Navratilova won 43 of her 80 matches with Evert, 14 of 22 Grand Slam Finals, and gained advantages on carpet (22 wins vs. Evert's 14), hard court (8 vs. 7), and grass (10 vs. 5) surfaces. Chris did dominate on clay (she won 11 of 14), but that wasn't enough to make up for Martina's advantages.

Final: Navratilova, 40–30.

WHAT WAS THE GREATEST U.S. OPEN OF ALL TIME?

 Certain people just don't like sports, and those poor souls' lack of interest may be due to a lack of appreciation for the deeper meaning involved.

On the surface level, the contests are about some guy hitting a ball with a stick, tossing a ball down a field, sliding a puck across some ice. They're pretty trivial in the grand scheme of things. At the same time, die-hard fans know that a stadium or arena can be a stage, an absorbing place where personalities are revealed, historical legacies are forged, and human dramas are played out. Pretty compelling stuff, that.

Fans know that great sports can be defined by great stories. Take the U.S. Open. Over the years, the tournament's had enough plotlines for a fair-sized anthology, so picking out the single greatest year is sort of like finding the single best passage from a master storyteller.

The 1976 Open, for instance, presented a thriller in the Jimmy Connors/Bjorn Borg Finals. Evenly matched in skill but wildly different in style, Connors used near-perfect power-hitting to counter Borg's beautifully angled ground strokes and cross-court play. At one point during a 11–9 third-set tie-breaker, Connors somehow survived no less than four set-point cliffhangers. His was the happy ending, though, in a final score of 6–4, 3–6, 7–6, 6–4.

The '84 Open, on the other hand, presented the interconnected storyline of "Super Saturday." It opened with Ivan Lendl prevailing over Pat Cash in the men's semifinal—a pitched, seesaw battle won by Lendl at 3–6, 6–3, 6–4, 6–7, 7–6. Soon after, Martina Navratilova defeated her great rival, Chris Evert, in another three-set battle (4–6, 6–4, 6–4). Yet another star, Stan Smith of the Over-35 bracket, followed up with a win over John Newcombe. Improbably, it was the third straight match to go the distance.

All those back-and-forth duels were mere preludes to the grand finale, though—a men's semifinal pitting Connors against his hated rival, John McEnroe. Connors came to Flushing to avenge an embarrassing 6–1, 6–1, 6–2 loss at Wimbledon, but McEnroe, playing at the top of his game, deployed serve-and-volley artistry to counter Connors' expert backhands. McEnroe took it by 6–4, 4–6, 7–5, 4–6, 6–3, in what would prove to be his last ever Grand Slam victory.

In Lendl's precarious victory and Martina's triumph to Smith's pride and McEnroe's coda, "Super Saturday" amounted to episodes of a single action story, one lasting more than 12 hours in all.

Another year, 1991, gave fans a comeback tale—this one authored by Connors. The former No. 1 in the world had appeared to be fading as a championship-level player, but Connors, nearly 39 years old, once again showed flashes of his old brilliance, defeating Patrick McEnroe in the opening round after being down 4–6, 6–7, 0–3, 0–4 (the final tally was 4–6, 6–7, 6–4, 6–2, 6–4). On his birthday, Connors rallied again, outlasting Aaron Krickstein in a match going nearly five hours. He was finally eliminated by Jim Courier in straight sets, but not before proving how desire and guile could overcome declining physical tools.

An even more improbable comeback run occurred when Andre Agassi shook off a long layoff before the 1994 Open. Against all odds, Agassi knocked off five straight ranked foes (including No. 4-ranked Michael Stich) to become the first unseeded player to win the tournament in the post-1968 professional era. When he took the No. 1 ranking for the first time shortly afterwards, Hollywood couldn't have served up a more improbable tale.

In 1995, Agassi's Cinderella story was transformed into something more bittersweet. Having run off a career-high seven titles (including a career-best 26 winning matches in a row) in the previous year, Agassi met up with his longtime nemesis, Pete Sampras, in the Open. Neither protagonist backed down, but 1995 was Sampras' turn to star—his booming serve and running forehand prevailed in the Final by 6–4, 6–3, 4–6, 7–5. Agassi never did recover his advantage in the rivalry.

The 1996 tournament gave the crowd a more tearful story of mourning and perseverance. Sampras lost his longtime coach and mentor, Tim Gullickson, to cancer a few months prior to Flushing, then came down with a stomach flu just hours before his quarterfinal match with Alex Corretja. The nauseous Sampras somehow found the mental and physical resources to beat the tenacious Corretja in a four-hour contest, however, and later battled his way to a fourth Open title.

To die-hard tennis fanatics, the very best of the best U.S. Open tournaments have featured matches displaying thrills, action, comebacks, bittersweet setbacks, and inspiration. More and more memorable shows come to mind—the moment in African American Arthur Ashe's victory in 1968, the promise in a young Sampras' first Open victory in 1990, the finality in Sampras' 14th Grand Slam in 2002. A lot of great sports, a lot of great stories.

But the single most dramatic of the Opens' many dramas? That may have come in 1980.

The buildup started in the year before, when McEnroe first came on the scene. The 21-year-old American became the youngest Open winner in 31 years, then reeled off 27 title wins in 1979–80. When he met the always-remote, stoic Borg at Wimbledon in 1980, he seemed prepared to break the Swede's four straight titles on grass, but the resulting showdown—featuring five saved match points in a fourth-set tie-breaker—had the defending champ winning out in the end (1-6, 7-5, 6-3, 6-7 (16-18), 8-6).

By the time McEnroe and Borg met for a rematch in the '80 Open, both players had everything on the line. McEnroe, who had already overcome spirited opposition from Lendl and Connors to the finals, was set on redemption. Borg, for his part, was motivated to finally take his first Open title while defending his new No. 1 ranking.

When it was over, the McEnroe/Borg confrontation lived up to its advanced billing, providing an awed crowd with multiple aces, drop-shots, and power backhands. McEnroe, a Douglaston, Queens native, won a five-set shootout in front of the hometown crowd, 7–6, 6–1, 6–7, 5–7, 6–4.

The 1980 U.S. Open, great enough in itself, has been even more memorable for the way it proved to be a one-of-a-kind display. The two antagonists met just twice more before Borg walked off the court and out of tennis in 1982. After Borg's retirement, what looked like the opening of a special rivalry turned out to be a peek at a future that never materialized.

John McEnroe and Bjorn Borg couldn't top the drama of the 1980 U.S. Open, and that somehow seems fitting. No one could have topped it.

RINGS

"THE LONG-COUNT FIGHT" —DID JACK DEMPSEY DESERVE TO WIN?

 There'll never be another controversy like it. Just imagine this setup:

After seven years at the top, the heavyweight champion of the world loses his title to a highly disciplined, power-punching challenger. The ex-champ and the new champ, one an adopted New Yorker and the other a native, are set on a collision course for the most eagerly anticipated and lucrative sporting event of the year.

The rematch is a ferocious bout, one with the fighters exchanging punishing blows for round after round. Finally, in the seventh, the wily veteran surprises the younger man with a devastating left cross to the chin.

The fighter goes down, but his attacker rejects the referee's order to retreat into a neutral corner. By the time the ref pulls him away and starts to count out the dazed man on the canvas, crucial seconds have passed. The felled boxer does get up, but only at the count of nine—the bonus seconds in the neutral corner scuffle allowed him just enough time to avoid a 10-count knockout. In the remainder of the fight, the newly energized champ rallies, wins on points, and retains his title. Only, his victory is forever clouded by the controversial seventh round's count.

The story does sound like boxing-by-way-of-Hollywood, but the truth was stranger than fiction. It actually happened. The dethroned heavyweight champ was Jack Dempsey, who lost a heavyweight belt to Gene Tunney through a 10-round decision in September 1926. The rematch, held in Soldier Field, Chicago, produced both Tunney's victory and the legend of "the long count."

The most memorable notion to come out of the bout was that Dempsey was robbed in the whole mess. It's been said that the final decision shouldn't have happened, because Dempsey effectively knocked out Tunney, fair and square, in the all-important seventh. It was the neutral-corner technicality, not Tunney's ability, that allowed the victory.

It's a notion that makes sense at first glance, but only at first glance.

For starters, it's important to remember that it was Dempsey who screwed up in setting up the "long count"—he could have sidestepped the whole matter by simply obeying the ref's direct, repeated orders. He didn't follow the fight's official rules, and that can hardly be pinned on referee Dave Barry, much less the dazed Tunney. That was on Dempsey alone.

Why didn't Dempsey move the 10 feet or so into a neutral corner? Well, it's possible he just lost his cool in the heat of battle, but then again, Dempsey didn't build a championship reign by flying off the handle very often.

More likely, he failed in an attempt to gain a competitive advantage over Tunney.

The neutral-corner rule was an important safeguard in the way it provided felled boxers with a small cushion of distance from their opponents. Without it, attackers could "hover" over a knockdown, then just pounce back at the first possible moment. Tunney, a technician, insisted on the rule as a pre-condition for the rematch, very likely because he knew about Dempsey's reputation with the tactic (once, in a fight against Luis Firpo, Dempsey hovered his way into seven knockdowns in a single round). In effect, the neutral-corner rule was designed to prevent cheating, and that's how it worked in the Dempsey-Tunney fight.

The pro-Dempsey crowd has a tougher point against the decision, though, when they point out that the referee didn't follow the official fight rules. OK, they'd admit, even if Dempsey was to blame for the original delay, Barry should have joined the official timekeeper's count as soon as Dempsey retreated to the corner. If he did, Tunney probably would have been out according to the normal 10 seconds and no one would have had heard a word about some strange long count in the first place.

You know, the Dempsey partisans have a point. As writers like William Nack have pointed out, the Illinois State Athletic Commission's bylaws did read that way:

When a knockdown occurs the timekeeper shall immediately arise and announce the seconds audibly as they elapse. The referee shall first see that the opponent retires to the farthest corner and then, turning to the timekeeper, shall pick up the count in unison with the timekeeper, announcing the seconds to the boxer on the floor.

It's this lapse—in the way that Barry unfairly allowed those extra few seconds—that gave the controversy its staying power.

Tunney always insisted he could have gotten up before he did, that he just stayed down to the last second to give himself time to regain his balance, but that was a pretty self-serving statement, wasn't it? Jack Dempsey was Jack Dempsey because once he hit someone, that someone stayed hit. It's possible that the dazed Tunney barely escaped through the ref's mistake.

"THE LONG-COUNT FIGHT" —WAS DEMPSEY ROBBED?

Even if you allow that, hypothetically, Dempsey could have won by strict application of the rules, he still wasn't robbed in the "long-count" fight.

The better fighter did end up winning the bout. Tunney won a unanimous decision in the first fight, then dominated the rematch before and after the knockdown controversy.

He was younger, faster, stronger, and deployed some of the best technique ever seen in the squared circle. It was only fitting that he should walk away with the title belt.

There's another reason why Dempsey wasn't robbed by the final outcome. As it turned out, it's hard to imagine someone could have walked away from a loss with more to show for it.

After Dempsey refused to place blame for the Tunney fight's outcome, fans hailed his graciousness and insisted he was still "the people's champ." Sympathetic sportswriters stopped bringing up longtime allegations of dirty fighting and draft dodging. A legend grew. Decades after the fact, the retired old man was still holding court in his famed Manhattan restaurant, greeting strangers with a hearty "hiya" and giving daily recaps of his last pro fight, the one where he could-a or would-a knocked 'im out. Gene Tunney grew up in Greenwich Village but, in time, it was "the Manassas Mauler" who became New York's favorite boxer.

Was Jack Dempsey robbed? Heck, Shirley Povich once wrote that the Tunney debate was "the best and luckiest thing that ever happened to Dempsey." In the long count's long run, he won.

LOUIS/SCHMELING II VS. ALI/FRAZIER I—WHICH WAS THE "FIGHT OF THE CENTURY"?

89 & 90

When the Muhammad Ali vs. Joe Frazier bout was being promoted as "The Fight of the Century" in March 1971, a ring event finally seemed to live up to its advanced billing. That night, Madison Square Garden drew immense energy from contrasting personalities, politics, societies, and celebrities. It was an epic clash. It was a "fight" in the truest sense of the word.

Ali vs. Frazier was great, all right, but it may not have been the very greatest. Another New York fight, the Joe Louis vs. Max Schmeling heavyweight bout of June 1938, may have been just as intense and memorable. Consider the scored cards for the "Fight of the Century" contenders:

THE ANTICIPATION

Ali vs. Frazier I was the first time two undefeated heavyweights decided a championship title. Ali was 29 years old and came in with a 31–0 record (25 knockouts) while Frazier, 26, climbed through the ropes at 26–0 (23 KO's). It was matchless grace and speed against unequalled force. Of Ali and Frazier, one commentator said "this wasn't David vs. Goliath as much as it was Goliath vs. Goliath."

Louis vs. Schmeling II was a rematch of the duo's 1936 bout, in which Schmeling knocked out a previously undefeated Louis in the 12th round. It was the only fight the 24-year-old "Brown Bomber" had lost to that point, going 35–1 before the rematch. Schmeling, 33, was a former world champion, and entered at 52–9 (three disqualifications).

The round goes to . . . Ali vs. Frazier. There were so many questions about how two feared, very different fighters could match up. Schmeling, on the other hand, was eight years older than Louis and had suffered previous losses to Jack Sharkey and Max Baer. He came in at a 10-1 underdog because many suspected that he wouldn't be able to surprise his fearsome opponent once again.

Ali/Frazier I–Louis/Schmeling 0.

THE MOTIVATION

Ali, the reigning champ, was stripped of his title in 1967 after refusing military induction during the Vietnam War. In 1971 he was out to prove that prosecution and persecution had stripped him of something he still deserved. Frazier, who claimed the vacant title in the three years it took to resolve the Ali case, was out to prove his legitimacy as more than a paper champion—like the former champ, he'd already won an Olympic gold medal and taken on all available contenders.

In the other fight, Louis sought revenge, plain and simple. Even after he took the heavyweight belt from James J. Braddock in '37, he said he wouldn't feel it was real until he finally defeated the only man who'd ever defeated him. For his opposite number, Schmeling, the rematch was a means to prove that the previous Yankee Stadium result was no fluke.

The round goes to . . .draw. By all accounts, the fighters involved were immensely proud athletes, and they couldn't have had more incentive to give their very best.

1–0–1

THE POLITICS

The Ali vs. Frazier bout, inevitably, got tangled up in the highly charged politics of the time. The challenger was seen as a draft dodger by some, and a militant member of the Black Muslims by all (he was among the first prominent athletes to convert religions or change his name). Frazier looked like a conservative by comparison, a stance that was infinitely magnified by Ali's insults regarding an "Uncle Tom" and "white man's champion."

The issue of race played an immense, overshadowing role in Louis vs. Schmeling as well. Louis was only the second black heavyweight champ in history (and the first in 22 years), while Schmeling hailed from an avowedly racist Nazi Germany. In an era where racial discrimination defined many of the injustices of American life and helped spark World War II, a confrontation between a black

American and a white German had an all-too-important, all-too-relevant meaning.

The round goes to . . . Louis vs. Schmeling. No one can minimize the passion involved in the antiwar movement and the cultural frictions of the early 1970's, but the Louis vs. Schmeling bout had a backdrop of black and white, America and Germany, freedom and tyranny, war and peace, life and death. *Nothing* will ever top it.

1–1–1

THE BUILDUP

Historian/scribe William Nack once called Muhammad Ali "the most gifted carnival barker in the history of sports," and he was at his rhetorical best in the weeks and months leading up to Madison Square Garden. His incredibly dismissive, cruel comments were joined by a customary bravado when, for instance, "the greatest of all time" called the upcoming fight "the biggest sporting event in the history of the whole planet earth." The cameras and microphones ate it all up.

With pugilism in its peak popularity in the 1930's, however, Louis vs. Schmeling didn't need any special theatrics. Joe Louis received a pre-fight telegram from President Roosevelt and starred in multiple movie newsreels as a hero to all races. Max Schmeling, who was no Nazi, nonetheless received a good luck telegram from Adolf Hitler and billing as a fascist poster boy. By the time they met, the two fighters were among the most famous men in the world.

The round goes to . . . Louis vs. Schmeling. Again, nothing against Ali's showmanship, but the '38 fight just couldn't be beaten. For the first and only time, a heavyweight fight was treated as a world-historical event.

1–2–1

THE ELECTRICITY

Ali vs. Frazier garnered record multimillion dollar purses and an instantaneous sell out at the Garden. Ticket scalpers took four figures for bad seats. An estimated 300 million watched from closed circuit TV. As the fighters made their way to the ring, the live crowd let out a roar that veteran commentator Bert Sugar had never heard before.

The Louis vs. Schmeling test of wills attracted the same kind of bedlam. More than 70,000 witnesses walked into Yankee Stadium as a then-record audience of 100 million listened through radio. One author said it attracted more media attention than any previous event in human history, including the Versailles peace conference of 1919.

The round goes to . . . Ali vs. Frazier. Call it a copout, but the mass media had expanded so much in the years between 1938 and 1971 that the "Fight of the Century" almost had to have a bigger, more charged-up audience. We may never see another fight with so many New York celebrities (Leonard Bernstein, Count Basie, Miles Davis,

Woody Allen, Dustin Hoffman) in one place. Burt Lancaster helped out in the broadcast. The ringside photographer was a fight fan named Frank Sinatra.

2–2–1

THE FIGHT

Ali/Frazier I was a battle of upper cuts, crosses, jabs, and body blows, one going the distance to a bloody 15 rounds. Well before Smokin' Joe won a unanimous decision, fans were calling it one of the most painful, punishing bouts of all time.

Louis vs. Schmeling, for all its buildup, didn't have nearly the same kind of payoff. The challenger barely landed a couple of punches before Louis returned murderous combinations, taking out Schmeling via a first round technical knockout. At 124 seconds, Louis/Schmeling II was one of the quickest pro bouts of all time. Ringside writer Bob Considine called it "short, sharp, merciless, complete."

The round goes to . . . Ali vs. Frazier. While the Louis fight will go down in history as an example of one man's fury, the '71 fight was a duel of sheer talent and will. The fact that Muhammad Ali survived his first pro defeat was a victory in itself.

3–2–1

And there you have it. Muhammad Ali and Joe Frazier did, indeed, fight the "Fight of the Century." They win on points.

WAS MIKE TYSON EVER A GREAT HEAVYWEIGHT?

91 When substantial numbers of people routinely refer to you as "The Baddest Man on the Planet" for a good long while, OK, there's a special something going on.

Sure, for a few years there, Mike Tyson seemed to be the baddest man on earth or any other planet. When the Brownsville-born teenager stormed into professional boxing in 1985, he routed opponents in a series of fights that amounted to a series of first-round demolitions. By the time he disposed of reigning title holder Trevor Berbick in 1987, the 20-year-old established himself as the sport's youngest heavyweight champion and was well on the way to a perfect 37–0 record (34 by knockout).

Basically, though, that was it for Tyson's claim to invincibility. Iron Mike was knocked out by a journeyman in 1990 and called out by federal prosecutors in 1992. When he was released from prison in 1995, Tyson fought a couple of punching bags, then lost two Evander Holyfield bouts, the first through a technical knockout and the second through a gruesome ear-biting disqualification. After that, Tyson's career amounted to some punch-up wins over overmatched underachievers and defeats to legitimate challengers, interspersed with various arrests and disgusting personal episodes. The disgraced champ was 43–1 before meeting Holyfield, 7–5 in the years afterwards.

Tyson trashed his own career and life after 1990, but even so, many still look back in wonder at that early career, when spectators asked when, not if, he would stage his next knockout. Proponents still hold on to the image of a time Tyson could claim to be a great heavyweight.

Well, image was one thing, reality was another. Iron Mike's world-beater reputation was always phony—it just took a little while for it to be exposed.

The fact is, by the mid-1980's, the sport of boxing had already deteriorate, to the point where experts like Bert Sugar lamented the disappearance of quality heavyweight fighters. No one believed otherwise, or would claim that the forgettable likes of Tony Tubbs, Pinklon Thomas, Marvis Frazier, Jose Ribalta, Frank Bruno, and Tyrell Biggs did anything much before or after their Tyson fights. KO's over that sad bunch weren't statements on the winner's superiority as much as they were evidence of the losers' inferiority.

Some might say that Michael Spinks, who Tyson knocked out in 1988, was a notable exception to the lineup of canvasbacks. Not really. Spinks was an accomplished champion in his time, but when he met Tyson he was 32 years old and had endured nearly 130 amateur and pro fights. The former champ was fighting out of his natural weight class (light heavyweight) and stepping into his professional finale. Mike Lupica, for one, declared the veteran simply "didn't want to fight that night." Only Michael Spinks knows if that 91-second knockdown was about one last easy paycheck rather than Mike Tyson's inherent ability in the ring.

Even if you want to credit Spinks as a single semi-exception, Mike Tyson was never truly tested during his late-1980's peak. He was muscular enough to deliver punches alright (*Ring Magazine* ranked him #16 in all-time power), but his hammering masked weaknesses in all other areas of his craft. Tyson, who lost mentor Cus D'Amato when he was just 19 years old, never developed fully effective combinations, for instance, or balanced defense, footwork, or the technique needed to overcome his relatively short stature and reach. The 1980s-era demolitions were brief enough that Tyson never really learned to take a punch, either, or develop the stamina needed to last into late rounds. Funny, for a braggart who once derided his opponents' "primitive skills," he wasn't too sophisticated about his craft, either.

Comparing Tyson's bullying, puncher's game to that of undisputed champions like Gene Tunney, Joe Louis, and Rocky Marciano . . . any historian will tell you there was no comparison. Tyson didn't belong in the same conversation. Until he met Holyfield, he was a Sonny Liston brawler in a world without a Muhammad Ali boxer.

If no one could claim that the young Mike Tyson was a test-ed champion, even in the 1980's, why did he develop such respectability among commentators? In a word, money.

Don King, the casinos, the pay-per-view people, and cable companies made out with tens of millions for Tyson's one-sided spectacles, of course, and the media had their own reasons for going along with them. Most commenta-tors had come of age with tales of legitimate wars like "The Fight of the Century," "The Thrilla in Manila," and "The Rumble in the Jungle," and they desperately yearned to cover a real fight in their own time. It wasn't much of a leap to pump up circulation numbers through Tyson hype, especially since he was the only fighter capable of provid-ing a good show. It wasn't too hard for writers to buy into the standard storyline, either, the one that said Tyson's demons somehow fired his fighting greatness. The only thing missing from Iron Mike's press clippings were close looks at the champ's piñata opponents.

It was all fun while it lasted, but it just took a few years for it all to fade into oblivian. Tyson's lack of heart and technique was first exposed in the 1990 loss to Buster Douglas, but became undeniable when he finally tangled with a fundamentally sound and conditioned boxer in Holyfield. Tyson suffered convincing losses in both bouts—his only "victory," if you want to call it that, was the way he managed to distract attention away from his lousy performance an onto his ear-biting and various other crimes and misdemeanors. It wasn't until later, as Tyson's skills eroded even further, that fans finally realized he had too many serious mental and emotional disorders to put up a great fight. A few still don't realize that, in all likelihood, he never had what it took to put up a great fight.

At this point, the Tyson Show, complete with various felonies, lawsuits, bankruptcies, face tattoos, etc., is such a complete train wreck that it seems churlish to tarnish the man's early career. So many prefer to see him as a tragic figure, a talented prize fighter who fell from glory. It rings hollow—Mike Tyson never had any real glory to lose.

THE SWEET SCIENCE— WHY IS BOXING SO SCREWED UP?

92 There was a time.

There was a time when boxing stood out as one of the most popular of American sports, an attraction that captivated fans among the rich and poor, all ethnic groups, and both genders. Title fights regularly attract banner headlines, network television audiences, live sell outs, and multimillion dollar purses. Jack Dempsey was treated as a celebrity equal to Babe Ruth in the 1920's, and later champs became household names.

Working-class kids from around the country climbed through the ropes in pursuit of that vast fan base, big money, and glamour. Terry Malloy couldah been a contendah instead of working on the waterfront.

There was a time. But it was a long time ago.

In the new millennium, the sport of boxing staggers along on the fringes. It can't draw the mass audiences needed to move beyond status as cable television filler and secondary Vegas events. Big title fights are lucky to attract a paltry few thousand fans in Cleveland or Boise. Current belt holders like Wladimir Klitschko, Hasim Rahman, Segei Liakhovich, and Nikolay Valuev may not be household names in their own households. Obscure foreigners, ex-cons, and aging fat men fill the ranks. Athletes don't grow up dreaming of big-time prize fights anymore.

The transition from yesterday's power to today's punchline was a long time coming, but the roots of the sport's decline were there all along, in the sport's central administration. The problem is, it never existed.

Unlike baseball, football, and every other major sport in the land, boxing never established a singular authority capable of setting sensible competition rules and schedules. Instead, nominal power was held by a dispersed, sleepy collection of state government regulators. Meanwhile, the true power was held by various fight promoters, most of them drawn among hustlers and lowlifes who were already well acquainted with all kinds of big city violence (sporting and otherwise). A convicted killer named Don King was only the most notorious of a whole bunch of notorious characters in that world.

With that makeshift, ad hoc system in place, boxing was always set up to fail. By the 1960's, various connivers had already set themselves up into competing federations, each of them maximizing their "championship" sanctioning fees by creating an ever-expanding list of weight divisions. Meanwhile, pugilists were left unprotected from promoters, who busied themselves in either:

A) defrauding their fighters through lopsided contracts, if not outright theft, and,
B) defrauding their customers in mismatches featuring questionable judging, if not outright fixes.

And there you have the mess that's still with us today. Four bureaucracies with an unintelligible jumble for "championship" titles and inside politics for mandatory defenses. Brutalized fighters left "punch-drunk" (read: "brain damaged") from their opponents and penniless from their thieving reps. Fans ripped off in one overpriced bout after another after another. A wave of potential boxers turned way, way off by all the above.

THE SWEET SCIENCE— CAN IT MAKE A COMEBACK?

For boxing to move away from a sad present and into a hopeful future, it simply has to throw the works into reverse.

The powers that be must consolidate the alphabet soup federations into a central commissioner's office. The first order of business would be cutting down on unnecessary weight divisions, providing rational rules of procedure, and arranging for orderly challenges. Fighters' health and finances must be shielded and fans' confidence must be won by quality competitions and competent judges. If and when that happens, the sport's successes will, slowly but surely, start drawing quality talents back into the gyms and weigh-ins. Those who would have become tight ends and linebackers will become the cruiserweights and heavyweights.

Unfortunately, if boxing's solutions are relatively simple, its working realities are anything but simple. No tin-pot dictator will voluntarily give up his piece of the action, and Congress hasn't shown the will necessary to force the issue. With no good guys in sight to drain the swamp, most fans may have to make do with pseudo-events like ultimate fighting, pro wrestling, and celebrity boxing.

A comeback seems very, very improbable. But not impossible.

It's important to remember that there's a reason why the sweet science has somehow survived so much mismanagement for so long—the sport has an incredible, primal power all its own. It brings two men into pitiless one-on-one confrontations, all alone in the squared circles, stripped of virtually everything except their visceral urges to attack and defend. It involves instincts anyone can understand, which is why grown adults seldom forget the overwhelming physicality involved in long-ago schoolyard fights. Is anyone so civilized that he'd turn away from the sight of a pummeling on a bar's sidewalk? Well, if a drunken punch-up brings people running from all around, think about what two highly trained, highly motivated professionals can bring when they spill a little blood.

And you can't dismiss boxing's potential comeback because you can't ignore the sport's vast, resilient place in American culture.

The sweet science can still draw on a literature and mythology matched only by baseball for its depth—past chroniclers include Ring Lardner, Ernest Hemingway, Normal Mailer, Pete Hamill, and A.J. Liebling, among others. Old Muhammad Ali, ravaged by Parkinson's disease, was *Sports Illustrated's* "Sportsman of the Century" and remains one of the most recognized, admired men alive. Fighters like Oscar de la Hoya still draw attention among

Latino populations and foreign-based audiences. *Requiem for a Heavyweight, Rocky, Raging Bull,* and others are recognized movie classics, and big-budget Hollywood fare like *Fight Club, The Hurricane, Million Dollar Baby,* and *Cinderella Man* still draw audiences.

The fight game has been so incredibly screwed up for so long that it's too easy to forget its past greatness and future potential. A renaissance may be unlikely, but boxing can't be counted out. There was a time. It may come again.

TRACKS

THE TRIPLE CROWN— WHY IS IT SO TOUGH TO WIN?

94 In the sport of kings, the Triple Crown is the most regal of sports titles. Exactly 10 thoroughbreds have won the Kentucky Derby, Preakness Stakes, and Belmont Stakes in succession since 1919, making winners from Sir Barton to Affirmed the rarest, most elite performers in all of sports—animal or human.

The elite, rare nature of the Triple Crown is hardly an accident. There are very good reasons why it hasn't had a winner since 1978.

The Triple Crown's unmatched tradition, obviously, acts as a magnet for the very fastest three-year-olds from around the world and, beyond that, contestants must complete three contests in a mere five week span—a challenge compounded by the fact that rested, fresh horses invariably join the field for the second and third races. In going from the Derby to the Preakness to the Belmont, a prospective winner also has to maintain peak form in unfamiliar distances ranging from 1 1/4th miles to 1 3/16th miles to 1 1/2 miles. The last leg is the most grueling of them all—Belmont has the longest track in North America.

By the time Belmont ("the Test of a Champion") comes up in early June, fans are looking for a near-perfect combination of speed, versatility, and stamina. The tiniest mistake or piece of bad luck, whether it comes in a bad post position, early gridlock, a bump or a jostle, a tiny stumble, unfavorable track conditions—almost anything—is enough to cost a contestant the split-second that can make all the difference between winning and losing.

THE TRIPLE CROWN— WILL WE SEE ANOTHER WINNER?

95 Horse racing fans know that the Triple Crown is the most elusive achievement in sports, but still argue about its future. With a continuing, 26-year title draught in Crown winners, has an always-difficult achievement become almost impossible? Will fans ever get to see another Triple Crown champion?

Well, if you go by recent events, there's some reason to believe we might see another big winner sometime soon. Since 1978, 10 horses have won both in Louisville and Baltimore before faltering in Elmont, with three of the near-misses—Silver Charm (1997), Real Quiet (1998), and Smarty Jones (2004)—coming up within a recent eight-year period. With candidates coming up so close so often, sure, it's possible that some thoroughbred will break through and win it all at some point.

That's the sunny scenario, but it may not be a realistic one. The fact is that racing's been transformed over the years, and in ways that have made Triple Crown odds longer than ever.

More than anything else, money's changed the sport. As racetracks have attracted bigger audiences over the years, they've offered bigger and better rewards for their winners. Skyrocketing purses and stud fees, in turn, have encouraged millionaire/billionaire owners to dramatically increase the number of registered foals born per year (in North America alone, the number of potential Triple Crown contestants has gone from 5,800 in 1945 to more than 35,000 in the new millennium). Naturally, the very best of the new horses have benefited from detailed, generations-long pedigrees as well as the kind of painstaking prep and fine-tuning otherwise seen only in world-class race cars.

There was a relatively simple time, long ago, when a dark horse like Seabiscuit could sneak up and repeatedly surprise a relatively unsophisticated breeding world. It was possible as late as the 1970's, but that time may have passed. With so many more quality competitors available in the twenty-first century, it's never been tougher to take on the world time after time after time.

Eugenics, also, may well have made it impossible to

improve on the scorching 40+ mph track speeds of the modern era. While there's no such thing as a perfect animal, there is a certain point where half-ton animals have been bred to run as fast as their fragile bones, ligaments, and joints can possibly bear. We may have already seen that point, and with it, the end of breakthrough, Triple Crown-level performers.

Significantly, the "two-third" horses that have come along since Affirmed don't really disprove this—all but a couple were so spent by Churchill Downs and Pimlico that they were also-rans at Belmont Park. The two horses that have come closest to the Crown since '78, Real Quiet and Smarty Jones, may have been flukes rather than important exceptions to the larger trend. The may have used up a considerable amount of luck just to fall somewhat short of the final achievement.

For all that, though . . . betting men never say never.

No one predicted Man o' War and no one predicted Secretariat. Once in a rare while, fans witness ultra-special athletes who match a champion's physique with an indomitable urge to surge forward. Finding a new Triple Crown horse may be a long shot, but everyone who's had a good day at the track knows—sometimes long shots do come in. That's the thrill.

SUPERLATIVES

BABE RUTH VS. AIR JORDAN—WHO WAS THE BETTER PLAYER?

96 When Michael Jordan first gave up on pro basketball in 1993, he didn't quite quit his career in sports. No, he told the gasping reporters, he just had a new dream—one that involved stardom in Major League Baseball. Unfortunately for Jordan, though, the next season had a reality involving a .202 batting average in the low minors and, from then on in, Air Jordan stuck to the athleticism involved in slam dunks and passes rather than grand slams and pitching.

It wouldn't be fair to hold Jordan's baseball bust against him, though. It's hard enough to excel at the very top level of any one sport, let alone two. For all we know, the slow, stout Babe Ruth may have been just as rotten of a baller as Jordan was as a ballplayer.

That doesn't mean Ruth-Jordan comparisons are impossible, however. After all, the superstars did have well-established track records in their chosen occupations, so it's more than possible to judge where the Bambino stood relative to his fellow ballplayers and just how Jordan compared to other basketball stars. The question is, "Who was the better player?"

Elsewhere in this book, it's been argued that Babe Ruth is still the greatest hitter and all-around performer the Major Leagues have ever seen (#11, 13). 'Nuff said.

Was Jordan, on the other hand, the best NBA player who ever lived?

Well, Larry Bird once said he saw God disguised as Michael Jordan, but surely the Lord could have managed more than 5.3 career assists per game. No, He would have played less like Michael Jordan and more like Wilt Chamberlain.

The Big Dipper was Jordan's superior in offense, certainly. Both scorers averaged 30.1 points per game, virtually tied for the best in NBA history, but Chamberlain led the league in field goal percentage nine times to Jordan's zero. Chamberlain's .540 career shooting average towers above MJ's .497, actually, because Wilt's scoring was the product of power dunks and accuracy rather than ball-hogging and "Jordan Rules" officiating. Wilt also had far more games when he dominated in scoring, putting up 50 or more points on 118 occasions, compared to Jordan's 37.

And defense? Forget it. Chamberlain led the league in rebounding 11 times on the way to becoming the NBA's all-time leader. Jordan ranks #96. No one knows how many shots Wilt blocked in his career, because the stats weren't kept from 1960 to 1973, but newspaper accounts had Chamberlain rejecting as many as a dozen per game. Jordan was a nonfactor in blocks. The Big Dipper played more suffocating defense, and played it longer—he averaged 45.8 minutes per game over 14 campaigns while MJ averaged 38.3 when he decided to play from 1984 to 2003.

It can't be said that Michael Jordan was unsurpassed on the court in the way that Babe Ruth was unsurpassed on the diamond. Numbers aside, though, the two super-duper stars' vastly different status can be heard in the language of their respective sports.

No sane scout has gazed upon some bright young prospect and uttered the words, "You know what? That kid's the second coming of Babe Ruth." Even the most devoted, moony fans of record-breakers like Hank Aaron and Mark McGwire haven't claimed that they enjoyed superior all-around careers. The thought would never occur to them. More than 70 years after the Bambino's last ball game, finding "the next Babe Ruth" is an effective impossibility.

Basketball fans, however, are on a perpetual hunt for a worthy successor to a certain bald Bull. Some have said it's Kobe Bryant, who collected three championships at an age (23) when Jordan hadn't won a single playoff game. Or LeBron "The Chosen One" James, who averaged over 24 points per game at ages (19 and 20) when Jordan was taking college classes in North Carolina. Less than seven years after Air's last game, finding "the next Michael Jordan" is more than possible—it's likely.

To be the "Michael Jordan of _____" has a meaning akin to being the "Babe Ruth of _____," at least among some commentators, but that doesn't mean the superlatives are roughly the same. The greater player didn't wear red and black. He wore pinstripes.

BABE RUTH VS. AIR JORDAN—WHO WAS THE BIGGER INNOVATOR?

97 In the closing months of 1999, ESPN aired a documentary series devoted to the top athletes of the previous 100 years. As the list slowly dwindled down from #100 to #1, the contest for the single greatest "Athlete of the Century" came down to Babe Ruth and Michael Jordan. In the end, Jordan was honored. Ruth was robbed.

Babe's first claim to the title is based on his athletic achievements. As argued in the preceding chapter, Ruth was even greater as a baseball player than Jordan was as a basketball player.

Beyond the Babe's superior career accomplishments, though, was his once-in-a-century ability to utterly transform his sport. Before the Bambino's arrival, Major League hitters tried to score by slapping singles and bunting— few tried to swing for the fences, much less succeeded with the long ball. Ruth was the first who possessed 1) the vision to see power hitting's potential, and 2) the prodigious skill to score with extra-base swings.

With that insight and ability, Ruth revolutionized the Pastime. When he set a home run record by hitting 29 home runs in 1919, the rest of his team totaled four. When he hit 59 in 1921, the runner-up had less than half as many (24). When he became the career leader in homers (139), he broke his own mark another 575 times over. As late as 1927, he was out-homering every team in the American League. By the time he'd retired in 1935, he had more than twice as many home runs as the second-greatest home run hitter (Lou Gehrig) to that date.

Ruth was the very first to prove that a single swing of the bat could change everything, and today's long-ball hitters are still playing the mighty, unpredictable game he invented.

For a modern-day hitter to follow Ruth's lead in creating a whole new ball game, he'd have to hit more than 150 home runs in a season or 1,500 in a career. He'd have to put up more home run crowns than Barry Bonds, Alex Rodriguez, Vladimir Guerrero, Albert Pujols, Manny Ramirez, Jim Thome, Carlos Delgado, Jason Giambi, Gary Sheffield, David Ortiz, Andruw Jones, and Mike Piazza . . . combined. Don't hold your breath waiting.

Now, Michael Jordan was an outstanding player in all phases of the game, but he didn't come close to transforming basketball. He's mostly hailed for bringing an inventive verticality ("Air" Jordan and all that) to the game, but that had skyball precedents stretching back to Julius Erving and Connie Hawkins. It was Dr. J., not M.J., who first proved that basketball could be an aerial art form, even if his early soaring wasn't broadcast to the masses. To his credit, Jordan's never pretended he invented a thing. He was the one following in the footsteps of giants.

BABE RUTH VS. AIR JORDAN—WHO WAS THE BETTER AMBASSADOR?

Apart from his achievements on the diamond and status as an unparalleled innovator, Babe Ruth bested Michael Jordan as "Athlete of the Century" because he was a sports ambassador par excellence.

No one's done more to cement baseball's grip on America. Organized ball was wracked by the "Black Sox" gambling scandal until it was lifted by the Babe's popularity. In the year he broke his first home run record, league attendance doubled and only increased as the years went on. In the off-season, the "Bustin' Babes" barnstorming club won new fans in every corner of the country. Ruth never stopped mingling with ordinary fans, especially his admirers among the kids. His tour of Japan captured a new nation's imagination and ignited their ongoing obsession with the game. He was the first to give the Yankees Franchise the championship halo it carries to this day.

Julia Ruth Stevens and Dorothy Ruth Sullivan, now in their 80's, say their late father's memory resonates today just as it did during his own lifetime. They're right. In the new millennium, Babe Ruth is as universally recognized and influential as he ever was. Epochs removed from his last game, the Bambino's amassed the kind of goodwill that will never die.

Jordan? Jordan's been a corporate media presence in an era when the corporate media reigns. No one's soaked in more attention in *Sports Illustrated* covers, cartoons, commercials, TV shows, posters, you name it. Jordan's also been a busy salesman in an era overrun by salesmen, too, selling himself in sneakers, overpriced clothes, underwear, fast food, perfume, pastries, the list goes on. "Just Do It," "Be Like Mike," yadda, yadda, yadda. The spotlights and endorsements were all very lucrative.

Apart from that, though, his Airness didn't have a Ruthian impact. The NBA was reinforced by labor compromises, revenue sharing, and marketing strategies well before his first day in the league—he didn't save anything. Basketball's popularity increased during his career but dipped as soon as he left. Jordan mostly confined himself to mingling with bodyguards and admirers among the entourage. He won new fans in America and Asia, true, but not nearly enough for the sport to attract more than a fraction of baseball's annual attendance or year-round media ratings. Just as soon as he retired, the Bulls fell apart and haven't been heard from since.

No one knows if Jordan's fame will endure for future fans, but it wouldn't be too smart to bet the mortgage on it. After a while, yellowed magazines do get shelved and outdated ad campaigns are downsized. Corporate packaging, branding, and synergy wait for no man.

It was Babe Ruth, the one and only, who truly changed and transcended twentieth century sports. Michael Jordan was no slouch, but he wasn't "The Athlete of the Century," either.

WHY IS THE "MIKE AND THE MAD DOG" SHOW SO INCREDIBLY AWESOME?

99 The thing about New York is that it can't be easily categorized.

It's as busy as Times Square at dusk and as quiet as Staten Island at dawn. It's as frustrating as bumper-to-bumper LIE traffic and as tranquil as a stroll through a Central Park meadow. It's about as artsy as a Chelsea gallery opening and unaffected as a neighborhood block party. It's a Democratic metropolis that elects Republican mayors.

That's the thing about New York's favorite radio show, "Mike and the Mad Dog"—it can't be easily categorized, either. When Mike Francesa and Chris Russo chatter through their 1–6:30 afternoon gig on WFAN-AM, they're all over the place.

#1. THEY'RE FAR-RANGING

Baseball, football, basketball, the Olympics . . . if it's within shouting distance of the tabloids or the *Times*, they're talking about it. Anyone tuning in gets reviews, previews, who's winning, who's losing, who's coming up, who's going down, who's in, who's out, who's hurt, who's healthy, who should be hired, who should be fired, histories, futures, upcoming prospects, Hall of Fame prospects. The list goes on.

Beyond the fact that they talk about any sport and any topic, the show's terrific in the way they tackle subjects in different ways. At any one moment, they're zipping around from host commentaries to beat reporting to experts' dissections to insider interviews. "Mike and the Mad Dog" calls to mind that old joke about New England weather if you don't like it right now, just wait a minute.

#2. THEY'RE INFLUENTIAL

Front offices claim that New York's most popular talk show doesn't influence their decisions. Front offices lie.

Huge ratings give "Mike and the Mad Dog" an automatic say on organizations' bottom lines, because if these two aren't happy, it's a pretty good indication that the ticket-buying public isn't happy, either. The show's pull forces accountability—whenever things go south, higher-up's tend to pop up on 660 AM's air with their best explanations, justifications, and rationalizations. Fans may not like the answers, but they do get them.

(Sometimes, rarely, the show crosses the line between influencing decisions and making decisions. It's no secret that the show prodded the luckless General Manager Steve Phillips into some disastrous trades and signings after the Mets' pennant in 2000.)

#3. THEY'RE REAL

Listen to other cities' sports talk, and you'll find a bunch of arm-wavers screaming about nothing and fake-laughing at each other's jokes and generally going way over the top to be outrageous and controversial rather than, say, interesting and smart. Not Mike and the Mad Dog.

At this point, they've done so well for so long that they'll just do their own thing, providing some meat-and-potatoes analysis and off-the-cuff entertainment. It's not *Masterpiece Theatre*—the Noo Yawk accents, run-on grammar, and Russo's *creative* pronunciations ensure that much—but there are no gimmicks, either. They respect the fans' intelligence and the fans respect them right back.

#4. THEY'RE UNPRETENTIOUS

Talk isn't exactly cheap nowadays—both Francesa and Russo reportedly pull down seven-figure salaries while starring in a coast-to-coast cable show. Their faces smile down from billboards and they've hit the bestseller list. When they show up for remote broadcasts, they're hounded for autographs.

To hear Mike and Chris talk, though, they're still a couple of working stiffs arguing at the nearest Astoria bar. They don't come off as media-creation "personalities," and if the thought ever crossed their minds, their daily call-in's would be more than happy to knock them down a couple pegs. Even as they've moved up in the world, they're still the voice of the everyday fan.

#5. THEY'RE FEARLESS

The big numbers and big money have evidently freed the hosts up to say whatever the heck they want whenever they want. Mike's feuded with Jeremy Shockey, Chris' feuded with Al Leiter, and both have had their issues with *Monday Night Football* poobah Al Michaels. They certainly don't hesitate to jump all over the Mets 'n Jets 'n Nets, despite the fact that WFAN has always had multimillion-dollar contracts to carry their games.

The show never gets too nasty, and they always give targets chances to talk back, but, chances are, if New Yorkers are booing something somewhere, Mike and the Mad Dog have no problem in talking it over.

#6. THEY'RE MEN OF THE PEOPLE

Bruce from Bayside. Al from White Plains. Chris from Stamford. The late, great Doris from Rego Park.

WFAN's airwaves are big enough for a regular cast of callers and dozens of first-time call-ins, all of them offering their own takes on the show's take. Sometimes the segments are so much hot air, but the listeners regularly come up with some good points and, rarely, they do stump Mike (these are moments worth waiting for). The show's a five-day-a-week town hall for sports junkies.

#7. THEY'RE ORIGINALS

Give them the credit or the blame, but WFAN invented 24-hour sports talk radio back in 1987, meaning the station and show are the founders of the nation wide sports talk phenomenon that's exploded since. Worth noting. It's always nice when New York leads and America follows.

#8. THEY'RE AN INSTITUTION

When "Mike and the Mad Dog" launched in September '89, there was apartheid in South Africa, Communism in Eastern Europe, and another George Bush in the White House. In the time since, they've outlasted 64 (and counting) managers and head coaches and way too many players, executives, and assorted other notables to count. Pretty soon their microphones will be named New York City landmarks.

#9. THEY'RE DIFFERENT

Francesa and Russo are local Italian Americans and as nutty as sports nuts get, but they represent an Oscar-and-Felix match, too.

One's all about cerebral, sober analytics and detailed historical context. The other's about off-the-wall humor and from-the-hip energy. One's a beefy guy from Manhasset. The other's a lanky type from New Canaan. One's a lifelong subject of the Evil Empire. The other's a born Yankee hater.

Basically, their angles are so divergent that they're guaranteed to come up with lively debate on a regular basis. Their solo shows are good, too, but there isn't as much gin in the tonic when they're on their own.

#10. THEY'RE NOT QUITE CHUMMY

Maybe it's those personal differences or the stir-craziness involved in partnering up for hundreds of hours a year, year-in and year-out. One way or the other, shows sometimes reveal that Mike and the Mad Dog don't enjoy being Mike and the Mad Dog every single moment of every single day, so there's just enough unease to keep things lively. They may be working dream jobs, but they're still in the real world.

#11. THEY'RE UNIVERSAL

Fans turn on afternoon radio in skyscrapers and tenements, in luxe shops and bodegas, in limos and cabs, in the five boroughs and the suburbs . . . the same show unites 'em all. For all those who love New York sports, "Mike and the Mad Dog" is the shared soundtrack.

#12. THEY'RE FAMILIAR

You hang out with a couple buddies long enough, and you learn what to expect. The ever-present jingle ("Sports Radio 66 . . . THE FAN! . . . W!-F!-A!-N!"). The intro ("They're going at it as hard as they can! Mike and Mad Dog on the FAN! . . .").

Russo's unchanging opening ("Ahhhhhhhhhh . . . Goooooood afternoon every-body! How are you toooo-day?"). First-time callers and longtime listeners chipping in with the "first-time, longtime" shorthand.

By now, most listeners have heard from these guys more often than their siblings. Still, it never gets old.

In the way they're all the above, Mike Francesa and Chris Russo have been the perfect talk of the town. They're all over the place. They're New York.

IS NEW YORK CITY THE GREATEST SPORTS TOWN IN AMERICA?

An interview with Gothamite T. Metropolis, the biggest sports fan around

100

Is New York the greatest sports town in America?

Absolutely. I'm telling you, if you don't like New York sports, you don't like sports.

You want history? Our pros go back to the earliest days of the Majors, the NFL, the NBA, and the NHL. If it's been worth doing, it's been worth doing in New York. Don't bother trying to find a town with more traditions and memories.

You want action? We've got nine big-time teams, almost double what you've got in LA, and that's before you count U.S. Open, racing, title fights, and the rest. Events come round like subway trains.

You want winners? New York's got 10 championships over the last 20 years alone. Sorry, Green Bay—this is Titletown.

You want fans? Hey, we've got fans, millions of 'em. They're the ones who have been ringing up attendance and ratings records since forever, too, packing the rafters from the Coliseum to the Garden to the Stadiums.

Yeah, but that's just because New York has a bigger population. Some say they've got more passionate fans in Boston, for instance.

Hey, more great people, more great fans. That's the way it works.

Boston, Boston. Ah, Boston's got some nice qualities. They've got some things going for them, but I'll put New York fans up against them any day—rating point for rating point, turnstile click for turnstile click, decibel for decibel, no problem.

They say Chicago fans are more knowledgeable, too.

Ah, come on, who's "they"? Chicago fans, probably.

Walk down Madison Avenue and, within a couple of minutes, you'll find fans who've memorized the play-by-play on Super Bowl XXI. You got nutcases who know Phil Simms' college, the backups on the '73 Knicks, and Mike Bossy's career points total.

What was Phil Simms' college, the backups for '73 Knicks, and Mike Bossy's career points total?

Morehead State, Jerry Lucas, Phil Jackson, Dean Meminger, Henry Bibby, and Dick Barnett, and 752.

C'mon, gimme something tough. Challenge me.

OK. A lot of critics say that that the media's too pushy around here, that they ruin sports with constant, overbearing coverage.

No one's gonna give you bigger money, a bigger stage, and more space in the history books—when you make it in New York, people notice. And when you don't make it in New York, people notice. Whaddayagonnado? That's life in the bright lights, big city.

Are New Yorkers front runners?

This definitely isn't the Midwest, where they'll be cheering on the Cardinals or Vikings even if they lose every game of the season. I guess, over there, losing's adorable or they're more into loyalty or whatnot.

I know plenty of New York die-hards and they're in it for a love of the game. But, generally, to really make it, you gotta win, and that's all there is to it. Around here, if you've got a lousy restaurant, or shop or office or whathaveyou, people always have options for a better deal on the next corner. Same goes for sports—with these ticket prices, you better produce. Life's too short and there's too much to do around here.

Sports Illustrated recently published a list of "The 25 Best Sports Bars in America," and none of them were in New York.

SI's office is on West 50th. I guess the grass is always greener, huh?

I'll give you a list of a dozen great sports bars within the next few blocks if you want it. My cousin Tony tends bar at one of them. Last Saturday, my buddies Chris, Chris, Louie, Sully, Mike and I were there, having some beers while arguing over the Mets' rotation, watching a couple middleweights, and handicapping the Belmont. At the same time. *That's* what I call a great sports bar.

What about the lack of big-time college ball?

You used to have St. John's, but they haven't done anything in a while. I guess you can have Manhattan, Kansas for the pom-poms and rah-rah. I'll take Manhattan, thanks.

I'll give you that, but we've got great amateurs, though. Take the New York area, let's say New Brunswick in Jersey to Stamford, Connecticut and from Yonkers to Syosset on the Island. I'll bet you, dollars to donuts, you've got the most Little Leagues, pee wee football, basketball programs, junior hockey, training centers, etc., in the United States of America. Throw in miniature golf, bowling, and wiffle ball. You can find rugby leagues and cricket if you look. Anything at all.

The best athletes in America come out of the area, too. You don't even have to go the Stadium or the Coliseum or the Garden to see a superstar—just walk down to the nearest youth league.

But New York's never hosted the Super Bowl. The All Star Game hasn't been in town in nearly 30 years.

[laughs] Who needs 'em? We've got enough. I say spread the wealth.

What about the World Cup and Olympics?

You know what? We don't need a special occasion to welcome the world. That's what the airport's for.

Hey, case closed—we're the best. I love New York.

INDEX
By Subject

THE BEST NEW YORK SPORTS ARGUMENTS

THE BEST NEW YORK SPORTS ARGUMENTS

THE BEST NEW YORK SPORTS ARGUMENTS

INDEX
By Name

396

Q

Qualls, Jim, 205

R

Rahman, Hasim, 356
Raines, Tim, 59
Ramirez, Manny, 371
Randolph, Willie, 128
Raschi, Vic, 83
Ratner, Brett, 303, 304
Real Quiet (horse racing), 363, 365
Redford, Robert, 9
Reed, Willis, 287, 288
Reese, Jimmy, 55
Reese, Pee Wee, 78, 97, 190
Reiser, Pete, 29, 187
Reynolds, Allie, 82, 187
Rhoden, Rick, 181
Rhodes, Dusty, 191
Ribalta, Jose, 352
Rice, Glen, 299
Rice, Grantland, 61
Rice, Jim, 180
Richardson, Bobby, 149
Richardson, Michael Ray, 33
Richardson, Quentin, 298
Rickey, Branch, 76, 78, 80, 100
Rijo, Jose, 181
Riley, Pat, 292–95
Ripken, Cal, Jr., 70–76, 221–22
Rivera, Mariano, 175, 202, 223
Rivers, Mickey, 35, 36, 190–91
Rizzuto, Phil
  Hall of Fame, 81
  nickname, 187
  number retired, 12
  "Paradise by the Dashboard Light" and, 220
  quotes, 33
  Yankee tradition and, 224
Robbins, Tim, 30
Robertson, Charlie, 96
Robinson, Brooks, 61, 147
Robinson, Frank, 25, 147, 166
Robinson, Jackie, 64, 76–81, 87, 97
Robinson, Nate, 298
Robinson, Rachel, 119
Robinson, Wilbert, 127, 189
Robustelli, Andy, 272

Rodriguez, Alex
  clutch hitting, 162–67
  image of, 175–76
  intangibles, 172–74
  leadership, 168–71
  Mara, Wellington, 277
  power hitting, 167–68
  Ruth, Babe, 371
  Yankee spending and, 208
  Yankees–Red Sox rivalry, 212–13
Roe, Preacher, 191
Rogan, Bullet Joe, 65
Rogers, George, 269
Rogers, Kenny, 95
Roosevelt, Franklin Delano, 348
Rose, Jalen, 298
Rose, Malik, 296
Rote, Kyle, 236, 272
Roth, Allan, 92
Rozelle, Pete, 273, 284
Rozier, Mike, 269
Ruel, Muddy, 49, 191
Rupp, Adolph, 80
Ruppert, Jacob, 44–45, 216
Russo, Chris, 375–81
Ruth, Babe
  abdominal surgery, 178
  baserunning, 58, 59–60
  Bonds, Barry, 52–70
  Curse of the Bambino, 16–17
  death of, 218
  Gehrig, Lou, 217, 218
  historical era comparisons, 64–68
  Huggins, Miller, 189
  integrated games, 65–66
  Jordan, Michael, 367–74
  Maris, Roger, 109–12
  McGraw, John J., 45
  nickname, 191
  number retired, 12
  on-base percentage, 54
  OPS, 55
  pitching, 62–63
  playoff performance, 166
  Seinfeld sitcom and, 183
  slugging percentage, 53
  Sylvester, Johnny, 19, 22–23
  Toot Shor's, 23
  uniforms, 10

.ABOUT THE AUTHOR

Peter Handrinos is a syndicated columnist and author of the "Baseball Men" interview series. He lives in Norwalk, CT.